JULIA MORGAN

Design B

JULIA MORGAN

An Intimate Biography of the Trailblazing Architect

BY VICTORIA KASTNER

With photography by ALEXANDER VERTIKOFF

CHRONICLE BOOKS
SAN FRANCISCO

TO RUTH,
WITH ABIDING GRATITUDE

*"Life shrinks or expands in
proportion to one's courage."*

ANAÏS NIN

Library of Congress Cataloging-in-Publication Data:
Names: Kastner, Victoria, author. | Vertikoff, Alexander, photographer (expression)

Title: Julia Morgan : an intimate biography of the trailblazing
architect / by Victoria Kastner.
Description: San Francisco : Chronicle Books, [2021] | Includes
    bibliographical references and index. | Identifiers: LCCN
2021027691 (print) | LCCN 2021027692 (ebook) | ISBN
    9781797205632 (hardcover) | ISBN 9781797205816 (ebook) | ISBN
    9781797215952
Subjects: LCSH: Morgan, Julia, 1872-1957. | Architects—United
    States—Biography. | Women architects—United States—
Biography.
Classification: LCC NA737.M68 K37 2021 (print) | LCC NA737.M68
(ebook) | DDC 720.92 [B]—dc23
LC record available at https://lccn.loc.gov/2021027691
LC ebook record available at https://lccn.loc.gov/2021027692

Manufactured in China.

Design by Kayla Ferriera.
Typesetting by Frank Brayton. Typeset in LTC Californian,
LTC Record Title, and Copperplate.

Cover photographs courtesy Alexander Vertikoff and California
Polytechnic State University, San Luis Obispo.

Title page photograph: Julia Morgan's drawing for one of San
Simeon's bell towers, inspired by a church tower in Ronda, Spain.

Copyright page photograph: A ceramic della Robbia wreath Julia
purchased in Italy for display in the Chapel of the Chimes in
Oakland, California.

10 9 8 7 6 5 4 3 2 1

Chronicle Books LLC
680 Second Street
San Francisco, California 94107
www.chroniclebooks.com

CONTENTS

Introduction
7

Julia Morgan in her late forties, circa 1920. Like most career women of her era, Julia never married, nor is there evidence of any romantic relationships. Her passion was architecture.

Introduction

During the past several years, both critical and popular regard for Julia Morgan and her architecture has skyrocketed.

One reason for this expanding interest: the American Institute of Architects' decision to posthumously award her their highest honor, the Gold Medal, as their first-ever female recipient. No longer is she associated solely with Hearst Castle at San Simeon—the vast and glamorous country house she designed for William Randolph Hearst in the 1920s and 1930s. Julia Morgan is now justly celebrated for her work in its entirety. Over the first half of the twentieth century, she designed an estimated seven hundred structures throughout the western United States. They vary widely in purpose (schools, churches, office buildings, clubhouses, hospitals, stores, modest family dwellings, and grandly opulent estates) as well as in architectural style. In the 1960s and 1970s, when modernism was in its ascendancy, critics either ignored her or derided her for not having adopted one signature style of her own. Today she is acclaimed for her skill in employing disparate styles, and for her steadfast commitment to creating buildings that met the needs of each individual client. Julia Morgan's designs are all alike in one way. Large or small, they exemplify the three characteristics propounded by the ancient Roman architect Marcus Vitruvius: *firmitas* (strength), *utilitas* (functionality), and *venustas* (beauty).

In spite of her widening renown, some misconceptions about Julia still linger. One enduring myth holds that she burned her papers before closing her San Francisco office in 1950. Perhaps this legend derives from her having asked former clients if they would like to keep the drawings and blueprints that she no longer had sufficient space to store. In fact, Julia personally preserved an enormous amount of material, including hundreds of letters from her family, staff, and friends; more than two thousand letters that she exchanged with Hearst over thirty years; school notes and sketchbooks from her studies at the École des Beaux-Arts in Paris; and the half dozen diaries she kept on her travels. These last items are perhaps the most remarkable, since they alternate between mundane record-keeping and surprisingly personal disclosures—and since they have been so rarely read or quoted by scholars. Julia's papers are located primarily in the Robert E. Kennedy Library's Special Collections and Archives at California Polytechnic State University in San Luis Obispo. There are also significant holdings—including invaluable interviews with her family, friends, and employees—at the University of California's Bancroft Library and its College of Environmental Design in Berkeley, as well as in the archives at Hearst Castle.

Another durable misconception concerns Julia's private life. Many have wondered whether she remained unmarried because she was a lesbian. Abundant historical evidence confirms that she had no romantic relationships of any kind. Though she cultivated many warm friendships with her clients and her staff, Julia's lifelong love affair was with architecture. She once offered this reasoning when declining a request to visit long-distance friends: "Thank you for your invitation, which sounded so pleasant. . . . One trouble about an architect's work is that there is never a period when things do not overlap and to get any real time away, it means the closing of one's office."[1] Her nephew, Morgan North, and his wife, Flora, knew her best. He explained, "I don't think she ever got close to marriage. . . . I don't think the subject ever entered her head, really." Flora continued, "I think she found immediate interest in her career, because she pursued it twenty-four hours a day, thoroughly. . . . [When she was with you], it was full focus," but the rest of the time, her attention was on her architecture.[2]

When Julia died at age eighty-five in 1957, Morgan North served as the executor of her estate. He and Flora carefully preserved her archives and protected her legacy. In the 1970s, not long before his death, he also recorded a "Message to the Historian." He was worried that authors of the time seemed to be focusing on Julia's architecture, but not on Julia herself. "[Her] personal background [is] going on concurrently with the business background," he explained. He stated that no author thus far had "described what Miss Morgan was, or what she really did, or what she was trying to do, or why." Without addressing these motivations, he continued, no book would be complete. He concluded by saying that if a biographer sticks with it long enough, they will eventually develop insight.[3]

This book is described as "an intimate biography" because it is the first volume to thoroughly examine Julia's private life as well as her career. In Morgan North's phrasing, I have "stuck with it." During the decades I spent as the official historian at Hearst Castle, I developed a deep knowledge of Julia Morgan and William Randolph Hearst's inimitable architect-client relationship. I was already very familiar with her environs, having, like her, grown up in the San Francisco Bay Area. I spent many years reviewing her papers, exploring her buildings, and studying her drawings. In short, I have developed the insight and knowledge necessary to reveal the woman behind the architecture—as a complex individual, as well as a brilliant artist.

Perhaps the one word that best describes Julia Morgan is "strength." This might seem odd, considering her diminutive appearance. But her strength helped her conquer endless difficulties—stubborn misogynists; family troubles; personal health struggles; demanding clients; and more logistical and construction challenges than we can possibly guess. She led a passionate life, albeit one that was devoted to creativity rather than to romantic love. She believed in herself and in her ability to solve problems, and this was the secret of her greatness. She gave her all—invariably with determination, and

often with joy. When she was about to return to San Simeon after a long illness, her first missive to Hearst concluded: "It is a great pleasure to be able to play at work again."[4] The story of Julia Morgan's inspiring life will encourage us to do the same.

Julia with her niece and nephew, Judith Avery Morgan and Morgan North, circa 1918.

CHAPTER ONE

GLIMPSING THE FUTURE

IN THE SPRING OF 1919, WHEN JULIA MORGAN first visited San Simeon, she saw a quiet shoreline bordered by rolling hills. She didn't realize she was looking at the site that would preoccupy her for nearly thirty years. It was a time of new beginnings. World War I had ended, and America was on the brink of the Roaring Twenties—a decade of unparalleled prosperity. Julia had traveled to San Simeon at the invitation of William Randolph Hearst, a prominent press lord whom she knew well. His mother, Phoebe Apperson Hearst, had introduced them fifteen years before, and Julia had already designed three projects for him: a lavish estate in Sausalito, north of San Francisco (which was never built); a modest cabin on the south rim of the Grand Canyon; and a large Mission-style headquarters for one of his newspapers, the *Los Angeles Examiner*.[1]

Earlier that week, W. R., as Hearst was known, had walked into Julia's office at the end of the day. Years later, her longtime employee Walter Steilberg related the conversation he'd overheard:

"I was at my table, after five o'clock. I often worked late because it was interesting work, whatever it was. I heard this voice, which I had heard before, but I didn't realize what a high pitch Mr. Hearst's voice had. For such a large man, it seemed to me his pitch was very high, so it carried. I heard him say to Miss Morgan, 'I would like to build something up on the hill at San Simeon. I get tired of going up there and camping in tents. I'm getting a little old for that. I'd like to get something that would be more comfortable. The other day I was in Los Angeles, prowling around second-hand bookstores, as I often do, and I came upon this stack of books called Bungalow Books. Among them I saw one which has a picture—this isn't what I want, but it gives you an idea of my thought about the thing, keeping it simple—of a Jappo-Swiss bungalow.' He laughed at that, and so did she."[2]

A simple project, W. R. promised. It would take her less than six months, from start to finish.

A few days later, therefore, Julia boarded a train for the eight-hour, overnight journey to San Simeon—the first of what would become her nearly six hundred trips. When her train pulled into the San Luis Obispo station just before sunrise, W. R. was waiting. He led her to a black Model T Ford idling nearby. It was driven by young Steve Zegar, who would eventually amass a fleet of taxis for driving Hearst's guests the additional 40 miles north to San Simeon. They climbed into Steve's Tin Lizzie—as these cars were affectionately known—which he eased onto the narrow, bumpy highway.[3]

W. R. and Julia never had a romance, but they were old friends. They had much in common—including a passion for European art and architecture—though a casual observer would have been more struck by their dissimilarities. Hearst was fifty-six in 1919: a tall, stout man whom actor David Niven once described as "shaped like an avocado."[4] He typically wore a finely woven Panama hat, a light-colored linen suit, a necktie of startling brightness, and two-toned wingtip shoes. He had a large head and large features: big hands, big blue eyes, and a long aquiline nose. Surprisingly, he had a high voice. Many years before, the caustic writer Ambrose Bierce—whose column was syndicated in Hearst's newspapers—described his incongruous tenor as sounding like "the fragrance of violets, made audible."[5] Nevertheless, W. R. was a lively and amusing conversationalist.

William Randolph Hearst, who in 1919 approached Julia about a six-month building project at San Simeon. Construction lasted for twenty-eight years.

Julia was forty-seven, very slender, and not much more than 5 feet tall. Her large eyes were framed by round dark-rimmed glasses.

She typically wore a navy blue or charcoal gray woolen suit with a long skirt and matching jacket, a crisp, high-collared white shirt, and a bell-shaped hat pinned over her upswept hair. Though slight and soft-spoken, with just a trace of a lisp, she nevertheless carried herself with quiet authority.

From 1900 to 1950, Julia forged an unprecedented career. There were other female architects working in America during that time, but she was the only one who broke through the societal constraints that limited others to designing mostly private homes and women's clubs. In a profession that relied on social connections as well as ability, Julia competed on an equal footing with her male contemporaries, few of whom could match her energy or her skill. One of her employees described her: "A tiny woman, gentle yet formidable. Her manner was simple. Pleasant, yet rather reserved. Eyes very direct. A low clear voice. I've seen strong men tremble when she said: 'No, it won't do.'"[6]

As was fairly common among the career women of her day, Julia never married (nor is there any evidence that she had romantic relationships with other women). She devoted her life to architecture, but never became a prudish old maid. Her large social circle included family members, childhood friends, trusted employees, and admiring clients. One of her closest friendships was with the man she rode alongside on that day in 1919, and W. R. felt the same way about her.

Their conversation must have flowed easily on that two-hour drive, as they passed rugged green hillsides dotted with wildflowers and caught occasional glimpses of the windswept coastline. W. R. likely pointed out all the local ranches, where they saw far more cows than people; he knew the region well, having spent time there since his early childhood. They finally pulled up to a large white Victorian house, beyond which the road ended. Julia could see the start of a narrow trail, where two saddled horses stood waiting. This was a most unwelcome sight.

While they shared a love for the California landscape, they viewed it very differently. Julia was born in San Francisco in 1872 as one of five children, all of whom had a comfortable, upper-middle-class childhood, funded by her mother Eliza's family fortune. The Morgans moved to Oakland in 1874, when the city truly was an "Oak-Land" dotted with *Quercus agrifolia*, the native Coast Live Oaks that grew above California's shoreline and within its shady canyons. As a child, Julia had climbed the oaks that grew in her neighborhood, and had joined her family on summer camping trips to Monterey, Santa Cruz, and Catalina (monthlong adventures that made such an impression on her that she reminisced in her diary about certain stargazing and tidepooling trips a full fifty years later). But as an adult, though she loved the region's scenery, she admired it from a distance.[7]

W. R. was just the opposite. He was born in San Francisco in 1863, the only child of George Hearst, who ranked among the nation's wealthiest miners, and Phoebe Apperson Hearst, who was one of its most generous philanthropists. In 1865, the Hearsts took the money from George's stake in

San Simeon, located midway between San Francisco and Los Angeles, provided the dramatic setting where Julia and W. R. built the estate he christened La Cuesta Encantada (The Enchanted Hill).

Nevada's Comstock Lode—the richest vein of silver in the country—and invested it in 48,000 acres of ranchland along San Simeon Bay, a quiet natural harbor 250 miles south of San Francisco. Its nearby mountaintop became a favorite summer campsite, where the weather stayed sunny even when the coastline was blanketed in fog. W. R. learned to ride a horse when he was two, and later joked that as a boy, he found the climb up this mountain so steep that he only managed to keep from falling off by hanging onto the horse's tail.

Camp Hill, as they christened it, remained his favorite place in the world. It was too remote for a year-round home, but he escaped there as often as he could, to enjoy its dazzling views and cherish his happy memories. When he and his wife, Millicent, camped there with their five young sons in 1917, he wrote to Phoebe: "I love this ranch. It is wonderful. I love the sea and I love the mountains, and the hollows in the hills and the shady places in the creeks, and the fine old oaks—and even the hot brushy hillsides, full of quail, and the canyons, full of deer. . . . I would rather spend a month at the ranch than anyplace in the world."[8]

Riding a horse up a narrow, 6-mile trail was therefore second nature to W. R., who had been known to downplay the distances and difficulties of horseback rides before. He and Millicent had honeymooned in California in 1903. She was eager to see San Simeon, and anxious to establish her rustic credentials—which were few, since she was a twenty-year-old vaudeville dancer who had grown up in New York City. The forty-year-old Hearst assured her that San Simeon was very close to Monterey. In fact, it was 100 miles south, at the end of a rough overland trail. Many years later, Millicent could still recall that arduous ride: "One night, we slept in a cave that was full of bones and had a funny smell. An old codger we ran into later on the trail laughed at us [and] told us it was a well-known mountain lion den! The couple we started out with turned back after two days, but I stuck it out. . . . W. R. had told me it was a short ride!"[9]

On that spring morning in 1919, Julia looked sternly at the horses, then sternly back at Hearst. In a tone that brooked no argument, she informed him that she didn't ride. Furthermore, she didn't intend to learn. An ingenious solution seemed necessary. As Zegar tells it, he spotted some cowboys riding nearby and called them over. W. R. mounted his horse, but Julia remained inside the taxi, which Zegar drove straight up the steep grassy hillside. He gunned the engine and tried to avoid the largest rock outcroppings as they climbed from sea level to an elevation of 1,600 feet. The cowboys rode alongside, roping the taxi's bumper so they could pull it over the impassable stretches.[10]

It was a bizarre beginning to an incomparable project, over which Julia would preside in its entirety: as architect, interior designer, landscape architect, personnel manager, and overseer of every detail, from shipping enormous quantities of construction materials to housing the hundreds of exotic animals in Hearst's private zoo. She must have spent that long first day clambering over boulders, keeping a cautious eye out for rattlesnakes and scorpions, and marveling at the mountain and ocean vistas that stretched for hundreds of miles. As she listened to W. R. bubble over with ideas, she soon realized that his six-month construction estimate was completely impossible. By the time Steve had inched his taxi down the hill and completed the two-hour drive to the train station, it was late in the evening. Julia requested an upper berth, since she was small enough to sit upright and work on a lap board.[11] As her train clattered through the night, she sketched the first of what would become San Simeon's ten thousand drawings.

CHAPTER TWO

A CALIFORNIA CHILDHOOD

JULIA WAS A LIFELONG TRAILBLAZER. IN 1898, she was the first woman admitted to study architecture at the world-renowned École des Beaux-Arts in Paris (founded in the seventeenth century). Less than four years later, she became the first woman to graduate from its demanding program (which generally took six years to finish, though many never completed it). In 1904, she was the first woman licensed to practice architecture in California.

Few other architects could match Julia's output during her fifty-year career: an estimated seven hundred structures, including Hearst's two lavish residences—one at San Simeon and one in Northern California—which rank among the nation's largest. San Simeon alone contains approximately 110,000 square feet of enclosed floor space, divided among a half-dozen independent structures. Yet it receives only one number—Job 503—in Julia's records. Though the exact quantity of her designs may never be known, due to omissions in the historical record, it is fair to say that Julia ranks among the twentieth century's most prolific architects.[1] With so many groundbreaking achievements, therefore, the most recent one could be considered long overdue. In 2014, the American Institute of Architects posthumously awarded Julia its Gold Medal. She was their first female recipient in the prestigious award's hundred-year history.

Another distinction—of which Julia was very proud—greatly influenced her career: She was a native Californian. Most San Francisco Bay Area architects of her era were transplanted Easterners (including Willis Polk, Bernard Maybeck, and John Galen

Howard). Julia forged a deep connection with California's distinctive landscape, and considered it "a decided advantage to grow up in the general environment one is to work in."[2] The majority of her buildings are located in California, and her thorough understanding of the spatial and visual interplay between architecture and setting is a defining element of their design.

When Julia was born on January 20, 1872, she was the second of Charles and Eliza Morgan's five children, and the eldest girl. Her parents were Easterners who moved to San Francisco soon after they married in 1869. Within a few years, the Morgan family relocated to Oakland, where city records list them living first at 716 Fourteenth Street, then in a house nearby at 1363 Castro Street. Both homes were in an excellent downtown neighborhood around the corner from the mayor's mansion. In 1885, the Morgans commissioned their finest residence, located at 754 Fourteenth Street. This three-story Victorian house featured towers, gables, balconies, and abundant exterior ornament, including stained glass, fish-scale shingles, and wooden spindlework. Julia lived in this elegant home for forty years, then moved back to San Francisco in 1925, where she spent the last thirty years of her life.[3]

Oakland was a wealthy enclave during Julia's childhood. Its weather was milder than San Francisco's; its gentle topography made construction much less difficult; and

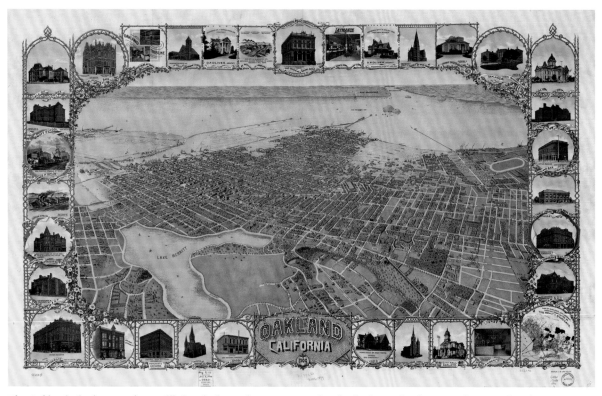

The Oakland of Julia's youth was filled with elegant homes. It was also the final stop for the transatlantic railroad.

The Morgans lived on Fourteenth Street at the opposite end of this block, across from the Baptist Church on the left.

its lack of congestion meant that lot sizes and house sizes could be significantly larger. San Francisco was an easy ferryboat ride away, and horse-drawn streetcars provided efficient transport down to the pier. Most importantly, Oakland's Central Pacific Depot was the termination hub of the transcontinental railroad, which had been extended south from Sacramento in 1869 to facilitate agricultural shipments. Because the railroad reduced the cross-country journey from several weeks to a mere ten days, its most important repercussion was bringing hordes of wealthy, sun-starved Easterners flocking to Oakland's abundant hills. They were lured by its reputation as a garden city, as one new arrival described: "The green lawns, the bewildering luxuriance of roses, fuchsias, callas, heliotropes, geraniums, poppies, larkspurs, chrysanthemums, and a host of other flowers, the hedges of cypress, ivy, and privet, the palms, olives, oaks, magnolias, laurels, eucalyptus, madrones, as well as the blooming fruit trees of every variety of color, are a perpetual glory."[4] Julia's mother Eliza—an enthusiastic gardener—wrote to her in Paris, where Julia was studying architecture while shivering through the harsh Parisian weather: "It has not been a cold Winter—you never saw such loads of violets as there are and very pretty roses in the garden. All the girls that pass the house have long stemmed violets pinned on their jackets."[5]

During Julia's childhood, the Morgans stayed a few weeks most summers in one or another of California's most beautiful locations, including Santa Cruz, Catalina, Pacific Grove, and St. Helena. In 1938, when she was sixty-six, Julia reminisced in her private diary about two childhood trips when she had

Julia—shown at age eight, in 1880—was energetic and determined. She was the second of five siblings and the eldest girl.

Her nephew, Morgan North (hereafter referred to as "North" to avoid confusion), recalled his mother, Emma, saying: "As a young girl [Julia] was rather inclined to be athletic and like trapeze things and bow and arrow." North's wife, Flora, added: "In the garden of her family's large and formal home . . . , she was caught doing somersaults on the gymnastic equipment erected for her three brothers. Her very proper Victorian mother was shocked at this unladylike behavior, and made her do penance by practicing the violin an extra hour a day."[7]

Julia became an accomplished violinist, and, like her sister Emma, also studied piano. Their brother Avery—who had the most musical talent—played the violin, piano, and organ. Late in life, Emma recalled the horror of being compelled to practice the piano hour after hour: "The front living room . . . had these old sliding doors . . . and they would pull the doors all closed while [everyone else] went into the parlor or stayed upstairs, so the pianist [wouldn't disturb] the household."[8] Though Julia didn't continue to play the violin as an adult, she pursued it seriously throughout her school years, performing a Haydn violin quartet for her graduation from Oakland High School in 1890. North called it part of her finishing-school upbringing: "[Aunt Julia's] house [after her death in 1957] was full of her violin [sheet] music." Flora continued, "[The] Oakland High School of those days was pretty select . . . [Its teachers were] impecunious widows . . . who were forced to give [music] lessons, and all the young ladies were forced to subject themselves. And [the Morgans were] a very proper family, very well

gone tidepooling: "That wonderful summer at Catalina . . . and those lovely water pools one hung over in the early Monterey days, [where we] saw all these kinds of life—[and] took in too the quietness and peace under those mighty breakers . . . and these most delicate & beautiful forms of life,—like those nudibrancs [sic] or those anemones—or the spider-like stars . . . quietly waving of millions of mouth feelers . . . to bring food one could not even see. [Others] certainly missed much we children had."[6]

At home in Oakland, the Morgan siblings frequently played outside, which Julia enjoyed.

mannered." The school's curriculum was so renowned that students throughout California moved into nearby boarding houses in order to enroll there. Julia had notable local classmates as well, including Gertrude Stein and her older brother Leo.[9]

As well as Julia knew and loved Oakland, she also spent a significant part of her childhood on the East Coast, at her grandparents' spacious home in Brooklyn Heights. Widely regarded as the most aristocratic suburb of New York, this half-mile-long enclave was affluent, elegant, and quiet—but its residents could board the Fulton Street ferry and arrive in Manhattan only twelve minutes later. Julia's maternal grandparents, the Parmelees, resided in an elegant five-story brownstone on Remsen Street, which boasted one of the finest views of the city. From her earliest years, Julia was familiar with Brooklyn Heights's distinguished Greek-Revival and Italianate mansions, ornamented with Corinthian columns, arched doorways, and projecting cornices. She was baptized in one of its most impressive Gothic churches, Richard Upjohn's 1847 Grace Church, located around the corner from Remsen Street. She also witnessed portions of the Brooklyn Bridge's thirteen years of construction. When the world's first steel-wire suspension bridge opened in 1883, Julia was eleven years old.[10]

Albert Ozias Parmelee, Julia's maternal grandfather, could afford to live in Brooklyn Heights thanks to his generous income as a cotton broker before and after the Civil War. He was born in Litchfield, Connecticut, in 1806, the fifth of David and Lucy Lewis

Parmelee's six children (three boys and three girls). Their father David reportedly held many civic offices, including Justice of the Peace and Registrar. Like his father, Albert was ambitious. Instead of remaining in Litchfield like his siblings, as a young adult he relocated to the South in order to pursue his cotton speculations. In Columbus, Georgia, at age thirty-six, Albert married nineteen-year-old Sarah Emma Woodland, who had grown up in Kent County, Maryland, in her family's stately eighteenth-century Federal-style mansion, Woodland Hall.

Though Albert regularly returned to the South for business, the young couple moved to Brooklyn Heights soon after their marriage. North recalled: "He was a cotton trader—I guess you'd call him an out-and-out gambler. His whole life was in buying and selling cotton futures."[11] Albert and Sarah sent their daughter Eliza to the refined and formal Brooklyn Heights Female Seminary. Founded

Julia's wealthy grandparents, the Parmelees—whom the Morgans visited frequently—lived in Brooklyn Heights, New York's most fashionable suburb.

in 1851, its objective was "in the fullest sense of the word, to educate … not only the culture of the intellect, but the moulding of the character and manners."[12] Eliza's determined personality was likely shaped by this highly moral curriculum, and she certainly passed her disciplined work ethic on to her eldest daughter. When writing to Julia, who was away on a college excursion, Eliza used personal stationery emblazoned with the motto *Vincit Qui Patitur* ("He conquers who suffers"), and advised her: "I hope you are having a pleasant time. Let a sense of duty animate you, if you are inclined to droop."[13]

The paternal branch of Julia's family was also financially comfortable. The Morgans were distantly related to J. P. Morgan (1837–1913), the nation's wealthiest financier, though there is no evidence that their respective families ever met. Julia's great-grandfather Avery Morgan was born in 1781 in Colchester (now Salem), Connecticut, and served in the Connecticut legislature. He married Jerusha Gardner, from nearby Groton, and they had seven children, including Julia's grandfather, William Avery, who was born in 1812. William co-owned a dry goods store in Brooklyn. He died in 1848 at the young age of thirty-five, and his wife Sarah died only two years later, leaving three children behind. Julia's father, Charles, was an orphan at age nine. Avery and Jerusha presumably raised their three grandchildren thereafter. They also had a daughter, Lydia, who in 1830 married Eliphalet Adams Bulkeley, an attorney and Connecticut state senator who founded Aetna Life Insurance.

Julia's family later benefited from financial opportunities provided by their wealthy Bulkeley relatives.[14]

Charles Morgan met Eliza Parmelee in Brooklyn while they were both still in high school. At eighteen he was hired as a clerk for the 1st Ward of Brooklyn, but he had higher aspirations. After training as a mining engineer, he decided he wanted to become a sugar broker in the Hawaiian Islands (one of many goals he never realized). This aim brought him as far as San Francisco in 1867, where he worked for Blanchard, Williams, and Co., the largest shipping merchant on the West Coast.[15] Charles continued wooing Eliza, and on June 10, 1869, they married in Grace Church on Remsen Street.

Their wedding occurred one month after the completion of the transcontinental railroad, a mode of transport the Morgan children knew well (since the family traveled to New York on at least three occasions before Julia's tenth birthday). Throughout her life, Julia spent many hours watching the American landscape flash by from the window of a moving train. Though rail journeys were a vast improvement over wagon travel, during Julia's childhood they could still be quite uncomfortable, as one female traveler explained: "You don't know what it is to live day and night for 8 days in one of those [rail]cars, with all sorts of people, and surrounded by what one may call all the indecencies of a civilized life. I often hear people say they enjoy it, but it is quite incomprehensible to me."[16]

The Morgans' trips to Brooklyn Heights were funded by the Parmelees, who were a very close and generous family. Throughout his marriage to Eliza, Charles was ambitious but unsuccessful in attaining his grandiose dreams. The Parmelees wanted the young couple to move back to Brooklyn Heights, where they could keep a closer eye on their daughter. Sarah wrote Eliza a few months after the wedding: "You are on my mind all the time nearly. I pray for it earnestly, and hope to live to see you back here with us. Your father is terribly worried about you all the time [and] he wishes you back. I try to keep up his spirits and Julia's [Eliza's younger sister] all the time." Albert's frequent letters to Eliza enclosed either $75.00 or $100.00 in gold (equivalent to $1,500 to $1,800 today). In 1874, the Parmelees offered Charles and Eliza an even more tantalizing prospect. Her sister Julia had admired a nearby house in Brooklyn Heights, and wrote Eliza later that day: "We went home and mother said she'd tell father about [buying] it, ... and in two hours he came back ... and said, 'Well, I've bought you the house!'" Albert also offered to buy the house next door for Eliza and Charles. Sarah added her entreaty, writing that Albert "cannot yet [be] reconsiled [sic] to your living so far away. He thinks he is growing older all the time and that the few more years that he may be spared ought to be spent with you, your family and Julia's. I only wish you could, but Mr. M[organ] knows best."[17]

In spite of these pleas and enticements, Eliza and Charles didn't move back to

Julia's mother, Eliza Woodland Parmelee, was strong and decisive.

Julia's father, Charles Bill Morgan, often pursued unsuccessful business schemes, and therefore Eliza's parents frequently provided financial assistance.

Brooklyn Heights. They lived in San Francisco's lavish Palace Hotel while searching for accommodations. Their firstborn child, a boy who arrived in 1870, was given the family surname, Parmelee. Eliza's parents paid for their trip to New York for his christening. For the next few years the Morgans rented spacious homes in San Francisco, entirely funded and furnished by the Parmelees. When Julia was born on January 20, 1872, the family again headed east for her Grace Church christening. Their third child, Emma, was born in 1874, and another son, Avery, arrived in 1876. Their youngest son, Gardner Bulkeley, nicknamed "Sam," arrived in 1880. The Parmelees could afford to support their eldest daughter's young family, because Albert's cotton-trading business was booming. The 1870 U.S. census valued his real estate holdings at $50,000 (equivalent to $1.5 million today).[18]

These prosperous times unfortunately didn't last. In 1873, a worldwide financial panic was triggered when Germany ceased minting silver coinage. In response, the United States passed the Coinage Act, moving the country entirely onto the gold standard. Silver prices fell by half as a result, and what became known as the Long Depression began. Overspeculation in agriculture and other commodities had caused prices to soar after the Civil War, and between 1872 and 1877 the price of cotton fell by 50 percent. Times were tight in New York as well as in Oakland, where one resident wrote: "I hear and read everywhere of the bad times.

Notwithstanding the low prices of everything, nobody seems the richer. . . . The only people who seem to be rich here are those who cheat or steal in some way. Of course they don't call it by such names, but that is the truth."[19]

The Parmelees lost a substantial sum on cotton, but the plight of the Morgans was much worse, since Charles had been unable to succeed even during the previous boom years. North explained: "He [Charles] was in airplanes, balloons, nails, farm machinery, sugar—most anything that didn't work, he was in."[20] Retrenchment was imperative. In the fall of 1878, Eliza and the children moved into her parents' home in Brooklyn Heights, while Charles attempted to rent out their house in Oakland and find work. The large number of letters that Eliza sent Charles at this time are very revealing; she is the powerful one in the family, and he is submissive to her demands. Eliza had the additional challenge of taking care of four young children (Parmelee was eight; Julia was six and was nicknamed "Dudu," based on Parmelee's failed attempts to pronounce "Julia"; Emma was four; and Avery was two). In addition, Eliza was caring for her ailing mother, whose poor health had been another reason for their visit. This was difficult enough, but Eliza also had another concern. She was ashamed of how badly she and Charles were doing financially, and desperate to conceal this fact from her parents.

Julia kept these letters all her life, and they provide a fascinating portrait of her family during an exceptionally stressful time.

Eliza wrote to Charles late in October 1878: "I kept Dudu [Julia] here—as Parm is carrying on high at Julia's [Eliza's sister]; he insisted on Cake every day for dinner—said he <u>always</u> had it at home and such like actions as declining to accompany Julia to N.Y. Father was up last night—he offered me some money—as he paid my board but I declined, and said <u>you</u> would send me some money next month—he kindly offered to write you not to send it— which I also declined."[21] Charles had gone to Chicago to try to sell his stock in a silver mine, but had returned home empty-handed. Eliza responded: "I know you must be very lonely and I wish I was with you—I am very sorry for you—but you know I did not willingly leave you, that I love you dearly and if it's God's will we will all meet again and it will not be very long to wait—so keep a brave spirit, go out all you can and try to be cheerful and don't nurse your wrongs." Charles was able to find a tenant for their home, which pleased Eliza: "I'm glad the house is rented and agree with your reasoning—there is little damage can be done—and we are not paying anything out for it—What money you send next month I will make do—I am glad you have a room that suits you." Unfortunately, even this plan went awry: The tenant paid less rent than Charles had expected, and left after only a month.[22]

Julia and Parmelee enjoyed several New York excursions with family and friends, including trips to the circus and rides on the ferry, but Emma soon fell ill, to Eliza's concern: "I've no confidence in [Dr.] Johnson and

were I in funds should not have him." As the weather worsened, Eliza grew impatient with Charles: "I trust you are well—We all send you our love—Father is well and very kind— he always wants to know how you are—What is the number of your boarding house—and the name—do you continue to like it—If I can I'll write more Sunday—I know I neglect you—but you can survive it."[23]

Eliza reported on the children's daily activities when she could, but she was preoccupied by money shortages. She could afford to send Parmelee to school, but not Julia. At age six, Julia was occasionally clumsy at home, perhaps due to poor vision: "Dudu fell down the upper flight of stairs this morning— Mother's nurse picked her up and laid her by her Grandma on the bed—but on examination no injuries of a serious nature were discovered, she strained her arm and bruised her hip but not worse than at home, she has fell [sic] short distances twice since—and the way she useses [sic] her legs is simply bewildering."

Eliza was frustrated to learn that their new tenant had left, and they weren't going to be receiving his rent. She issued crisp instructions—both business and personal—to Charles:

"I am <u>real</u> sorry about the house. Why did He leave it?—If that man that has it now don't keep it until April—perhaps it may be for the best—you could store the furniture—<u>mind</u> you don't sell it—for it's mine. Does the Ranletts new house [their nearby neighbors] spoil ours?—I am sorry you are feeling blue but cheer up and be a man—you ought to be above such weakness. I observe by the papers that Scorpion [another of Charles's mining investments] is to be 2½ shares for one—what's the assessment? Turn an honest penny and be a good Boy and we will all send you lots of love."[24]

When Charles (whose letters to Eliza don't survive) expressed doubt or disappointment, she rebuked him:

"Yesterday I received your letter telling me, you were back in your room again and the house given over to that Mr Van Lassell. It was a very pleasing letter and I was much releaved [sic] that you'd written me a rational letter. The last two that I received befor [sic] were so weak and mawkish I did not intend acknowledging them at all. I do not like sentimental letters—you can write me decent letters if you will, and I'd like to remind you, that you are supposed to be a man—and I wish you would write like a sensible one. If your life and business does not suit you, it's no worse than it has been—and you ought to enjoy a rest from family cares and domestic duties. You should be thankful for your liberty to go and do as you please. Don't be a bad Boy and quarrel with your mercies."

Her tone was not shrewish, but authoritative, like a captain encouraging the troops. She concluded: "Write me a good letter you bad old Boy and don't . . . do any bad things—but keep well and do your duty and grow strong against the time when I return to be your Girl."[25]

As Christmas preparations began in early December, Julia fell seriously ill:

"When I wrote you last I considered all the children well. That night Dudu came to me sick and I took her into bed with Emma and I. Next day (yesterday) she complained of her throat and threw up all day—had a headache looked miserable and finally went to bed in my bed—with Emma and Avery. I thought it one of her usual bilious turns, at the worst mumps—This morning when I saw her—I sent for the Doctor and sent the children down stairs—Dr Johnson said at once it was Scarlet fever—you can imagine my feelings—I don't know wheare [sic] she got it—Johnson says it's all over Brooklyn—The others have probably all got it and will break out between now and eight days—I will as you know do my best and if they die it will not be for doing all I can. Parm cries and says he is afraid of it, and he don't want to have it—I'm very sorry but he is none too well now and I've no hopes of his escaping. I can't send him to Julia and there is nothing I can do now as he was with Dudu yesterday. Dudu is very sick and too good—I will write you how she is tomorrow morning when I mail this. It's almost twelve and I am going to lay down a while . . . You could do nothing if you were here—more than I—so don't harrow me with such wild talk. . . . Mother continues to improve and expects soon to be down stairs. In all events you remain wheare [sic] you are and turn that honest penny to take us back with."[26]

As December wore on, Julia's scarlet fever seemed to be healing, and Eliza quoted their doctor: "If she don't take cold and get heart desease [sic] or rhumatism [sic] or dropsy or Brights desease [sic] of kidneys or an abcess [sic] in her ear or some other horror—she will recover." Unfortunately, Julia contracted a severe ear infection, which may have been the cause of her chronic ear problems later in life. Eliza wrote: "[I] find Dudu in tears with earache and she cried all last night and all today—she cries and goes into an agony of protestations when I put the drops into her ear.... She cannot turn her head—her actions are very fierce. Yesterday when Doctor wanted to look in her ear—she slapped at me like a cat and would not let me get near her to take off the dressings for the Dr. She yelled and screamed, pushed—and slapped at him," which was such unusual behavior for Julia that she must have been in terrible pain.[27]

New York was bitingly cold that winter, and Eliza struggled to keep the children warm inside the large house. She also tried to keep them separated to avoid contagion, and spent a considerable amount of her time scrubbing the floors and walls with carbolic acid. In spite of her efforts, Eliza's sister Julia's very young daughter, Jeanie, caught scarlet fever as well. Eliza wrote worriedly to Charles: "All last night Jeanie was very sick—I went around there today and sat with

her while Julia got her dinner—and she is a very sick child. I think it is scarlet fever.... I've warned Julia not to come here—so has Dr. Johnson but she will come—there is so much Scarlet fever now that Jeanie may have got it in the Street. Dudu had it very bad, and I am very thankful she is doing so well. She is looking very pretty—prettier than I've ever seen her look."[28] As Eliza had feared, Jeanie didn't survive. Four days after her previous letter, Eliza wrote to Charles: "The new year has open [sic] most awfully—Last night Julia's little Jeanie died—it was the most terribly fiendishly wild windy night I ever passed in Cal—or hear [sic]—The cold below zero and the highest wind blowing the sleet about—It was a heartrending night for the poor dear little soul to go out in—it's seem'd [sic] and seems all so cruel."[29]

Their worst nightmare had been realized; one child had died, and Eliza was frightened for the others. Two-year-old Avery screamed and cried for her, but Eliza refused to take him from the nurse, fearing she would expose him. She wrote Charles later that day: "I never have felt so low personally. I fear I have diphtheria—I don't say so—but my throat is bad. I'm fighting it with—Quinine—whiskey and potas[h]—but I feel very bad.... If I never see you again come get the children and marry some good kind of wife that will not be too young."[30]

Scarlet fever was killing adults and children alike that winter. Just as Julia started to recover, Avery and Emma both came down with it. Eliza wrote: "I don't know when I can go back [home]. There is much I think I cannot or had better not say—Emma sends her love and two kisses. Dudu sends hers and five kisses. Emma is very hard to take care of she yells and behaves so—but it's hard for her to stay in bed so long—<u>You</u> have no idea what a pest Scarlet fever is—I am sorry 'Scorpion' has turned so bad but suppose you'll not thank me for making any comments."[31]

Charles had been unable to find steady work, and though it seemed unlikely things could get worse, they did:

"Julia [Eliza's sister] wrote to you last week and I suppose told you how I'd clapped the climax of the foolish and disasterous [sic] actions of this year by setting fire to Father's house—Mother and I saved the house—my first though[t] was to put it out and I did not stop to choose what with, consequently my hands were burnt badly, the left one almost half off and the agony was unbarable [sic] that night—I'll tell you about it when I see you and you can bet I'll never put out a fire with my hands or clothes again.... I've no use of my left hand and it will be a long time befor [sic] I can have—the pain is terrible. I walk the floor all the time.... The Insurance Man gave Mother fifty dollars for the damage to the carpets and the blankets we burnt and fifteen dollars for my dress. Father will pay Dr. Johnson's bill."[32]

After nine months of separation, Eliza and all four children returned to Oakland in June 1879. Charles found a job managing a tool manufactory, and Albert may have subsidized their journey west. The Morgan family finances apparently remained precarious, however, as they continued to rent a home rather than build one for the next few years.

Eliza's correspondence during that grim winter of 1879 remains the only collection of family letters that has survived from Julia's youth. The Morgans were a close and loving group, with all the children living at home long into adulthood. The letters they each sent to Julia in Paris, twenty years later, also reveal their defining character traits: Charles was ineffectual, Eliza was strong, Parmelee was detached, Julia was determined, Emma was complacent, Avery was mercurial, and Sam—who was born in 1880—was carefree.

Charles described himself as "a capitalist," but his investments invariably failed. Among the schemes that went awry: buying shares of a worthless gold mine in Shasta City; staging an unsuccessful bid for the position of Oakland's city treasurer; running a luxury inn and resort in Mount Shasta; and launching a campaign to sell what turned out to be defective voting machines.[33] Julia's nephew North remembered Charles as a small, dapper man who was loud and bombastic—a backslapper and a salesman. But in private, Charles's feigned confidence evaporated. He wrote to Julia: "How I wish that my life had been more successful and that I might contribute to the happiness of my children. This is a subject which I cannot dwell upon."[34] Eliza had no illusions about Charles, writing Julia: "I have no hopes of his making anything out of that Shasta property, but he has—so that keeps him cheerful." She had considerable energy

Julia's older brother Parmelee's business attempts as a cotton broker were, like his father's, unsuccessful.

Julia was closest with her younger brother Avery— who, like her, was musical and studied architecture.

and did a fair amount of the housekeeping herself: "Saturday I swept and cleaned house and bought food—went to San Francisco on a hurried trip and got home late and had to hurry to get the dinner ready as Delia only does the kitchen part."[35] Delia was the live-in servant who cooked their meals, all of which everyone customarily ate together. Eliza was apparently not a fan of Delia's baking: "Delia is good—makes bread and biscuits—like lead, as treats for us."[36]

Parmelee was pleasant but remote, and like his father, an unsuccessful businessman. Charles helped his eldest son begin work as a cotton broker, an endeavor that quickly failed. Parmelee seems to have been somewhat socially awkward, and was certainly not a polished dresser, as Eliza disclosed: "Parm

. . . has gone Golfing—in black stockings with checked black & white Tops and tan shoes—grey Golf trousers—darkish blue shirt—plaid nectie [*sic*]—grey coat and brownish cap . . . tan belt—the more he mixes the happier he seems."[37]

The most conventional sibling was Emma (whose family nickname was "Baby"). She was very interested in boys and in new clothes (which were handmade for them by Miss Hines, a local seamstress who came to the house).[38] Emma felt that Eliza worked unnecessarily hard: "I think Mama has if anything been better feeling this week—You know I believe there is little need of her feeling so poorly—that a little rest is what was needed. But you also know that she will not make anything easier for herself. There is no more to do than there has been right along . . . but she wears herself out bringing home the fruit because the carts spoil it—& the bread—so that [the delivery] box won't get too full—etc—& no one can do it but herself."[39]

Avery could be moody and sensitive. He and Julia were closest among the siblings, and she often felt protective of him. Eliza related one of the conversations she had with Avery while they were staying at a rustic mountain hotel: "Avery is in bed—he just called out to me—'What is sleep?—it cannot be brain rest—for I always dream, so what is sleep?' I had to call back, that I did not know—nor do I, do you?" Avery also struggled with health problems, which may have brought him closer to Julia: "I have just spent a week today with an old friend and companion of yours, Mr. Mumps."[40] (Mumps are caused by an infection in the parotid gland, a salivary gland located below and in front of the ears. Julia's most serious health problems in adulthood derived from an infected mastoid process, the bones that connect the outer ear and the inner ear.)

Sam was the youngest and the most easygoing. He loved sailing and fishing, and volunteered for the fire department for years until he was old enough to be hired as a fireman. He also loved socializing. Eliza reported that Sam went to a "Senior Party (High school) with a girl friend who was on the Reception Committee Friday night—and danced 26 dances—with 26 different girls—was not that a record breaker?"[41]

Julia was always driven to excel. One of her earliest teachers at Oakland's Lafayette Grammar School described her sweet expression as "a gentle eight-year-old child, when the school prizes fell into your tiny hands."[42] Julia's independent, energetic spirit found a similar match in her childhood friend Mary Olney McLean, who lived in the neighborhood and reminisced many years later:

"We always walked the fences, and there were all kinds. Some were quite difficult to walk on; others were nicely planned for small girls. We always went along on the tops of the pickets. . . . There were a great many vacant lots, [some with] favorite oak trees that we children enjoyed climbing. . . . One of the things we little girls liked to do was to go over to Broadway and look in the windows. Some of the windows, like the harness shop, didn't interest us very much, but there were several other windows from which we 'chose' things that we'd like to have, especially in a certain small silver and jewelry store. . . . Then we'd come to a bookstore, and there'd be books opened to colored pictures. . . . Then of course the candy store—we used to look at the different kinds of candies and choose what we'd have. The funny part was that out on the edges of the sidewalks were racks for newspapers. . . . [and] a perfectly fascinating magazine called 'Police Gazette,' and it was illustrated by very lurid pictures—ladies and gentlemen who were getting themselves into trouble, one way or another, murdering each other and various things. We would squat down in front of these racks . . . and we learned a great deal."

This was a subject they never discussed at home.[43]

Like Brooklyn Heights, Oakland was filled with beautiful Victorian houses and imposing Gothic churches. The Morgans attended the First Baptist Church across the street. Eliza reported: "Our trees are so large and heavy you can just see the top part of the Baptist spire, but the Weather Vane is unobstructed, which is a comfort to me. I take great stock in its indications. It's very sensitive."[44] Their neighborhood Congregational church may have helped spark Julia's fascination with Chinese culture. Each week it conducted a special Sunday school for the many Chinese residents who lived downtown. Mary recalled the sight of dozens of Chinese men walking through their neighborhood in single file: "They had queues with tassels which dangled down their backs as they walked, and [wore] Chinese shoes with the thick padded soles and the loose pants and coat."[45]

Julia was an active member of the Baptist church, and was particularly fond of its stained-glass windows and its tradition of hymn singing. She taught Sunday school and proudly wore a white ribbon, meaning she had taken its Prohibition pledge (to which she adhered all her life). Julia apparently knew the Bible well. Her personal copy of the New Testament contains a verse from 1 John 3:18, written in Julia's hand: "Let us not love in word, neither in tongue, but in deed and in truth." Beneath a drawing in one of her sketchbooks, she jotted a phrase used by the nineteenth-century British author and architect G. E. Street: "The old paths, where is the good way," which comes from a fragment of Jeremiah 6:16: "Thus saith the Lord, stand ye in the ways, and see, and ask for the old paths, where is the good way and walk therein, and ye shall find rest for your souls."[46]

The Morgan household changed after 1880—Julia's eighth year—when her grandfather Albert Parmelee died of a stroke. Eliza's mother, Sarah, left Brooklyn Heights and moved in with them. Sarah may have paid for the Morgans' largest and most luxurious residence, constructed in 1885 at 754 Fourteenth Street. Julia lived in this house half her life, and its detailed ornament, outsize comfort, and dramatic design likely influenced her aesthetic vision. The Morgan home was at the vanguard of the era's fashion, combining two Victorian styles: Eastlake-Stick (named

REDWOOD FIREPLACE IN THE LIVING-ROOM OF C. B. MORGAN'S HOUSE.

The Morgans' living room was praised in this 1892 article— particularly the redwood arch framing their fireplace, flanked by inglenook seating (paired side benches).

In 1885, when Julia was thirteen, the Morgans built their large Victorian house at 754 Fourteenth Street in Oakland, where Julia lived for more than forty years.

for nineteenth-century British architect Charles Locke Eastlake, this style featured stickwork trim around the windows and doors) and Queen Anne (which was more ornate, favoring round towers, multiple gables, and steeply sloping rooflines). The Morgan house was also equipped with the latest technology: gas lighting and indoor plumbing.

Its entrance, located on the house's narrow front, consisted of six stone steps that led to a gabled porch ornamented with turned spindles. The front door opened into a hall that featured an imposing staircase with a large landing (leading to bedrooms on both the second story and the half-story that made

up the third floor). Downstairs were two living rooms—the sitting room at the front and the parlor at the back—which could be joined together by opening the sliding doors. The sitting room was the glory of the house, lovely enough to be illustrated years later in the *San Francisco Examiner* under the headline, "Fine Rooms in Big Houses: Artistic Decoration and Equipment of Oakland Homes."[47] Its chief attraction was the mantelpiece, spanned by a dramatic redwood archway that framed an inglenook (a pair of comfortable recessed benches running along each side of the fireplace). Heavy velvet curtains bordered the hearth, which was decorated with glazed ceramic tiles in dark diamond patterns. Atop the mantel were a case clock and various objets d'art, including a reproduction of the ancient Greek bust known as *Psyche of Capua*. Bookcases lined the walls, and a library table—equipped with lower shelves for books—stood in the center of the room, illuminated by a large gaslit chandelier.[48]

When Julia graduated from high school in 1890, she contemplated a career in either medicine or music, but ultimately decided to study architecture. One influential factor was the advice she received from her cousin Lucy Latimer's husband, Pierre LeBrun, a successful New York City architect whom she met on her East Coast visits. Pierre's father and brother were also architects. The LeBrun firm's best-known building was New York's Metropolitan Life Insurance Company Tower on Madison Avenue. Julia remained very close to Lucy and Pierre during her years studying architecture in Paris, confiding to them: "... some times [I] have played that I opened the door when the bell rang, and there you were.... I have much to thank you for ... and I do."[49]

Julia may have had another reason for deciding to become an architect. During the decade when Sarah lived with them, Julia heard her grandmother's stories about growing up at Woodland Hall. Built in Kent County, Maryland, in 1782, it was a large Italianate house, three stories high, originally called "The Mansion." Sarah's father, James Woodland (Julia's great-grandfather), purchased it early in the nineteenth century, adding ornate wings to double its size and renaming it Woodland Hall. It still survives and is largely unchanged, retaining its beautiful cast-iron fireplaces. Some are ornamented with *verre églomisé* (decorative glass panels, backed with gold and silver leaf, then etched from behind so the delicate patterns are highlighted by the metal foils).[50]

Neither Eliza nor Julia and her siblings ever stayed at Woodland Hall, however, due to a family disagreement from which Sarah never recovered. In March 1835, on the eve of Sarah's twelfth birthday, her mother, Elizabeth Wright Woodland, died at the age of thirty-five. A year later, Sarah's father, James, remarried—and Sarah's stepmother managed to force the sale of Woodland Hall to another branch of the family. Sarah never forgave her, and never saw the estate again.

During Julia's last year of high school, Sarah wrote sadly to another group of descendants who then owned Woodland Hall. She enclosed money for the maintenance of her family's graves, and more than fifty years later, she still seethed:

"Dear Cousin—I asked you all those questions about the church and graveyard because I want so much to know. My Mother's father, Major Edward Wright, and his three wives and a little boy, Benjamine [*sic*], are all buried there. [Also] my mother, 55 years ago [next] March, my father several years after, also a little girl when I was small, all [buried] on the left of the center walk; but thank heaven, not the wicked stepmother, her bones are not under sacred grounds. We are told to forgive, but memory clings to us. . . . Don't ever leave your lovely home for a new one."[51]

On another occasion Sarah wrote more cheerfully:

"[On] the thirteenth of January I'll be 73 [*sic*, 68] years old, my grandchildren will not believe me. Avery says I look young, all say my face is full and does not change. I have an abundance of hair and no false teeth; my memory as good as ever, also sight and hearing; but I am never idle, I read a good deal, do plain and fancy work. You asked about my grandchildren. . . . Mrs. Morgan has 5, 3 boys & 2 girls, smart, bright children & good-looking; the eldest [Parmelee] is 19; Julia, the eldest girl, draws & paints beautifully, she is a fine scholar, she speaks German well, three of them do, and are fine performers on the violin (Julia and Avery).

Emma plays the piano. They have the best of teachers. Gardner [Sam, at] 7 years old, is the youngest, is very bright & smart. . . . I should like you to see them."[52]

Sarah died in 1891 soon after writing this letter, never having had the opportunity to revisit her family's gravesite. Julia may have seen Woodland Hall in her later years—she was near Maryland's Kent County on several occasions—but if so, no record of it exists. Yet Julia carefully preserved Sarah's framed photograph of Woodland Hall all her life. Perhaps the loss of this great estate influenced her decision to devote herself to architecture. Throughout her career, Julia built many opulent and imposing residences for other families to treasure.

Julia treasured this photograph of Woodland Hall in Kings County, Maryland, which was her grandmother's childhood home until its ownership was transferred in a family dispute.

CHAPTER THREE

SETTING A COURSE

ONCE JULIA DECIDED TO BECOME AN ARCHITECT, she never wavered from her goal. Berkeley's University of California didn't have an architecture department when she entered as a freshman in 1890, so she became one of its first female civil-engineering majors. Though this may have seemed an unpromising start, in fact Julia's timing was fortuitous. She attended the university when it was on the threshold of expansion—and the two people most responsible for this growth became two of her closest friends and long-standing mentors: Bernard Maybeck and Phoebe Apperson Hearst.

The university was founded in 1855 as a small private college intended to continue the programs of the exclusive Oakland Academy. After initially considering a site in Berkeley, its trustees rejected the location due to fears of insufficient water, deciding instead to build on several acres of what later became downtown Oakland. The enterprise continually lost money, in part because of the Civil War. In 1868, ownership was transferred to the state of California, which was mandated to establish a public university in its northern region. The campus was relocated to the previously rejected 140 acres in North Berkeley, once the trustees were convinced of its adequate water supply.[1] Four main buildings were constructed around a large open quadrangle, one of which—the Second Empire–style South Hall—survives. The university admitted its first female students in 1870. By 1880, women made up one-quarter of the student body, but few resources were available to them outside the classroom. Among thirteen non-fraternity clubs on campus, only four were open to coeds: two literary societies and two women's glee clubs.[2]

Julia studied Civil Engineering at Berkeley's University of California from 1890 to 1894, when the campus consisted of only a few buildings.

Author Elinor Richey, who was a friend of the Norths, drew on family lore to describe Julia at this time:

"[She] commuted to classes in a neat coat suit and ribboned sailor hat via a horse-drawn streetcar, accompanied at her parents' insistence by her brother Parmelee. Male students were still trying to discourage females from invading what they considered *their* precinct . . . [but] the taunts of the black-suited and hatted collegians [did not] disturb her businesslike demeanor. . . . Taking her seat, the lone female, in the sacrosanct engineering lecture hall, she directed herself to studying such problems as analyzing building materials and structural stresses. One of her paper topics was 'A Structural Analysis of the Steel Frame of the Mills Building in San Francisco.'"[3]

Julia worked extraordinarily hard, often remaining at home while other family members went on vacation. This concerned Eliza, who wrote her during one such trip: "I hope you are not working yourself sick, and that Sam & Pa are well."[4]

To Eliza's satisfaction, Julia became a charter member of Kappa Alpha Theta, the university's first sorority (or "women's fraternity," as it was then called). When the Thetas rented a house near campus the following year, Julia moved in, as did newly pledged Emma, who had entered the university one year after Julia. Being close to the Berkeley campus not only saved the girls time, but also freed Parmelee from escort duty. Young women required chaperones as well as proper introductions to any male, as Eliza explained while accompanying Emma and a group of her friends on their Santa Cruz camping trip. She wrote Julia: "I've ordered Emma to bed at her [sorority] sisters' request—she having spoken to a person she'd not been introduced to, that person a young man, as old as Sam—[fifteen]—he passed with a fishing rod and she asked if he was going fishing?—Instead of minding, she has gone out." Eliza's letters to Julia increasingly became a compendium of news about various sorority sisters, who seemed to regard Eliza as their friend and confidante: "I was asked if your Fraternity had a Matron yet—as Mrs. Randolph was very anxious to get it... I said your Fraternity had a Matron but mentioned no name—as I know Mrs. Randolph would not suit your girls ... [At] your age [the] girls would resent the espionage."[5] Julia was president of the KATs (as they called themselves) during her senior year and maintained warm friendships with many members (some of whom became her future clients). The Thetas' high social status was discussed in the campus newspaper: "Of the three girl fraternities, the Kappa Alpha Theta is the oldest and has the best standing and the most members.... It prides itself on being 'nice,' ... nice in a quite particular and peculiar sense. All the members are pretty, flower-like girls, daintily dressed and coming from old, conservative intellectual families. They are recognized instantaneously. 'Ah, that is a Kappa Alpha Theta, in the blue shirtwaist with the golden hair and the graceful bearing.'"[6]

Julia graduated in May of 1894 with a bachelor of science in civil engineering. Three female students had previously completed the program, but none ever practiced professionally.[7] Her longtime engineer and colleague Walter Steilberg recalled: "Miss Morgan's training in engineering ... was pretty elementary. It was given by Colonel Soulé, a retired army colonel. It belonged to another century, really."[8] Julia still had much to learn after graduation, and this process began with her introduction to the visionary architect Bernard Maybeck.

Today Maybeck is renowned for his woodsy Bay Area houses—circa 1895 to 1930—now identified as seminal examples of the First Bay Tradition. His design philosophy was actually shaped by an earlier ideology: the academic classicism he studied in the 1880s at the École des Beaux-Arts in Paris. Born in New York's Greenwich Village in 1862, Bernard Maybeck (known as Ben) was

Julia joined the Kappa Alpha Theta sorority in 1891. She is in the front row, far right; her younger sister Emma is in the fourth row, far left.

sent to Paris at age nineteen to apprentice with the exclusive furniture company Pottier & Stymus. Imaginative and unconventional, Ben had an unwelcome habit of redesigning their furniture instead of constructing it. One day, as he stood in their Left Bank workshop, Ben noticed several well-dressed young men wearing capes and tall hats. They were students from the nearby École des Beaux-Arts, pushing their overloaded drawing carts into the school's gated courtyard. For Ben, it was a life-changing moment: He decided to apply for admission.

This world-renowned school of fine arts was founded in the mid-seventeenth century as a training center that supplied Louis XIV

The Sculpture Court of the École des Beaux-Arts in Paris, the school of fine arts founded in 1648 to supply Louis XIV with trained artists and architects.

with talented artists and architects. It soon evolved into two separate divisions—painting and sculpture was one, and architecture the other. Students did not receive grades; instead they entered design competitions. A typical assignment might be to delineate a war memorial, within a specific time limit. The winners of these contests earned points, which they needed to advance through the program.

Yet even these considerable challenges paled in comparison with the notorious entrance examinations students had to pass first. Most applicants prepared by joining an independent atelier—a professional studio where an experienced architect served as *patron* and advisor. There they could practice assignments and hone their skills before taking the test. Ben was a rarity, having scored high enough on his first attempt to enter the École in 1882.

Like all students, he also joined an atelier. Ben's *patron* was the celebrated Louis-Jules André, designer of the Museum of Natural History in Paris. Ben's fellow students—numbering sixty in all—derided him as a country bumpkin and made him stand in front of the atelier and sing nonsensical songs. (Though this part of the story went unmentioned, Ben was likely forced to perform in the nude, since public humiliation via disrobing was a vital part of these initiation rites.)[9] He faced this hazing with equanimity, and studied at the École for nearly five years, leaving in 1886 without a *diplôme* (since foreign students were not allowed to earn diplomas until 1887).

Ben nevertheless fully absorbed the École's central architectural principles. Most important was the requirement that each design must be defined by its plan, and all related drawings must derive from this plan. Every project should also be carefully organized around a primary location, known as the central axis (for instance, the long nave of a cathedral). There should also be a secondary axis (in a cathedral, this would be the perpendicular wing known as the crossing). Students should look to the past for their architectural inspiration, but they should conversely solve any logistical problems by using modern yet unobtrusive methods. And every project—in its layout as well as in its decoration—must exhibit *caractère* (the visual appearance of a building, which unites its purpose and its design).[10]

After leaving Paris, Ben worked briefly for the influential New York firm Carrère and Hastings. In 1888, he moved to Kansas City, Missouri, hoping to establish his own office. Though he failed to generate enough commissions to maintain the business, his time there was not wasted, since Ben met Annie White, whom he married in 1890. The young couple headed to San Francisco, where Ben had been promised a job by architect A. Page Brown. The Maybecks lived in a small house in Berkeley while Ben commuted to San Francisco on the ferry, joining Brown and several others (including architect A. C. Schweinfurth and artists William Keith and Bruce Porter) in designing the small but highly influential Church of the New

Bernard Maybeck studied architecture at the École in the 1880s. He met Julia in 1895 and immediately recognized her talent.

Jerusalem. (Also known as the Swedenborgian Church, this rustic masterpiece in Pacific Heights is now considered the first Arts and Crafts–style building in California.)[11]

Always easygoing and personable, Ben soon became friends with Professor Frank Soulé on their daily ferry ride. Soulé informed him that the university was seeking an instructor of descriptive geometry for its newly established Department of Instrumental Drawing. Maybeck started teaching at the Berkeley campus in 1894, and was soon involved with another university project, becoming director of the Architectural Section at the recently founded Mark Hopkins Institute of Fine Art (located on the current site of San Francisco's Mark Hopkins Hotel on Nob Hill). This is likely where he met the newly graduated Julia, who was taking painting and sculpting classes with Emma and Avery at the time. Their instructor was the influential Arts and Crafts painter and furniture designer Arthur F. Mathews. (Described as a man of "untiring industry, undeniable ability, sound judgment, and advanced ideas," Mathews maintained the controversial practice of hiring nude models to pose for his life-modeling class. In this, he was replicating the teaching methods of the École des Beaux-Arts and many ancillary art academies throughout Paris.)[12] Not long after Ben began teaching at the Mark Hopkins Institute, he established an advanced design class—structured like an atelier—which met in his home. He invited Julia to join, since even among his best students, her superior talent was unmistakable.[13] These additional studies with Maybeck gave Julia valuable hands-on experience. Under his supervision, she helped design a house in the Berkeley hills for university professor Andrew Lawson, and assisted with the remodeling of the Maybecks' own house, which her brothers Avery and Sam helped them build.[14]

Both a passionate innovator and a dedicated teacher, Maybeck could be powerfully persuasive, as evidenced by his influence on Phoebe Apperson Hearst, California's leading philanthropist. Born in the Ozark mountains in 1842, Phoebe was the eldest child of Randolph and Elizabeth Apperson, small

Phoebe Apperson Hearst, born in Missouri in 1842, married the wealthy miner George Hearst in 1862. They departed for California, where W. R. was born in 1863.

landowners in Franklin County, Missouri. Phoebe later described her birthplace as "a miserable country."[15] With social aspirations that transcended her uncultured surroundings, Phoebe taught herself to speak French and became a schoolteacher at age nineteen. When she met forty-two-year-old George Hearst, who had just returned to Missouri after a ten-year absence, she immediately recognized the benefits of marrying this wealthy local landowner and successful miner. In 1860, after a decade of fruitless prospecting, George had finally made his fortune by purchasing part of Nevada's Comstock Lode, the richest vein of silver in North America.[16]

Phoebe ignored George's rough demeanor and disheveled wardrobe, realizing that he was a man of intelligence and humor, with great business acumen. They married in 1862, then sailed through the Isthmus of Panama into San Francisco, where their only child, William Randolph Hearst, was born on April 29, 1863. Though Phoebe hoped for a close relationship with George, it didn't take long for her to discover that he would be away more than he was home, investing in mining properties that eventually included the Homestake gold mine in Lead, South Dakota, and the Anaconda copper mine in Butte, Montana. Phoebe therefore devoted her considerable energies to raising William, whom she took to Europe for eighteen months when he was ten (a trip that inaugurated W. R.'s love of collecting art). On their return, he attended the elite St. Paul's School in New Hampshire, then entered Harvard in 1881 (where W. R. first became enraptured with newspapers). George Hearst was appointed U.S. Senator from California in 1886, then was elected to the post in 1887, by which time Phoebe was socially sophisticated enough to oversee the construction of their lavish mansion in Washington, D.C., and commence her role as one of the capital's leading hostesses.

When George died in 1891 at age seventy, Phoebe inherited his entire $20 million fortune (equivalent to $540 million today). It was hers for life—George having directed her to share portions of it with W. R., at her discretion—provided that she did not remarry. Phoebe knew that education had helped her escape from the Ozarks, and she wanted to offer similar opportunities to others (long before tax deductions incentivized philanthropy). In 1895—the year Julia and Maybeck met—Phoebe approached the University of California's president, Martin Kellogg, saying she wanted to endow five women's scholarships. Her next suggestion was more ambitious: She also wanted to fund a campus building dedicated to the study of mining, as a memorial to her husband.[17]

They needed an architect to discuss the building plans with Mrs. Hearst, so President Kellogg summoned Maybeck (the only architect on campus). Ben's five years at the École had taught him how to effectively present a competition drawing. He made a quick sketch, then hastily arranged some draperies and potted geraniums to form a backdrop. Thus equipped, he greeted Phoebe Apperson Hearst for the first time. It was an auspicious meeting. Phoebe was wealthy and influential but not particularly impressed by conventionality—therefore Ben's unusual wardrobe didn't faze her (his clothes were handmade and his appearance decidedly "arty").[18] She was, however, captivated by his vibrant enthusiasm.

When they discussed where to locate the mining building, Ben saw his opportunity. Having learned at the École that the plan was the most important thing, he convinced Phoebe that in order to beneficially site her new building, they would first need to draft a plan for the entire campus. Maybeck's initial sketch had been quite modest, but he

Maybeck encouraged Julia to move to Paris and apply to the École's architecture program, even though female students were barred from admission.

argued for something larger, explaining: "The University is a city that is to be created—a City of Learning." Ben maintained that its architect should create a plan that would be useful for "centuries to come." His farsighted approach worked. On October 24, 1896, Phoebe wrote to President Kellogg: "I am deeply impressed with the proposition now before the University's Board of Regents, to determine upon a comprehensive and permanent plan for the buildings and grounds of the University of California." She offered to pay the expenses for a worldwide competition and award the prize money to the winner— on the condition that Maybeck be given a two-year leave of absence from teaching in order to prepare and publicize the contest. Her stipulation was granted, thus launching the first international architecture competition in recorded history.[19]

This event may have greatly influenced Julia's decision to apply to the École des Beaux-Arts. If European architects were going to compete to design a building for the University of California, perhaps a California coed could compete for admission to Europe's finest school of architecture. It would take substantial courage to even try. If Julia gained admission to its architecture division, she would be the first woman to do so since the École was established in 1648. Maybeck had observed her closely in his home atelier, and as an École alumnus, he was uniquely qualified to assure her that she had the talent to succeed. His involvement in the university competition would bring him to France, where he could lobby the École on Julia's behalf. Maybeck had remained in touch with the school's faculty, which may be why he requested that Julien Guadet—a Beaux-Arts professor who had designed the ornate Grand Palais exhibition hall in Paris— assist him with writing the competition's international program. Perhaps Guadet had told Ben the rumor that after more than forty years of campaigning by a determined group of women artists, the École seemed likely to accept female painters and sculptors for the first time. (No one considered the possibility that a female architecture student would even think of applying.)[20] Though the specific reasons for Julia's decision are unknown, her dream was to study architecture at the École des Beaux-Arts, and Maybeck was very good at convincing people to pursue their dreams.

Julia initially planned to travel to Paris in 1895 with Arthur Brown Jr., a longtime friend from Oakland High School, and his parents. It would have been an ideal situation, but Mrs. Brown became ill—depriving Julia of her chaperone—and though Arthur left for Paris to prepare for the École's entrance examinations, Julia had to postpone her trip.[21] She therefore continued to work with Maybeck, from whom she received a valuable introduction to an emerging architectural style. His home and the Lawson house (on which Julia had assisted) were two of the earliest residences constructed in the First Bay Tradition. These picturesque but humble cottages were perfectly suited to Berkeley's steeply sloping hillsides (precipitous sites that Maybeck colorfully referred to as "goat lots.")[22]

By the summer of 1896, Julia had found another traveling companion, Jessica Peixotto, who was leaving for Paris to study social science at the Sorbonne. The elder sister of celebrated Bay Area artist Ernest Peixotto, Jessica was several years Julia's senior, but they had both been in the same graduating class at the university. Jessica was a recognized leader, according to the press: "She was a moving spirit in the class of '94. It was she who originated the idea of presenting the customary spectacle [class play] underneath the open sky.... a modern form of the Druidical ceremonies of the ancient Teutons."[23] Only one letter survives from the girls' cross-country rail journey. Written hurriedly by Julia while in transit, and mailed from the train station

Julia's mother Eliza, at fifty-five, sits in the family's back parlor in 1898, surrounded by books, flowers, and objets d'art.

in Reno, Nevada, it reveals her excitement and her concern about not spending too much of her parents' money: "The [rail] cars were very, very hot and [we] were cooking last night with only one thickness of blanket.... The dining car is fearfully dear, but Jessie and I are going to half [*sic*] it. We get on very well. My wrapper [a traveling dress; likely a going-away gift] is 10X prettier than hers.... When I get to terra firma I will write better, also spell." In conclusion, Julia made a vow she largely stuck to for the next six years: "I am never going to write anything about homesickness. With love to every one of you, Dudu."[24]

A photograph of Eliza at home, taken around this time, shows the comfortable surroundings Julia had left behind. Needlework in hand, fifty-five-year-old Eliza sits in the back parlor facing a sunny window that looks out onto Brush Street. The photographer (who may well have been Avery, since he purchased a Brownie camera in 1897) stands in the sitting room with his back to the fireplace. In the foreground, a large jardiniere holding a plant rests on a late-nineteenth-century Aesthetic Movement bamboo stand. Nearby sits a carriage clock as well as other art objects, including a miniature copy of the famous ancient Roman sculpture of Diana (the original of which was displayed by Louis XIV at Versailles). A long bookcase equipped with a drop-front desk fills one wall. Vases of flowers and family photographs decorate the room in such profusion that they are even displayed on the floor. Tasseled portieres frame sliding doors that open into the back parlor, where a mirrored chest of drawers is artfully draped with an American flag. On the wall hangs a print of Heinrich Hofmann's famous 1890 painting, *Christ in Gethsemane*. Photographs of interiors were rare at the time. This one reveals that Julia's home featured both creature comforts and beautiful objects, which may help explain why her later designs so often united these two elements.[25]

Julia and Jessica first toured Boston, then paid a happy visit to Pierre and Lucy LeBrun in New York. There they were joined by Nina Thornton, Julia's nineteen-year-old cousin, who accompanied them to Paris, where she spent four months studying art. Though no letters survive from Julia's first transatlantic passage, several guidebooks from the era describe the experience. As soon as their steamship hit the high seas, passengers were advised to reserve a reclining chair on deck from the purser for a $1.00 fee. Between

Julia and her traveling companions stopped in Rouen on their way to Paris and admired the city's fifteenth-century cathedral, with its 440-foot-tall central spire.

meals, the ship's luxurious dining room was turned into a parlor where passengers could write letters and read. (The smoking room was open only to the men.) After six days, passengers could glimpse the Isles of Scilly off the coast of England. The next day, their steamship was towed by tugboat into Le Havre.[26] Passengers then boarded a five-car train for the four-hour journey to Paris. The highlight of the trip was a stop in Rouen to see its immense Gothic cathedral, often the first one Americans encountered. Consecrated in 1063 by William the Conqueror, it represented the epitome of Old-World architecture. Between its two tall unmatched towers, a delicate central spire rises 440 feet into the air, dwarfing all American skyscrapers of that time.[27]

Julia's first hours in France were confusing as well as inspiring, and quite taxing on her limited French vocabulary, as she explained to Pierre and Lucy: "We went to Rouen after all—There was a dense fog when we woke the morning of getting into Havre, so they could not find the entrance and so missed the morning train for Paris. As I did not want to get [a] bus here alone at night, we decided to stop at Rouen." After they had seen the cathedral and several of the city's most prominent buildings, Julia wrote, "Mr. Bachelor [one of two gentlemen accompanying them, whom the girls had presumably met on the ship] got two most disreputable looking cab drivers and by dint of brain wracking Nina and I explained we had seen the churches etc. and wanted to see streets aged and picturesque.—And I should say we did. Through every little narrow, evil smelling alley way,—through streets packed with market women who had to move their wares off, with words, down the Rue Eau de Robec and all the little ones near it." Their intrusive caravan elicited plenty of hostile reactions from the natives, and provided the girls with many unwelcome glimpses of Rouen's seamiest sights. Julia continued:

"We could not find words to explain our objections and finally Mr. B. said I must say something, so I got out that we would fini-à Restaurant—Probably it being very

late and we tired made it seem worse than it was really was.—We drove back by the Bouv'ld Gambetta to the Grosse Horloge [the city's fourteenth-century astronomical clock], hence supper and a feather bed. The next cheerfulness was reaching the train to find it gone a half hour before—the landlord's fault—so we walked up the Bouv'd Beauvoisine to the hill overlooking the town—and it did seem very lovely from there—All the squalid dirtiness gone. . . . We did reach Paris at last. (Only losing a purse by the way—how no one can see unless taken—it was not serious)—Long before we came in, it seemed as though I could tell nearly all the principal things, thanks to . . . [perusing Pierre's books]. Indeed, as you said, the place does not make you feel a stranger."[28]

Julia's 1896 arrival in Paris was splendidly timed. The city was at its height of glamour and vibrancy, an era known as the Belle Epoque, which represented an astonishingly rapid rise from its nadir twenty-five years before. France had been defeated in 1870 when the Prussians captured Napoleon III and his troops, marking the end of his Second Empire. The victorious Prussians then surrounded Paris, first shelling the city, then holding its residents under siege for five desperate months. After the city's surrender in January 1871, internal dissensions sparked the battles of the Paris Commune, during which tens of thousands died and many buildings were torched, including the Tuileries Palace and the Hôtel de Ville. Over the next two decades the governance of the

Julia drew this sketch of the American Girls' Club at 4 rue de Chevreuse, the fifty-room dormitory where she lived during her first year in Paris.

Third Republic—though riven by political unrest—brought relative stability to Paris. In 1876, novelist Henry James praised the amazing elasticity of the Parisians: "Beaten and humiliated on a scale without precedent.... Paris is today in outward aspect as radiant, as prosperous ... as if her sky had never known a cloud."[29] The Exposition Universelle of 1889, with its triumphant Eiffel Tower, signaled the returning eminence of French technology and culture. When Julia arrived in 1896, more Americans were studying art in Paris than ever before. They congregated in the most bohemian part of town, the Left Bank, where they could live inexpensively while attending classes at the École des Beaux-Arts, the Sorbonne, or the city's many private art academies.

In order to ensure the safety of so many impressionable young female arrivals, in 1893 Elisabeth Mills—the wife of American ambassador Whitelaw Reid—purchased a rambling eighteenth-century chateau at 4 rue de Chevreuse, three blocks from the Luxembourg Gardens, and established the American Girls' Club. With four stories and forty to fifty small rooms, the club functioned as a genteel dormitory. Tea was served at 4:00 each afternoon, and curfew was at 10:00 each evening. Cultural activities were not neglected; the club had a 600-volume library, and its modest art exhibitions gave residents their first Parisian "showing." Julia lived there reasonably happily for a year, writing the LeBruns: "The service might be a trifle more dainty, the rooms have a more convenient assortment of furniture .... But to make up for little failing of these natures [*sic*], it's a perfectly safe and proper place, [and] the garden ... is large and very pleasant, when you get used to it."[30]

After moving rooms a few times, Julia was pleased with hers, as she explained to Beatrice Fox, one of her former sorority sisters:

"I like mine because it's quite large and has plenty of fresh air, but it's not elegant in its furnishings. The narrow dark halls have most mysterious and unexpected steps. You get to know where they come and do it mechanically—but at first! They have the hexagonal tile floors all the old houses had, and many of the newer ones too. I always wanted a room with them, but those who have say they are very cold. We have funny little stoves too, like lard cans set up on three little legs. Very active little creatures which heat up most alarmingly. But the chiefest [sic] treasure is our Fauchette—our little maid. Would not you picture the name as belonging to a dainty little creature in cap and apron? Well our Fauchette has a white cap—but it rests on an iron rust-colored wig—which in turn covers a tiny weazened face, with many wrinkles, pale blue eyes, one single tooth at a most peculiar angle in the lower jaw—and a voice . . . whose nasal shrillness I have never heard the like of—and whose idea of cleaning is not remarkable. Never believe the French are neat! No mam! [sic] She has the best intentions—and I'll never forget the picture the old creature made as she came in, in one hand a new corked oil can, in the other a silver nail cleaner whose dainty mother of pearl tip was broken off—& with the most dejected air, she explained how she was filled with sorrow, dejected—forlorn—and showed how she tryed [sic] to take off the big sealed cork with it. 'Why Fauchette, why on earth did you choose that, of all things? Why, mademoiselle, I thought it was so strong.' I've not had the heart to scold; it was worth the funny little picture."[31]

One of Julia's first responsibilities was taking care of her young cousin, who upon their arrival at the club promptly became ill, as Julia explained to Lucy and Pierre: "We have had varying fortunes since last writing—a few days after, Nina was taken quite sick, and was in her room fully a week—which I did not write her mother. I had to get an American doctor, and look after her pretty sharp—Paris did not seem very lovely then, partically [sic] the distances to be traversed to get the things ordered for her. It is only recently she is herself again and I feel all right about going around without tiring her. Now the Programme is ½ day sightseeing and ½ Atelier."[32]

Even during those early days, Julia didn't lose sight of her primary goal, which was to secure admission to an atelier where she could improve her drafting skills before attempting the École's formidable entrance exams. She was accepted at the studio of Marcel de Monclos, who was not among the top *patrons*, as Julia explained to the LeBruns:

"M. de Monclos is young—as guessed. He could not show any pupil's work and but little of his own. The rooms are on the 3rd floor in a small court, are quite well lighted and clean. . . . [I] think probably I'll

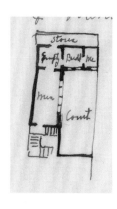

Julia joined the atelier of architect Marcel de Monclos to prepare for the École's examinations. Her floorplan shows her cubicle (right) alongside Katherine Budd's (center). To reach these, they walked through the men's studio, and Julia mentioned receiving their unwelcoming response.

work there ½ day ... and find out in the mean time whom I could have better. ... The Beaux-Arts is [expected] to be opened to Women in Architecture in the fall—but without separate ateliers—and I don't think from the few days I've seen here that that is a very possible arrangement."

This was probably because of the unfriendly reception she received. Julia—who was one of two young women at the atelier—had a small separate workroom, but was still made to feel unwelcome. She continued: "[One man] is very gentlemanly [but] the other two could be exchanged with advantage." Still, she concluded: "I'm glad I came—it wakes one up wonderfully more than Boston."[33]

In the late nineteenth century, American artists flocked to Paris not only to study art, but to study Paris itself. Julia was no exception. A historian of the era wrote: "Coming to Paris from ... America, as so many artists did, was unimaginably exciting. ... its beauty, its light, its myriad attractions, its vibrancy. The combination of old and new building, the splendors of the new boulevards and the Bois

de Boulogne, the profusion of cafes, the theaters, the contrasting opulence and seediness of the different neighborhoods, the smells of the city, its strange ways, indeed even the strangeness of the language: all these aspects of the city exerted a spell...."[34]

Most of Julia's time during her first year in Paris was spent working on assignments at the atelier. She missed California's sunlight, however, and occasionally allowed herself an excursion. The first spring-like day in the midst of an icy winter prompted just such an adventure, as Julia told Pierre and Lucy. She had gone "with Miss [Katherine] Budd [the other female member of the atelier] and a friend of hers to Versailles for the day, the first beautiful day, sunny, the trees just showing signs of budding out, and so bright after the two months of gray. You felt like living. The Palais and Trianons are becoming very familiar. The gallery of statues of the Kings of France—always impresses me anew with the sense of these really having been."[35]

Julia was also very fond of the hauntingly majestic Cathedral of Notre-Dame, which she described to Beatrice Fox as

"one of my favorite places in Paris—where you lean over the balustrade between some of these old, half nice, half wicked feind [sic] gargoyles, who have looked down the same way for centuries, watch the city as it spreads out with the river and its bridges, the towers and domes, and queer old roofs and courts—and try to look back with their

In 1900, Julia posed beside Notre-Dame. She was fascinated by the cathedral's grotesque gargoyles and liked to imagine them watching Paris change over many centuries.

eyes, and see the things they have watched happen in the big open space before the cathedral. It's the dreamiest, most fascinating place I know. The little dark corkscrew stairs, almost pitch dark in places, with mysterious corridors opening off here and there, into the darkness, make Victor Hugo's story very full of life and human feeling...."[36]

She found the panorama of Parisian street festivals fascinating, writing to the LeBruns about *Le Boeuf Gras* (literally "Fat Ox," equivalent to Fat Tuesday): "I have seen the Boeuf Gras fête—from a balcony on the Boulevard around the corner—[have] been nearly drowned in confetti which does not taste good when a hand full lands unexpectedly in your mouth, and after several brushings still shakes out of my coat sleeves. There were some very bright, pretty floats.... the white 'Boeuf' in state on his cart,... really very pretty, like some ballet march on a great stage."[37] Less stately and much more chaotic was a celebration Julia witnessed at the Place de la Concorde:

"The streets are packed with people, and getting on omnibuses is out of the question—I just stood and looked.... The perfect swirl of carriages, soldiers,... bicycles, people, men putting up flags, & electric things—I just calmly waited to see them, some or all, killed by collisions.... The whole 'Place' is strung from gas pole to gas pole with strings of electric lights.... One could watch all day there.... Every building on the 'Cité' is bright

Both Julia's atelier and the American Girls' Club were near the lively Luxembourg Gardens, where she ate her lunch each day.

with flags, even to the very top of the spire of Saint Chappelle. It's gay doings, but … to see [it to] advantage a brother would come in handy [since young women could not venture out in the evening unescorted]. I hope we can manage some way to see it at night, for it must be, as they say, 'féerié' [a fairyland]."[38]

Few things brought Julia greater pleasure than her almost-daily visits to the Luxembourg Gardens, very near the atelier. American painter Julian Alden Weir called these gardens "one of the loveliest spots I have seen … there are large fountains, fine old trees, beautiful flowers, fine statues, … everything to make a place attractive and

pleasant."[39] Julia recalled many years later: "I used to bring my lunch and picnic on a bench there, so as to watch the children with their nurses, the ducks in the little ponds, and all the fascinating daily panoramas of human & animal & vegetable life."[40]

Throughout those early months in Paris, Julia's hopes of attending the École never wavered. Her optimism stemmed from watching the ongoing efforts of a group of female artists who in 1889 had established their own *Union des Femmes Peintres et Sculpteurs* (Union of Female Painters and Sculptors). When they were banned from exhibiting at the biannual Parisian Salons (public art exhibitions that were the École's most important design competitions), they organized their own separate showings. Their first victory—obtaining permission for women to sit in on classes, though they were still barred from enrolling—occurred in the fall of 1896, just after Julia's arrival.[41]

The École's male students resented this feminine encroachment. They also objected in general to the increasing number of Americans who had gained admission. The *Boston Globe* reported: "Within and outside the school there are now about 100 Americans in Paris engaged in the study of architecture, and the number is constantly increasing from year to year. They outnumber several times over all the other foreigners combined." The school responded by reducing the number of foreign students it accepted during any examination to only ten, while guaranteeing entry to thirty French students, even if they scored lower than the other foreign applicants.[42]

Auditing classes at the École gave women artists a literal foot in the door. In April 1897, the *Brooklyn Daily Eagle* reported that they "are growing in will power, and they are slowly gaining ground each year and the admission of women students in the school of fine arts is only a question of time; the law is to be under discussion very soon." In addition to the many hours she spent each day working at her drafting board in the atelier, Julia could now enter the elegant Palais des Études, the École's main building, and audit its classes in history, art, and mathematics. Even better news followed. Though it occurred one year later than Julia had hoped, in May 1897 the École announced that women would be admitted to its painting and sculpture division for the first time.[43]

This news sparked a swift and hostile response from the male students, as the press reported:

"The admission of girls to the Paris School of Fine Arts has been followed by a disturbance of a highly discreditable character. No sooner had some girls, too poor to pay for private instruction, and anxious to avail themselves of the unrivalled advantages which the French Government offers freely to deserving applicants, presented themselves at the school than the male students in the *ateliers* of painting, sculpture, and engraving raised an outcry, and when the women came out of the classes, the men pursued them in a body throughout the streets, yelling and hooting, until the poor girls took refuge in some neighboring shops, and the police appeared and marched the most noisy of the men off to the station-house.... None of the students in architecture were implicated. The *Builder* attributes this simply to the fact that their classes did not happen to be dismissed in time for them to join the mob; but M. Anthony Wable, who is himself the *patron* of an architectural *atelier*, and who ought to know something of the subject, thinks they would hardly have been disposed to do so."[44]

The *patron's* explanation was evidently based on the presumption that it was impossible for women to be admitted into the architecture section, and therefore those students had no reason to protest.

Julia wrote very little about the misogyny she encountered, but veiled references occasionally appear in her letters and others' reminiscences. Her Berkeley friend Grace Fisher visited her in Paris in 1896 and later recalled "how they sneaked around to avoid the boys who looked down on them, because they did not like the idea of a girl studying architecture." Warren Charles Perry, who studied at the École a few years after Julia and then returned to Berkeley to teach at the university, recalled: "She had water poured over her head, and was pushed off the ends of benches." These were typical hazing traditions in the ateliers (which were funded and operated by the students—young men in their twenties—with the *patron* visiting only one or two evenings a week. As a state-sponsored entity, the École's classes were free to all). Julia's older brother Parmelee responded to a letter of hers that had discussed her "social work in the boys club," which apparently meant her efforts to gain the atelier members' respect. He sent her detailed instructions for a number of party games (sitting on a broomstick suspended between two chairs, for example), concluding, "You might use some of these in your high jinks," presumably following the principle, "If you can't beat 'em, join 'em."[45]

Instead she earned the atelier's grudging esteem in her usual way: by demonstrating her superior talent and its usefulness to others. She told the LeBruns about a prize competition—the only one her group was eligible to enter that year (since they were not officially enrolled students):

"Our Atelier was very anxious to at least get hung, though there was no chance for more— The men have been very 'polite' lately, if that does not quite express the idea—and said if all would try one day, [they would] then narrow down to the two best, and put them through to send in.... I had one, and worked from 6.30 P.M till 11.30 A.M.—with rests for coffee and rolls, ... as did Mr. Stokes [Isaac Newton Phelps Stokes, who later established an office in New York with architect John Mead Howells] who had the other—And they got in by twelve at the school. It was the quickest work I ever did."

Though their atelier did not win, Julia doubtless gained some respect, including from one instructor who "has been very kind, [but] always seems astonished if I do anything showing the least intelligence, *Oh-mais,*

c'est intelligente!, as though that was the last thing expected."[46]

Julia was careful to maintain an unintimidating demeanor in front of her male colleagues. The LeBruns sent her current issues of *American Architect and Builder,* which she shared with her fellow students: "I took the magazine to the atelier where it created much interest, for nearly all had seen the [U.S. Capitol] building at some stage." She continued, "I have carefully secluded the 'Gannon-Hands' extract from the eyes of the men's part of the Atelier—but one must own they have energy." (Gannon and Hands was the first all-female architecture firm in America, founded in New York in 1894 by Mary Nevan Gannon and Alice J. Hands.)

She had apparently been advised by the LeBruns to remain cautious at this volatile time of riots and protests, because she reported: "Until lately, I have had to stop ... the evening class, your advise [*sic*] applied, but have begun at the Colarossi [art academy] which is just around the corner, and so saves a good deal of walking."[47] The Académie Colarossi was located in the Sixth Arrondissement, very near the American Girls' Club. Founded by Filippo Colarossi in the 1870s, it operated on Beaux-Arts principles but was more liberal, admitting female students and allowing them to draw from nude male models. Julia studied there with one of the finest sculptors in Paris, Jean-Antoine Injalbert, as she recalled many years later: "Almost without exception the American students there were preparing for the competitive examinations for entrance to l'École des Beaux-Arts, but to my regret, these examinations were not open to women, and the best I could do was to enter the private atelier of M. de Monclos, drawing at Colarossi's and modeling with Injalbert,—an experience not entirely regretted as it rubbed one up against students of many nationalities and ideas, but giving more time to the allied arts than to architecture."[48]

Colarossi and Rodolphe Julian (who administered the Académie Julian) ran two of the finest independent art schools in Paris. Both men—alumni of the École—operated separate studios for men and women. The men were charged half as much, "as it was generally believed that women would be able to find a family member or an outside sponsor who would pay their expenses."[49] These art schools brought together a wider range of students than Julia encountered at the École: "From the Evening Class connections I have become acquainted with a number of Russian women, fine, strong workers, and very intelligent and good, but they smoke and drink tea—the first almost I've seen of bohemianism, and I immediately thought of the exhibition I promised Cousin Pierre of all I learned in that way."[50] (He must have teased her about the dangers of acquiring dissipated habits in Paris.) Julia was always moderate and careful, but it must have been nearly impossible not to feel intoxicated by the beautiful sights around her.

CHAPTER FOUR

REALLY MINE NOW

TWO MONTHS AFTER JULIA AND HER COMPANions arrived in Paris, the city shut down for its customary August holidays. During this lull, Julia, her cousin Nina, Jessica Peixotto, and fellow American Girls' Club resident Clara Kalisher had their first look at another country when they journeyed through Switzerland by train. Julia was apparently the group's treasurer: She saved their travel receipts for more than sixty years.

The girls left Paris for Geneva, where they stayed at a hotel beside the lake (still in existence, and now known as the Hotel des Bergues). They likely visited the city's twelfth-century cathedral and doubtless admired the lake's towering water jet, installed in the harbor a few years before. They made the brief journey to Montreux, also located on the lake, where they lodged at the grand hotel across from the train station. Then they stopped at Bern, Switzerland's capital, and likely explored its old city, built in the twelfth century. When they rode on to Interlaken, they doubtless enjoyed the mountain railway, which had only been completed six years before. They must have marveled at the spectacular scenery, which until recently had been inaccessible to all but the hardiest alpine explorers.

Julia wrote later of Switzerland's many train tunnels: "Before [your] eyes clear from one, whisk, it's into another." Climbing ever higher on the curving tracks, the train streamed "all along, fairly chasing itself." They spent a few days in Meiringen (made famous by Arthur Conan Doyle just three years before, when he set Sherlock Holmes and Moriarty's desperate battle at its tumbling Reichenbach Falls). Julia was especially fond of Lucerne, their next stop, which she later described as "bright, clear, [and] sparkling ... her towers, her rushing river, the old bridges, the shining lakes, the old fountains. I'd like to stay." They ended in Basel, at the Grand Hotel Euler, still in operation today. After two months of admiring the muted colors of Paris's beige and gray stone buildings, they must have been shocked to see Basel's bright red sandstone cathedral and sixteenth-century town hall.[1]

Julia also visited the crowded exhibition rooms of the celebrated Paris Salon during that summer of 1896. There she could view the work of students in the École's painting and sculpture division. She wrote afterward to Pierre and Lucy that during the two days she spent at the Salon des Champs Élysées, "I only saw ½ the rooms. The sculptures are more fine and numerous, the paintings on [a] larger scale & more finished—with a very large number of most horrible subjects—actually one room made me so faint I had to leave.... You would have had all sorts of gore to your heart's content." She preferred the smaller Salon exhibition at the Champ de Mars, which "had better water colors, smaller canvases, and [in] some way gave very much more interest and pleasure."[2]

But neither sightseeing nor attending exhibitions erased Julia's homesickness, especially at Christmastime. She confessed to Beatrice:

"Over here at best, it's a trifle lonely, and it gives its tinge to even the most wonderful of things—not that I'm homesick—<u>oh</u>! no. You are nice enough to understand that.... I speak French very badly, though I understand quite well—enough to follow sermons, lectures, critisms [sic] though there is much yet [for me to learn]. I have little time for study, and hear really very little, except as the servants or shopkeepers speak—I go to three series of architectural lectures at the Beaux Arts, very fine courses, and it all helps its little. The stores are full of Christmas toys—never saw such dolls, mechanical toys etc.—it seems very hard to have no chance to buy or give this year. I keep seeing some special thing some of the children [at] home would just be wild over. I expect a church service will be all my celebration this year. Thanksgiving was a miserable failure."[3]

Though she longed to buy toys in the shops, Julia was not impressed by Paris's famous department stores. The finest—Le Bon Marché—featured a huge iron-and-glass skylighted roof engineered by Gustave Eiffel in 1876. This temple of fashion left her cold, as she tersely explained to the LeBruns: "[Went] to the Bonne Marché (first and last time)." Julia was immune to Parisian fashions, and regarded buying new clothes as an unpleasant necessity: "Just now I have been rudely awakened to the fact that clothes, especially sleeves on drawing boards, wear out, and wish you [Lucy] could help me over the choosing—The blue suit is cleaned as fresh as new, was a splendid buy, but my waist is gone—even the shirt waists [long-sleeved blouses, worn tucked into skirts]—I suppose tomorrow I will simply have to face it, and do the best I can."[4]

She also found it difficult to adjust to the perpetually gray skies and persistently cold rooms: "We went [to Notre-Dame] in fog and rain, that being the normal condition of things. It's an utter surprise to see the sunlight. My drawing boards at the atelier are all mildewed where they rest on the floor at night, a most cheerful condition truly!" She struggled against homesickness, writing Lucy about a letter she'd received from Nina, who was back in New York: "Nina wrote of her visit to you, and it gave a sort of *heimweh*." This is German for "homesickness." When she left California, Julia had vowed not to mention that word (and she hadn't—technically).[5]

Julia completed the École's competition assignments even before she became a student. Her design for a colonnaded passageway is a typical example.

Throughout her years in Paris, Julia was seldom solitary. Nevertheless, she was frequently alone. When she sat in on the architecture classes at the École, she was often the only female student. Though her atelier included another young woman, Julia was the one whose talent allowed her to compete on an equal—or superior—footing with her male colleagues. When she took the evening drawing and modeling classes that were open to women at the independent art academies, she focused on improving her skills as an architect rather than as a sculptor or painter.

Although Julia was friendly with her fellow students—especially the women—she did not possess many society connections. In an effort to establish herself, she paid a few social calls not long after her arrival. Relying on an introduction from Lucy, Julia met John van Pelt, a slightly older student who later became a distinguished professor of architecture at Cornell. He lived in Paris with his mother. Julia wrote the LeBruns:

"I went with the letter to Mrs. Van Pelt who was very kind and pleasant, said her son was working with someone on the competition for the new Palais's [*sic*] for the Champs Élysée, and so could not call, but would I come to dinner the next Sunday and me[e]t him—She has a very nice Pension, but too expensive entirely for a student, and far from the work. It did seem very nice though after here—<u>He</u> proved very thin and lame, in spectacles for eyes that looked troublesome, but was very kind, thought M. de Monclos good, until I could get into the ways of work and see just what I would like to, and could, do. He also said he would look out himself, gave me a kind offer of the use of his books and a card to the American Ambassador to get from him a Letter to the Director of the Beaux Arts, asking permission to have such priviledges [sic] for Library and Lecture work as are open to women."[6]

Her former Oakland classmate Arthur Brown Jr. (with whose family Julia had initially hoped to travel to Paris in 1895) had also obtained formal recommendations from well-connected officials. Arthur Jr.'s mother, Victoria, provided him with additional social contacts. Mrs. Brown was so fond of Paris that she lived there with her son for almost the entire six years he spent at the École.[7]

Julia's one important social connection was with the Maybecks, who arrived in Paris during the summer of 1897. This cheering circumstance assuaged some of Julia's home-sickness, and also presented her with an opportunity to leave the American Girls' Club. An apartment directly beneath the Maybecks' flat at 7 rue Honoré-Chevalier became available, and Julia moved in along with her friend Sara Whitney, a sculptor who had also grown up in Oakland. Julia explained to the LeBruns:

"It seemed the pleasantest solution possible, so now it's ours. It sounds extravagant to say one has four pretty rooms, kitchen, hall, big closets, fire places in each room, all with street views, but in reality it is no dearer than the one furnished room apiece at the Club or elsewhere. We have one chair for each

The École stressed drawing skills, and Julia honed hers by taking night classes at the Académie Colarossi, where she also studied sculpture and painting.

room, and [only] the furniture absolutely necessary, which will not make much house-keeping, and will get our own breakfasts and dinners, with lunch out, as now. It's the location which takes my especial feelings, right one block from [the church of] San Sulpice, and half-way between the Atelier and the Beaux Arts, the trains all right at hand, and [a] very healthy neighborhood."[8]

Julia had now been in Paris for a full year, studying nearly every day, and Ben encouraged her to tackle the École's entrance examinations. These multiple-day ordeals began with the students executing a timed drawing assignment on-site, then returning on the following days for tests in descriptive geometry, mathematics, and history—all conducted in French—as well as modeling and drawing. With very little time to prepare, Julia signed up to take the examination in July 1897.

Like most applicants, Julia failed the École's examination on her first try. Afterward she rested in the countryside, where she painted this watercolor.

She wrote the LeBruns afterward:

"I was about ready for a vacation from the winter's work, and did not go into it very fresh and vigorous, and had I known they had changed and [there] would have been another [test] in October, [I] think I might have waited, though as they say it is necessary to fail once, to know how to take the examinations, perhaps it was best any way. I did pass them all, but not with high enough rank. Perhaps it would amuse you to tell you of some of them. The first was in Architecture. You are given from 8 A.M. to 8 P.M.—en loge [sequestered], . . . It was very hot weather, and it was impossible to close an eye the night before, so was up before five, got breakfast, and was down at the school a little after seven, as the head guard had said if I came early he would let me up before the men began to arrive. . . . But when I got there,

it turned out the other was a myth. . . . They had made a mistake, and I would be let in last. So as people began to arrive, I went up to the Quai and walked up and down and up, seeing the students arrive, in all sorts of regalia, by ones, in groups, until it seemed an almost endless time and number. It was nearly half past eight before things quieted down & one ventured back. I was put in a loge—a little 6 x 8 room in the roof . . . [with] a table & stool & stove as furnishings, with a window out on the court. . . . I did not notice partically [*sic*] just then that the entire ceiling was skylight, with no way of covering it, but when the sun arrived a few minutes later, and looked through on your head all day with no escape, then, being an exceeding hot day, you did notice. . . . The Programme was very difficult for the 12 hours, for it has to be drawn very carefully. I was very tired, and got so nervous I absolutely could not keep the ink in the drawing pen or get a point on a pencil. In spite of that I had my plan finished and the elevation about penciled [in] by 4 o'clock, when I took up the scale with a sudden suspicion, and found I had made a mistake calculating, as I cannot yet think in the meters [sic], and the whole thing was too low, though in proportion. That just finished all hopes—I rubbed out the 1st story, and simply put in the quickest and only thing I could—Utterly bad. . . . I went home and sat down on a sofa to rest a minute before dinner as I had not had a thing all day—and woke . . . at half past three in the morning.

"A couple of days afterwards they exhibited the Concours in the Salle Melpomène [a room named for the ancient Greek muse of tragedy], as always, and you should have seen M. de Monclos' face. He said I'd never done anything so bad since with him, and he was sure I'd not passed though the plan was good—So I went home and was so sure I never went to see if I had or not, until a couple of days after I met one of the students and heard by accident that I had [passed], by two points more than necessary. There were 376 drawings entered, and only 30 or 40 students to be admitted—small chance—especially for foreigners as they are limited to 5 or 10. . . . The next two [examinations] I was not ready for, for the drawing [class] at night has been from life only, and I had not touched clay since home, but they came out pretty well, but you should have seen the French of the history paper, or seen the twinkle in the examiner's

eyes in the oral. The oral mathematics broke down about a hundred at least. It's the most trying ordeal for its simpleness, and seems to depend more on the amount of nerve than of knowledge. There were thirteen examined before me the day I came up, and every one failed entirely—those being strong fellows would get up, tremble, turn white, clutch their hands, and seem to have no thinking power left at all. It seems very silly, but I think you would do the same—it seems a sort of contagion. Being the last [on] the list, I'd hoped to be almost alone, but probably from mischief, though they were perfectly polite and gentlemanly, and have been throughout, the room kept filling up all the morning, until when I was called there was a room full.

"I tried to pretend I was not afraid, and perfectly steady, and actually believed it until at the end of the first problem I discovered that my hand was rattling in the air, and the discovery so surprised me, I could not do any more mathematics—it was enough for a pretty good mark, but you see so many did nothing. The list has not been made out officially yet, but the students get their values [score] by going to the Secretary. He said this morning only 30 would probably be taken—and I am about 42 or 43—so you see it would be impossible in any case. None of those received have tried them less than twice, many 3—4—5 or 6 times. Every one takes their defeat in the most cheerful way, for you are always with the majority at least. . . . Next time perhaps it will be better results—it does not seem that one could ever be so nervous and tired again, even when some of these Frenchmen up for their 6th trial do the same thing . . ."[9]

Though Julia made light of her ordeal, it in fact had damaged her health, as she explained to Pierre and Lucy the following month: "The next day [after the examinations], the heat or reaction from the work was so surprising in results, that I could not do even the small things intended." The Maybecks intervened, and Julia was sent to the countryside to stay on a farm and recover, where "the last three weeks have been simply lazying. . . . [The doctor] said any sight-seeing or traveling this summer if I expected to enter the Examinations in October was out of the question, but if I'd be quiet without any working till Septembre I'd be all right—which eases my conscience, for it seemed so wasteful of time and opportunity to actually be in Europe, and then settle calmly in one tiny little place—& do nothing."[10]

Charles wrote her consolingly in the examination's aftermath:

"I am afraid you are home sick, and if such is the case, I would not continue to stay away [from home] out of any mistaken pride in the matter. Life is not all architecture and while you may gain in one direction it is not needful to sacrifice too much for one object. If however, you find your life interesting and the home sickness is not abnormal, why then stay as long as you desire. . . . I hope that when you take the next examinations that you will have more confidence in yourself and will not worry over the result. Just show 'em what an American girl can do."[11]

Avery—who was four years younger than Julia—usually looked to her for comfort, rather than the reverse. Julia didn't mind; she had always felt protective toward him. He was uncertain if he should join his sister in Paris to continue his architecture studies, or remain at the University of California. Avery wrote gloomily:

"Am working now on the design of a railroad bridge in which I am quite stupid. There are nine in the class and this is the actual state of affairs—Six of them have all pretty good heads, of five of them you couldn't say which was the best, they work rapidly and stay together. The other three consist of myself, one who is repeating the work and a third whoes [sic] name is a signal for laughing. We keep about together. Now, what do you think of your brother? This cannot be much of a surprise to you, if you traced back my record you would find nothing more encouraging. My work with Mr. Maybeck and Prof. [Herman] Kower [in the University of California's Department of Drawing] was awful poor and in the High School where I might have done . . . lots there is hardly any record to show that I did anything. . . . When people speak of my going to Paris, I am at a loss what to say and so say nothing. When Beaux Arts is mentioned I have to laugh—it seems so ridiculous! If there was anything

In 1897, Julia and a fellow student moved into the Parisian apartment below the Maybecks' flat at 7 rue Honoré Chevalier.

which I thought I could do better at, it wouldn't seem so hard, but there is not. It is hard to be a dissapointment [*sic*] to your family. I am sorry for you, who have always been so good to me. You have been no disappointment to anybody."[12]

This sad missive notwithstanding, Julia convinced Avery to join her in Paris and study at the École.

Julia's own best advocate was Bernard Maybeck. Three days before her second try at the examinations, she reported to the LeBruns that Ben had

"proposed my going to M. [Jean-Louis] Pascal [an instructor at the École], but only with his card of introduction, as he did not want to let it look like he was trying to use influence for me, Pascal being named [selected] for the French Competition judge. He is a bushy grey haired man, with a fine sensitive face, and very keen grey eyes—He thought I'd come to ask to be taken as a pupil, and began at once saying he would not take me, had no room, did not want the bother of only one girl, etc—before I'd even asked a bit—ending with advising me to enter with one of the Professors who have Ateliers in the Beaux Arts buildings themselves—He looked questioning[ly] at my roll of drawings before I left, so I mustered the courage to ask if he had time to give me his criticism—He did, a very careful, helpful one, ending by a most unexpected approval. He said any one of them at the Examination ought to have a very good mark, and some would bring one

out first—So if one fails utterly, there is still the sense that one can do better things in reality. When I told Mr. Maybeck he laughed, and said it was why he wanted to have me to know some really good man's opinion. That does not mean much, that is, that one can do any really good work, but it saves one's pride in case of failure."[13]

In October 1897, she went through the whole grueling round a second time, writing to Pierre and Lucy:

"There were 311 candidates for the thirty places, and only 8 places for foreigners out of these—I passed all the 'exes' [exams], each time sure that the work was better than before, each time with a lower note [score]—I felt very much ashamed and badly, for I thought I'd made mistakes I did not recognize, carefully avoiding the Ateliers and M. de Monclos,—he had been so ashamed of me before—I met him by accident on the street in the end—and he did not scold, and something he said made me suspicious all at once, and I asked him what had been the mistakes in the Architecture—He looked very funny, and said 'The mark'—explaining that the Jury had openly said they *Ne voudraient pas encouragé les jeunes filles*—[We don't want to encourage young girls], and that everyone said it would make no matter what I did— It was such a relief I did not care much—In the end as it was I did not rank with the first eight foreigners, so that ended it, but I'll try again next time anyway even without any expectations, just to show [them] 'les jeunes filles' are not discouraged."[14]

Once again she suffered physically afterward: "I have been doing little for some weeks of anything—though very well—It seemed to be a lazy fit entirely—coupled with a giving out of the eyes, whenever I would work the veins of the lids would swell until one simply had to stop—I am beginning gradually with them, and hope they will work regularly by next week—When all the rest of you is so willing it's quite aggravating."[15]

Julia was apparently at an impasse. Her examination results appeared destined to fail, no matter how well she did; and her attempts to gain admission to other ateliers were unsuccessful. Furthermore, the de Monclos atelier seemed to be coming apart: "The Atelier has fallen almost to nothing through a number of the students being called back to America—In fact, there will be no one in a month, unless there are recruits." Her one heartening prospect was Avery's imminent arrival. She moved into a flat that they could share, at 15 rue de Guénégaud—around the corner from the École—and vowed to conserve her spending money: "I'm going to save up till Avery comes, [since going to plays] will be so much more enjoyed together—I did not realize how [much] I'd like to see someone I care for, till the possibility really becomes strong." They intended to travel together: "The plans now are very indefinite, but probably we will work here until March, and then begin traveling very slowly down the South of France to Italie—and spending the rest

of our time to our money's limit in studying that way."[16]

As Julia awaited their reunion, she learned she would be welcomed into another atelier:

"M. de Monclos's other students have gradually all left, there have been none for months in fact, and as they left he lost interest, and came very seldom—I staid [sic] alone till a month ago, when M. Laloux told Mr. Maybeck that M. [François-Benjamin] Chaussemiche had come back from Italie, and he had been talking it over with him, and he would like to take me with the idea of having charge of a women's Atelier at the B.A. if it is ever started—He was the Grand Prix de Rome of '91 or '92 and Laloux's favorite student—the head of his office—He is very small, dark and quiet and Mr. de Monclos says is considered the finest of the younger school of architects—especially as to draughtsmanship—He critizes [sic] from an entirely different point of view from M. de Monclos, and it feels like a sort of weight had been lifted—and one could work in a bigger, freer, happier way."[17]

Changing ateliers was almost unheard of—students who did so seldom recovered from the stigma. In Julia's case, de Monclos's atelier disintegrated around her, giving her the chance to begin again with a more sympathetic *patron*.

From then on, Julia's good news multiplied. Avery arrived in mid-November 1898, and—nearly simultaneously—after two years of effort, she gained admission to the École. Her final score was so high on her third attempt that the administrators were essentially shamed into accepting her at last:

"Avery did not telegraph, as he arrived at two A.M. at Bolougne [sic]—and reached here about six thirty, before I was up, and had a rather queer welcome, poor fellow.... for I was working for the examinations at the École again, and pretty hard.... The Judgment was given today only, and [I] am the 13th—ten French & two foreigners— they take ... [thirty] in all—It's not much but has taken quite a little effort—If it had been simply for the advantages of the École, I would not have kept on after M. Chaussemiche was arranged with, but a mixture of dislike of giving up some thing attempted and the sense of its being a sort of test in a small way, of work itself overcoming its natural disadvantages—made it seem a thing that really had to be won."[18]

Her achievement was lauded in the press, thus beginning her uneasy relationship with fame. The *Oakland Tribune* headline read: "Fame Comes to Julia Morgan. Enters the Ecole des Beaux [sic] Department of Architecture, Paris." The article continued: "The examination in mathematics is oral, given before a committee, and is of such a nature as to try the nerves of even strong men. Other examinations last from 8 in the morning until 8 at night, most difficult problems being required in specifications furnished by the examining board." After proclaiming her triumph, the

reporter hastened to assert Julia's femininity: "Personally, Miss Morgan is as pretty as she is bright. She is a charming conversationalist and has figured at many a swell social function in this city. She is decidedly effeminate and extremely modest."[19]

In the midst of Julia's elation, Phoebe Apperson Hearst arrived in Paris. Julia did not know her personally, but of course she knew of Phoebe through Ben, and they quickly established a warm friendship. Phoebe hosted a reception for American female students, then left for Antwerp, where the semifinalists for her university competition were to be announced. Charles was dazzled by his daughter's prestigious new connection, writing Julia proudly (and, as it turned out, prophetically): "You must have astonished the French...[Mrs. Hearst] is not the only one who has taken notice of your success at entering the Ecole, as I am congratulated on every hand by those I meet. Like Avery is, I shall be known through you as Miss Morgan's Pa."[20]

As was her frequent habit when she met a talented student, Phoebe offered to pay for Julia's entire education. Julia gratefully refused, writing:

"If I honestly felt more money freedom could make my work better, I would be tempted to accept your offer—but I am sure it has not been the physical work which has been or will be hardest, for I am used to it and strong, but rather the months of striving against homesickness and the nervous strain of examinations. Now my brother is here, and a place is won at the Beaux Arts, really mine now it seems, the work ought simply to be a pleasure whether housekeeping or study. Your kind words at the depot were so unexpected, so friendly, they gave and still give, more help than you can guess and I will thank you for them always."[21]

In describing the École's demanding curriculum as "a pleasure," Julia was overly optimistic. She had spent the past several months resigning herself to returning home empty-handed. Instead, she was flung into this exacting regimen with little chance to rest or mentally prepare. The École's nearly continuous competitions were meant to simulate an architect's professional duties, which typically entailed creating a design, then vying with other firms to obtain the commission. Working architects did this only intermittently. Students at the École were expected to compete again and again, with no respite save their annual summer holiday.

Typical of Julia's challenging projects were assignments to design a museum or a hotel. The competition procedures seldom varied. The site's conditions and the client's stipulations were included in the specifications, but only in general terms. First Julia was shut in a small room for twelve consecutive hours (known as being *en loge*), to determine the basic plan (the *parti*) and create a sketch (the *esquisse*), which she then turned in, keeping only a rough copy for reference. Over the next six weeks, she elaborated on her sketch by creating ornately detailed drawings (the *projets rendus*) in plan, section, and elevation. On the final day, she

placed these large drawings in a cart, which had to be wheeled through the cobblestoned streets (a process known as *en charette*) to the École for judging.

If Julia's elaborate finished drawings had differed in any way from the initial sketch she had turned in six weeks before, the judges (the École's faculty) would have eliminated her submission. The student entries that remained were evaluated on technical skill, artistry, creativity, and the effectiveness of the plan. A runner-up and a winner were then chosen and respectively awarded one or two points.

In order to be promoted from the Second Class to the First Class, students had to earn sixteen points. To receive the *diplôme*, they needed to accrue twenty-six points. This competition process—repeated many times over—taught them to work quickly, determine their design's layout from the beginning, and solve any subsequent logistical problems as they went along.[22]

While difficult, these scholastic requirements were minor when compared with the École's other limitation. All competition entries had to be completed, and all points awarded, before a student reached the age of thirty. After that, they were barred from the program. Julia was already twenty-seven by the time she was finally admitted. She now had less than three years to produce what normally required six years' worth of work.

She confessed to the LeBruns that this deadline had put her under considerable emotional and physical strain: "I was very much pressed for a few weeks . . . at the

Avery arrived in Paris in October 1898, soon after Julia made history as the first woman accepted into the École's architecture program. During the summer they happily traveled to Switzerland and Italy.

Julia poses (likely for Avery's camera) on a Parisian balcony with the Palais du Trocadéro (an exhibition hall built in 1878) behind her.

Spring examinations—and succeeded quite satisfactorily—to the amusement of the other students. . . . then came down with a most peculiar malady which has just been recovered from—it sounds very funny, a boil in your ear, but it inflamed the whole head like mumps & was painful in addition—It's quite well now—but 'boils' is a sore subject."[23] This condition may have marked a re-emergence of the severe ear infections she had experienced in childhood.

The counterbalance to all this stress was Julia's joy at reuniting with Avery. She wrote Pierre and Lucy: "He is the kindest fellow always, and you can hardly imagine how different it makes the life here—You would be amused at our house keeping, & the efforts to learn to buy enough of things not to have them reappear too [*sic*] often—or spend too much time on them—then too we are limited by having only charcoal hobs and no oven—There were great struggles deciding where our trip should wander—there are so many plans, so many ways. . . ."[24] His quirky personality delighted her: "He concluded at first that I'd changed a great deal—but when he casually asked, 'How did my nose get so crooked?' it quite relieved me, for that member certainly is the same as always. He now says perhaps he never really looked at me—well—but the extent of my appetite really alarms him a little—that, he owns, is quite new."[25]

With Avery as her escort, Julia could finally enjoy Paris at night. They saw Sarah Bernhardt perform the title role in *Hamlet*, at her newly remodeled eponymous theater, equipped with 5,700 electric lights. They attended the opera, as she explained to the LeBruns: "Avery is more content, though still homesick I'm afraid, though we neither of us say anything of it. His French is progressing very well—enough to grasp 'Lakmé' at the 'Opéra Comique'.... We enjoyed the evening very much indeed."[26] Music had always united them. After hearing the Easter Vespers service at Notre-Dame, Julia wrote: "At last I got into the Triforium. The effect from there is simply fine and I don't think the nave will ever seem narrow and cold again.... [I] played I was a gargoyle until the music made me forget myself and the services became all absorbing—a 'candle' procession with the archbishop and other dignitaries, more than around the entire church in length.... It never seemed more grand, more ungraspable."[27]

They also caught glimpses of the preparations for Paris's spectacular world's fair, the 1900 Exposition Universelle, under construction on both banks of the Seine:

"It seems almost impossible for the Fair to be ready in a year! The Grand and Petit Palais's [*sic*] are up in the rough ... but the carving out is hardly more than begun.... The whole plan is surrounded by a very high fence so you can't see much except from the tram top or a chance glimpse [*sic*] through an open gate ... We gaze with wonder at the scaffoldings and false work they use.... There is great activity on the [Right] bank, building out a sort of platform up to the waters' edge all along—from the new bridge to the Champs [*sic*] de Mars—There are even two newly (replaced/restored) statues above the outer of the doors at Notre Dame—so white and clean they send a sort of shock through one even when some way off—AB [Avery] thinks every day helps tone them down a little."[28]

Julia and Avery were fascinated by the city's preparations for its lavish world's fair, the 1900 Exposition Universelle.

The 1900 Exposition Universelle covered a sprawling 250 acres. It utilized the Eiffel Tower (constructed for the 1889 Exposition) as one of its many entrance gates, while introducing several other wonders, including the cavernous Palace of Electricity, which featured elaborate light shows each evening, and an electrified moving sidewalk (the Marche de Trottoir), which conveyed standing visitors to the major sights. Both the Grand Palais and the Petit Palais were built as the fair's art-exhibition halls. The Pont Alexandre III—the world's first single-span bridge—connected them both to Les Invalides (the city's grand seventeenth-century hospital) across the river. The exposition opened on the fourteenth of April and closed on the twelfth of November. During those eight months it was visited by an astonishing 50 million people.[29] The Gare d'Orsay (today's Musée d'Orsay) was a magnificent train station constructed adjacent to the École, with the initial purpose of transporting millions of fairgoers. It must have been of special interest to Avery, since it was designed by his *patron*, Victor Laloux.

The only gloomy circumstance was the cruel treatment Avery received from his fellow students at Laloux's atelier. Avery was emotionally sensitive and physically small, which made him a vulnerable target. (Eliza wrote to Julia while Avery was in transit: "We miss Avery. I do all the time—knew I should—but I'd not have kept him if I could—as he is a man for all he is so small and he ought to go out for himself and see what the world is like and what he can do.")[30] As the younger brother of the infamous Julia Morgan, who had the effrontery to gain admission to the architecture division, it was almost inevitable that he would be taunted. Julia explained to the LeBruns:

"Avery likes his work, though he finds the atelier habits pretty trying. When I was *en loge* this week, he asked one of the men to lunch, and five came and insisted on staying—he went out and laid in more lunch, but when he came for me at night he looked as though he had had a pretty hard time. He's going to the country next loge day—for he says he's sure they will keep watch—and the whole atelier will come. Some days he comes home wet through, others with a hat crown out, or something hopelessly torn—yet they seem to like him, and only give him his share of the general disaster. He says the queerest part is that the men who do the most water throwing—and mischief making, do the best work!"

These unfortunate circumstances can't have helped Avery tackle the École's entrance examination, which he passed, but with a score insufficiently high to qualify for admission.[31]

A welcome respite for them both came in August 1899, when they traveled by train through Switzerland to Italy. Julia kept a diary of this trip, which they enjoyed so much that they repeated it the following summer. Their initial departure from Paris was complicated by their having been unaware of the consequences when everyone essentially

Though Avery was not admitted to the École, he studied architecture in the atelier of Victor Laloux, where he endured frequent hazing.

begins their summer vacation on the first day of August, as Julia explained: "Could not sleep [due to a] little baby with its hot head against my knee & the train overcrowded, terribly hot and dirty." Zurich also struck them as hot and dirty, but as the elevation rose, so did their spirits.

They enjoyed Lucerne and Lausanne, and stayed in the small town of Brugg along the border of the Italian alps, where they were "much amused [at] the knifes [*sic*] before fingers propensitys [*sic*] of all the table.... The German opp[osite]... put in everything that way, from salad to cookies." In Brünig, between Lucerne and Interlaken, Julia wrote: "The church bells rang from very early, and when I went up after breakfast, the big church was full, and [what] a quaint sight it was ... [women] all [on] one side [in] the

white & silver head dresses and all [on] the other the weather beaten men & all so quiet & reverent in the natural bowing of body and spirit."[32] Her diary ends with an account of their arrival in Venice. Julia described the three men who shared their train compartment as "Big, young, [and] fit.... The one opp[osite] a fine, thin, but keen-looking man with [a] very long thin nose—[who] looked really interesting. But as we came near Venice they forgot they were opaque ... so ... we could not catch but glances under their coat sleeves of the so much written of approach to Venice. Bits of marsh, gay boats, and reflections of red buildings & [then we] were in the station. The water was there & the gondolas. Bumpy in motion."[33]

Avery's company and their second journey to Switzerland must have been some consolation the following summer, when they were unable to return to Oakland for Emma's at-home wedding. She and her husband, Hart North, had had a long and somewhat combative courtship. (In a typical incident, Eliza wrote to Julia when she and Emma were on a camping trip: "Emma . . . had a long letter from Hartle which threw her into the usual rage.")[34] Hart was an attorney who was serving as a state legislator when they married and moved in with the Morgans. Parmelee, who was relocating to New York in hopes of improving his unsuccessful business as a cotton broker, wrote to Julia: "Sam always had me bringing a bride to the attic—it is amusing to have Emma bring a groom. . . . With the addition of a bathroom on this floor and the big front room made into an upstairs sitting room, they will be well enough fixed."[35] On the morning of the wedding, Emma wrote: "Mama looks ever so nice in her dress—and she has gone & done everything for me that could be thought of. The house is extraordinarily pretty with ferns and hydranagias [sic]. . . . Everything has been perfect so far except your & Gib's [Avery's nickname] absence, & I [will] regret it always."[36]

With no prospect of admission to the École, Avery decided to return home late in 1900. Julia remained alone in their flat and soon obtained a job, in addition to her school responsibilities. Though she had proudly turned down Mrs. Hearst, Julia was in fact very worried about money. Morgan North explained: "Aunt Julia felt very guilty that there were four other children in the family

and yet that her education was going on and on and on because they wouldn't accept her at the Beaux-Arts, and she was [studying in France] a lot longer than she [had] planned."[37] Julia ignored Eliza's frequent instructions to buy new shoes, take excursions, etc., and when she and Avery lived together in Paris, they got by on the sum she had budgeted just for herself.[38]

It must therefore have been a relief when she began working with Chaussemiche. The wealthy American expatriate and socialite Harriet Travers Fearing had hired him to add a *grand salon* to her large eighteenth-century home in Fontainebleau, 50 miles south of Paris. Julia must have served as translator in addition to her other duties, because Chaussemiche's English was not good. They designed an elegant ceremonial *salon* in eighteenth-century French style. Julia benefited from the experience, though Eliza was unhappy at the additional stress it caused her: "It was real low down mean of Mrs. Fearing to make you [do] all that extra work—and I wish you won't have anymore hitches or changes to bother you—from what I've known of Architect's work—I fear that thing often happens, especially when working for ladies, but it was sad to deprive you of your vacation—I hope you left that starvation convent and found good food and clean rooms—and got a little good of your trip." Eliza concluded with this advice: "Just you get in on your 'Projects'—'Esquisse's' and win mentions—medals—prises [sic] and honors galore! Hope your health will hold out."[39]

The pressure was increasing every day, since Julia would turn thirty on January 20, 1902, and therefore have to leave the École. Winning enough points to finish the program seemed an impossible task, and Eliza tried to console her: "I hope your 'Project' was not thrown out—It's too bad you have such struggles to finish—It's also sad about your age limit—but you can stay and work as long as you wish to. I feel real interested in all you write about the Fearings and trust things will continue on to the finish serene. . ."[40] Earning the *diplôme*—which required a long apprenticeship in an architect's office after the student had completed the necessary coursework—was out of the question. But Julia hoped to obtain the next best thing, the *certificat*, and this too seemed out of reach. After she failed to win a competition that autumn, Eliza wrote: "I am very, very sorry indeed after all your work and hopes that you lost. . . . I hoped so much that you could 'make' your Diplome. It's a comfort that you got that new suit and I hope it will fit good and be becoming and warm. I do not like to think of you alone there in the long cold dark days. . . . Whenever you can, you get all the Automobile rides the Fearings offer you and all the French Plays and everything entertaining possible."[41]

In December 1901, mere days before her birthday, Julia's elegant design for a theater in a palace won a first mention, earning her slightly more than the required twenty-six points, and allowing her to receive the École's graduating *certificat*. Eliza wrote: "I was delighted to know that you'd won that 'medaille.'. . . We all congratulate you and hope you will have a Happy Christmas and a Glad New Year and that those Fearings will invite you to their house for Christmas. They'll be shabby mean if they don't. You just do your work, and let Mrs. Fearing wait. I am very glad you will get your 'certificate,' whatever you don't get."[42]

It was an unprecedented achievement. When Julia became the École's first female architecture graduate, she broke a record that had stood unchallenged since 1648. Her determination and talent were praised in newspapers throughout the English-speaking world. Some of the articles were of questionable accuracy, for instance when the Jackson, Mississippi, *Clarion-Ledger* declared: "Miss Morgan displayed a talent for building, since [she was] a small child, her bloc [sic] houses being marvels of originality and genius."[43] A reporter for London's *Pall Mall Gazette* underestimated her future professional activities, claiming, "Her work in practice, like that of other women architects in America, will be largely confined to the office, and the preparation of plans." This article ended accurately, however: "Miss Morgan has been annoyed and embarrassed by the popular interest of which she has been the object here."[44] To her immense irritation, Julia realized that she was now famous.

Shortly before her thirtieth birthday (the age at which students must leave the École),
Julia submitted this competition sketch (esquisse) *for a theater in a palace.*

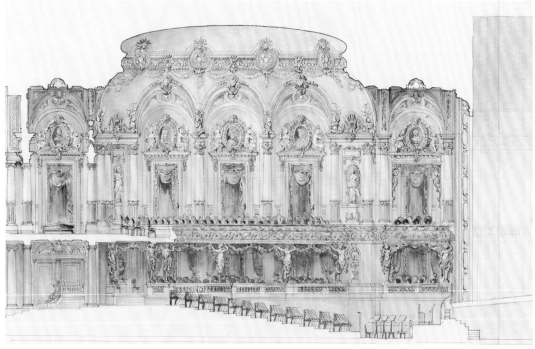

Six weeks later, Julia's formal drawings—the projets rendus—*won sufficient points for her*
to make history as the first woman to earn her certificat *from the École des Beaux-Arts.*

CHAPTER FIVE

MAKING A NAME

AFTER RECEIVING HER *certificat* IN FEBRUARY 1902, Julia remained in France to work alongside Chaussemiche, this time as his colleague. Their first task was to complete Harriet Travers Fearing's elegant *salon*, which was lined with *boiseries* (narrow panels of painted wood, decorated with delicate gold-leafed carvings), offset by two stately marble mantelpieces topped by mirrors extending to the ceiling.[1] In May Julia left for Southern Italy, where she likely spent the next two months assisting Chaussemiche in the coastal town of Terracina, where he was overseeing the restoration of the ancient Roman temple of Jupiter Anxur. Built in the first century B.C.E. near the Appian Way, the temple was dramatically sited on the edge of a 745-foot-high rock promontory overlooking the sea. Julia concluded her European sojourn with these two very different commissions,

then sailed from Naples in July 1902. After visiting the LeBruns in New York, she returned to a greatly changed Oakland.[2]

From now on, she would have to contend with the press. Julia knew that her family had been pestered by reporters, as Eliza recounted:

"[I] had just come into the front hall—when I heard a nocking [*sic*] on the Front door—I opened it—it was dark outside—A very fat man leaned against the door jam [*sic*]—he remarked I'm Mr. Davis—reporter for the Chronicle—'We are going to write up Miss Jane Morgan—City Editor sent me up for her Picture to put at its head, thought it would look kind of nice—also we'd like to know about any work she'd done here before she went and also—what started her on that track—seems to me an unusual one for a girl to take'—I corrected your name and refused Pictures or life history—and turned him over to Pa who he said he knew very well... I've refused so many of them."[3]

The Morgan household had also changed in the six years Julia was away. Parmelee had relocated to New York, and Emma and her new husband, Hart North, were now living upstairs. Julia had known her brother-in-law for decades, since he had attended Oakland High School and the University of California. After serving two terms as a Republican state legislator in 1894 and 1896, Hart was nominated by President McKinley for the post of commissioner of immigration at the Port of San Francisco. Soon after taking the position, he was implicated in a scandal, when the *San Francisco Chronicle* charged him and several other legislators with attempted interference in the granting of an exclusive contract to supply voting machines. No charges were filed, but by appointing Charles Morgan to serve on the supposedly impartial selection committee, Hart placed both his father-in-law and himself in a compromising position. Hart later experienced other career difficulties, some resulting from his own obstinacy; after numerous complaints, he was fired as port commissioner and then founded his own law firm.[4]

There was some discussion about Emma joining her husband's law practice. Though this didn't occur, she would have been well qualified, since she earned her bachelor of laws degree in the spring of 1902. Avery wrote: "Mrs. North vows up and down that when her law examinations are over, she will never go to

school anymore. One of your fraternity sisters said, wouldn't it be a great joke if Mrs. North took all her husband's law business away from him?"[5] The two high-achieving Morgan sisters were praised in the press: "Though so very quiet and retiring, [Julia] comes of a rather remarkable family of women. Her sister, Mrs. Hart North, is quite out of the usual run of women, also. Mrs. North has been taking a course at the Hastings College of the Law, and she goes about it as quietly and with as little assumption as though it were the most usual think[ing] in the world for married women to have enough ambition to undertake a really exacting and arduous course of study."[6]

In 1900, Emma was not particularly uncommon: Women often earned professional

While Julia was in Paris, her younger sister Emma earned a law degree from the University of California, but she married soon afterward and never practiced law.

degrees without intending to pursue a career after marrying. Before reliable birth control, marriage meant a family, and a family meant that women remained in the home. Eliza assumed that Julia would also eventually marry, writing: "Your [sorority] sister Brewer is going to be a real old maid and so is Sister Fisher—and I think it's too bad, for they are nice girls.—You be looking out for a nice young man for yourself. I don't want all my children old maids."[7] But Julia's "marriageable years" were over by the time she left the École. In her era, a woman of thirty was considered a lifelong spinster.

The point was moot. No evidence exists for Julia's ever having formed a romantic attachment with anyone. Despite Eliza's wishes, she clearly did not intend to marry, have children, and end her career. There were ample cautionary tales to support her decision, including the experience of Sara Whitney, one of her Paris roommates. An aspiring sculptor, Sara was so talented that the world-renowned artist Auguste Rodin accepted her as his student. After three years, when Sara faced returning to Oakland due to a lack of funds, Phoebe Hearst paid for her to continue studying with Rodin for a fourth year. During that time, Sara became engaged to Boardman M. Robinson, an American portrait painter, whom she married in France in 1903. They moved to New York, where Boardman became a magazine cartoonist and later an instructor at the Art Students League. Sara and Boardman had two children, which apparently marked the end of Sara's artistic career. No further mention of her appeared in the press.[8]

Since Julia evidently wrote or spoke very seldom about being a female architect—focusing instead on simply being an architect—it is easy to forget how many obstacles she must have encountered. Even her proud mentor, Professor Chaussemiche, did not believe Julia was capable of performing all the physical tasks required of a male architect:

"She will make a good architect. Her taste in ornamentation, however, will require correction. In common with her compatriots, Miss Morgan mixes styles a little too much, but this slight fault will pass away and I have no doubt she will succeed in her country. I would have no hesitation in confiding to her the erection of a building, as in the science of the profession she is far superior to half of her male comrades. It is true that an objection can be made that a woman cannot climb scaffolds to oversee the work or come in contact with the laborers and mechanics, but an architect's functions do not consist exclusively of these disagreeable duties. His office work, such as preparing plans and sketches, is more important, and for this women are well suited."[9]

The East Bay had also changed dramatically between 1896 and 1902, as California's Arts and Crafts movement transitioned from the fringe to the mainstream. In Southern California it evolved differently, as demonstrated by the restrained and graceful bungalows of Charles and Henry Greene, which were strongly influenced by Japanese architecture. (The Thorsen House, built in

1909 on Piedmont Avenue in Berkeley, is one of the few Greene brothers' commissions in the Bay Area.) Northern California's version of the Arts and Crafts movement was more rustic and more focused on the interplay between architecture and landscape.

Its three intellectual founders were the reclusive Reverend Joseph Worcester, who in the late 1870s built a simple barnlike wooden home for himself in the Piedmont hills; Bernard Maybeck, who in the late 1890s recognized the transformative potential of this house, and built a similar one for himself nearby; and Charles Keeler (Maybeck's first client), whose book *The Simple Home* codified many of the tenets of this emerging style. Keeler's affection for the local landscape inspired Annie Maybeck, who with several other women founded the Hillside Club in 1898. This East Bay group advocated siting buildings around the contours of the land, and also around the locations where mature trees grew (in contrast to San Francisco, which had been laid out on an exacting grid plan that ignored the city's varied elevations). The Hillside Club listed guidelines for residences as well, advocating unpainted wood inside and out, since "no colors are so soft, varied, and harmonious as those of wood colored by the weather." Consciously rejecting the convoluted designs of late-nineteenth-century houses, the Hillside Club advocated straight lines, simple furnishings, and "over-hanging eaves [which] add to the beauty of a house with their long shadows." This new focus on banishing Victorian complexity—in favor of simple architectural forms that deferred to the surrounding landscape—was as radical a movement as modernism became several decades later, when it sought to sweep away the timeworn examples of the Arts and Crafts era.[10]

Another major impetus for the East Bay's transformation was the philanthropy of Phoebe Hearst, whose funding of the campus expansion prompted a local building boom. In September 1899, Parisian Émile Bénard was announced as the competition's winning designer, but his selection soon proved controversial. Phoebe and many others found him argumentative and difficult when he visited Berkeley to collect his $10,000 prize. Ultimately the fourth-place winner, New York architect John Galen Howard, was chosen instead, and charged with implementing a modified version of the Bénard plan, as well as creating an official Department of Architecture on campus. Howard was a restrained and elegant man whose graceful design style was shaped by three experiences: a brief apprenticeship with the Boston firm of influential architect Henry Hobson Richardson; followed by two years working at the leading New York architecture firm McKim, Mead, and White; and concluding with two years of study at the École des Beaux-Arts (where he did not earn a degree, but distinguished himself nevertheless).[11]

The East Bay building boom also benefited Avery, who had no trouble finding work with the Oakland architect Walter J. Mathews. Unfortunately, however, Avery had begun to show signs of emotional instability. The constant hazing he'd received in Paris can't have helped. A girlfriend of his, whom Eliza and Julia had both briefly mentioned, no longer appeared in their letters. Avery was kind but impulsive—he overspent on gifts for the family and overworked himself while caring for Mrs. Sherman, their recently widowed elderly neighbor. Music had always been a joy for him, but now a simple trip to San Francisco for a concert might exhaust him for days. It had been nearly two years since Julia had seen Avery, and she surely must have noticed a change. With nearly all the Morgans once again living under one roof, there is no written record of her reaction.[12]

Within a month of Julia's return, she was working in John Galen Howard's office, which was initially located on campus in the East Hall building. One of her earliest projects was to install the iron gates that then marked the university's southern entrance. (They were replaced in 1908 by the familiar bronze portal known as Sather Gate.) With twenty-two buildings to design and construct, plus an academic department to establish, Howard was constantly busy. Within a few months, he had hired more associates and moved his firm off-campus to downtown Berkeley.

As his office grew, Julia took on more responsibilities, as the press noted: "Miss Julia Morgan is taking charge of the architectural classes [for] John Galen Howard ... who is at present in the east." She also assisted in the creation of what is arguably Howard's greatest project: his ornate Hearst Memorial Mining Building, the idea for which had sparked Phoebe's initial involvement with the university's expansion. Though she was not mentioned in the newspaper accounts, Julia was almost certainly present in November 1902, when Phoebe and William Randolph Hearst joined Howard to witness the official laying of its three-ton cornerstone. Jack London reported on the event for W. R.'s *San Francisco Examiner*: "Heads were bare more often than not and everyone seemed to feel the sacredness and solemnity of the occasion... The cornerstone was laid with a spirit very much like that with which the cornerstones of the old cathedrals must have been laid. The spirit of the new university, instinct with life, was in the air."[13] Phoebe paid for the mining building's construction in its entirety, spending a total of more than $1 million (equivalent to $30 million today). This formal Beaux-Arts building is somewhat deceptive: The historicism of its exterior conceals a decidedly modern interior, including a multi-chimneyed smelting furnace and a three-storied open lobby, illuminated by glass domes supported on slender iron columns.

Julia also served as construction superintendent for the open-air Greek Theater, which was inspired by the ancient amphitheater at Epidaurus. This ambitious project was not part of the original campus plan. The idea came instead from Benjamin Ide Wheeler, the university's president and a Greek scholar, who wrote in 1899: "In climate, in its comparative isolation, in much of its scenery, and in its location as a gateway to the Orient, California is strikingly like Greece.... The art, the love of beauty, the passion for culture, are all here in the germ."[14] The theater seated 6,500, and

*John Galen Howard—chief architect for the Berkeley campus—hired Julia in 1902.
Among other tasks, he put her in charge of constructing the Greek Theater.*

it was filled to overflowing on May 16, 1903, for spring graduation ceremonies, when the as-yet-unfinished arena was rushed into readiness. The press reported: "Few people know that many of the important details of the amphitheater were personally superintended by Miss Julia Morgan and under her direction men worked almost all night on many occasions to get the work finished . . ."[15] Its formal dedication on September 24, 1903, might have been when Julia and W. R. were introduced, though the actual circumstances of their first meeting are unknown. Hearst spoke briefly at the event, saying, "I am interested in this university and want to help it. This is no great thing, but it seemed to be a need, and I am happy to supply it." Howard also spoke, praising the theater's "monumental and festive character," and the way the "pure, simple, big classic forms harmonize exquisitely with the forms of hill and canyon."[16]

Since Bernard Maybeck oversaw the competition to redesign the campus, he did not create any of its initial buildings, with one significant exception. Before the winning architect was selected, Phoebe hired Ben to construct a home where she could "entertain the community in general and the women students in particular." His response was Hearst Hall, an extraordinarily innovative wooden structure whose immense central room—according to noted architecture critic Esther McCoy—represented one of the earliest uses of the laminated arch. For a few years, Phoebe resided there on her brief visits to Berkeley. In 1902 it was moved to the southern edge of the campus (onto Bancroft Way, near where the Hearst gymnasium is now located), a process made possible by disconnecting each of its 54-foot-high arches for transport. Flower-draped pergolas were then added to both sides of its entrance, and Hearst Hall became the gathering spot for the university's coeds, who formerly had nowhere but the basement of North Hall set aside for their use.[17]

Maybeck followed this tour de force by designing another remarkable residence for Phoebe in Northern California: a vast Teutonic lodge resembling a palace on the Rhine, which was christened Wyntoon (for the Wintu, the local Indian tribe, known for their beautiful beaded and feathered baskets). Built beside the rushing McCloud River, surrounded by fir and pine forest, and overlooked by a snowcapped Mount Shasta, Wyntoon was a sight straight out of a fairy tale. Around 1900, Phoebe first saw the region on a visit to Charles Stetson Wheeler, a fellow regent at the University of California. Entranced by his dramatic wood and stone hunting lodge, which had been designed by architect Willis Polk and sited on a bend of the river, she requested Wheeler's permission to lease some nearby property where she could build her own riverfront home. Wheeler somewhat reluctantly consented, with the

In 1902, Phoebe A. Hearst hired Maybeck to design Wyntoon, her enormous Bavarian-style castle in the forests of Northern California.

understanding that Phoebe's residence would be a modest one. When Maybeck subsequently designed a seven-story stone castle for her, Wheeler resigned himself to the inevitable loss of his isolated hideaway. Maybeck shared with Phoebe his picturesque vision of her reposing in Wyntoon's towering great hall: "The dark height of the room, the unobstructed archways, the deep blues, reds, and yellows of the cathedral window, to which time had given maturity, the tapestries, the little flicker of fire, and the roaring of the river outside; and you, satiated, tired, and inspired by the day's trip among hazel, dogwood, great aged pines, rocks, cascades, great trunks of trees fallen years ago . . . here you can reach all that is within you."[18]

Late in 1902, while Maybeck worked on Wyntoon, Julia undertook an independent commission to design El Campanil, a 72-foot-high concrete bell tower for Mills College for Women. It's likely that Julia was recommended by Phoebe, who was among the school's patrons. Founded in 1852 as a young ladies' seminary in nearby Benicia, it was sold in 1865 to former Christian missionaries Cyrus and Susan Mills. They purchased a large farm on the eastern edge of Oakland, where they constructed a four-story mansard-roofed building that they chartered as a college in 1885. Patterning its curriculum on Ivy League schools, Mills prided itself on being the only women's university west of the Mississippi.[19]

The tower's underwriter was college trustee Mollie Smith, who was married to the Oakland millionaire Francis Marion Smith,

the "Borax King." In 1902 Mollie noticed an idle set of ten bronze bells sitting on the campus grounds. They had been cast in 1893 for the World's Columbian Exposition in Chicago, then sent to San Francisco for the California Midwinter International Exposition of 1894, held in Golden Gate Park. The bells were donated to Mills College, which lacked the money to construct an imposing campanile until Mollie generously funded it. Her gift provided tangible evidence of the college's continuing success. A campus bell tower was rare at the time, having been previously constructed only at Cornell and a few other East Coast colleges. The tower was sited across the lawn from Mills's genteel administration building, which had been constructed in 1871 in proper Victorian style. In contrast, Julia's 1902 Mission-style design for El Campanil looked to the future, with its clean lines and graceful arches. Furthermore, it was designed by a woman.[20]

El Campanil was forward-looking in another way as well: It was made entirely of steel-reinforced concrete, regarded at the time as an experimental material. Julia had studied ferrous-concrete construction at the Beaux-Arts, and was confident that her design was structurally sound, but she soon realized she would have to contend with the doubts and disparagement of the project's builder, Bernard Ransome. He was the son of renowned engineer Ernest Ransome, who in 1884 had designed San Francisco's Arctic Oil Works, the nation's first building constructed entirely of reinforced concrete.

RIGHT: *In 1904, Julia designed El Campanil—the reinforced-concrete bell tower at Mills College for Women in Oakland—which survived the 1906 earthquake unscathed.*

Bernard Ransome asserted his superior experience by questioning the accuracy of Julia's calculations and denigrating her knowledge of steel-reinforced concrete construction.[21] Though the Mills contract had specifically placed Julia in charge, Ransome convinced Mr. Smith to challenge her authority. Julia's situation was complicated, since she did not yet have her license to practice architecture. Ultimately, Mollie complied with her husband's wishes, writing to Susan Mills: "It is needless to say that Mr. Smith has the greater faith in Mr. Ransome, and is thoroughly convinced that his statements are correct beyond the shadow of a doubt. And we desire that at the dedication, Mr. Ransome's work be recognized as fully as the architect's, if not more fully."[22] Ransome's name did appear above Julia's on the opening program. Nevertheless, her extensive drawings for El Campanil make clear that she had a thorough understanding of the materials (though Ransome reduced her specifications for 12-inch walls to his father's specifications for 6- to 8-inch walls between the buttresses).[23]

On the day of El Campanil's dedication—perhaps as a sign of her continuing confidence—Mollie hired Julia to design Mae Cottage, part of a charitable compound known as the Mary Smith College for Friendless Girls, located 4 miles south of the Morgan family home. In addition, Julia soon began working on the second of her six commissions for the Mills College campus, the Margaret Carnegie Library (another Mission-style building, with a dramatic open-beamed reading room on its upper floor).[24] Nevertheless, her experience with Ransome put Julia on her guard. While she was destined to contend with many men who treated her condescendingly, she was careful not to concede supervisory control on future projects.[25]

Julia's commissions for the Hearsts were generally devoid of such conflicts. Both Phoebe and, later, W. R. typically deferred to Julia's expertise and respected her authority. They had a harder time getting along with each other. Though Julia's first meeting with W. R. may have been in the fall of 1903 at the Greek Theater dedication, it is likelier that Phoebe had introduced them the previous summer at her Pleasanton estate, the Hacienda del Pozo de Verona (named in honor of the sixteenth-century Veronese limestone wellhead, or *pozo*, which stood at its entrance). W. R. began constructing this sprawling Mission-style mansion in 1894, intending to use it as his rural retreat. Instead, it became the site of a power struggle between mother and son (one that Phoebe, as the keeper of the family fortune, was destined to win).[26]

Born in San Francisco in 1863, William Randolph Hearst was the only child of the fabulously wealthy George and Phoebe Apperson Hearst. W. R. grew up independent, rebellious, and proud of being a native Californian. Father and son agreed on the topic of California's superiority. George was fond of saying that it was fortunate the pilgrim fathers hadn't discovered California before they settled on the East Coast, "or else nobody would have lived there." W. R.

attended Harvard but longed for California, as he confessed to his mother:

"I have had the 'molly grubs' for the past week or so. I am beginning to get awfully tired of this place, and I long to get out West somewhere where I can stretch myself without coming in contact with the narrow walls with which the prejudice of the bean eaters has surrounded us. I long to get out in the woods and breathe the fresh mountain air and listen to the moaning of the pines. It makes me almost crazy with homesickness when I think of it, and I hate this weak pretty New England scenery with its gently rolling hills, its pea green foliage, its vistas, tame enough to begin with but totally disfigured by houses and barns which could not be told apart save for the respective inhabitants. I hate it as I do a weak pretty face without force or character. I long to see our own woods, the jagged rocks and towering mountains, the magestic [sic] pines, the grand impressive scenery of the 'far West.' I shall never live anywhere but in California and I like to be away for awhile only to appreciate it the more when I return."[27]

Soon after penning this letter, W. R. got his wish, when Harvard requested that he leave at the end of his junior year. (This process was known as rustication, which differed from expulsion. The student was invited to depart with the option of returning to Harvard at some future time.) His banishment upset Phoebe, but didn't distress

W. R. was twenty-four in 1887 when his parents gave him the San Francisco Examiner. *His media empire eventually included twenty-eight newspapers.*

W. R., who later in life would say, with tongue firmly in cheek: "It takes a good mind to resist education."[28] In fact, W. R. was well-read, well-traveled, and highly intelligent, in addition to being active in politics. (One reason for his rustication was the uproarious party he staged on campus to celebrate the 1884 presidential victory of Democratic candidate Grover Cleveland.)[29]

Harvard made an indelible impression on W. R., even though he left without a diploma. He was appointed business editor of the *Lampoon* (a job that often went to the wealthiest student, since the college newspaper never made any money). He sold advertising, generated a substantial profit, and began his lifelong love affair with newspapers. In 1887, when he was twenty-four, W. R. received the *San Francisco Examiner* as a gift from his parents. It was little more than a third-rate paper, which Hearst family lore maintains George had won in a poker game. W. R. transformed it into "The Monarch of the Dailies," as its masthead declared, by turning San Francisco on its ear with his sensational journalism. The *Examiner* brought murderers to trial, staged a wedding in a balloon over the Golden Gate, published popular songs, and battled the city's corrupt administration. By the time Senator George Hearst died of cancer in 1891 in Washington, D.C., he'd seen his son turn the *Examiner* into a financial success.

George left his $20 million mining fortune (equivalent to $540 million today) entirely to Phoebe, requesting that she decide the amount their son should receive from the estate. W. R. was a spendthrift, as both his parents knew. His having to go to Phoebe to request funds gave her a measure of control over his activities, though never as much as she wished. W. R. worked conscientiously on the *Examiner* during the week, but he spent his weekends holding parties at the large home he leased in Sausalito. His hostess was his longtime girlfriend, Tessie Powers, a waitress whom he'd met in Cambridge. This situation infuriated Phoebe, as W. R. well knew. This may be the reason he avoided Sausalito when discussing a potential building site for his own home. Instead, he asked his mother for her consent and enough money to build himself a country retreat on their Pleasanton horse ranch 30 miles south of Oakland.

Phoebe gave W. R. her permission to begin the project. His chosen architect was a gifted thirty-year-old New Yorker named Albert Cicero Schweinfurth. W. R. gave his mother a progress report early in 1895: "Jack [Follansbee, his lifelong friend] and I went to Sunol [near Pleasanton] last Sunday. The men [working] up there have plowed over all those hills and done a lot of good work, so I imagine the ranch has been considerably improved and that the grass will largely take the place of weeds this Spring. Schweinfurth has completed drawings for the house and I will forward them in a few days." He had also

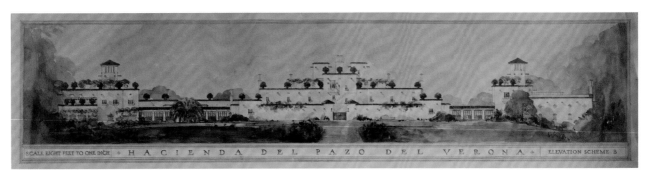

In 1895, W. R. hired architect A. C. Schweinfurth to build his Pleasanton retreat, the Hacienda del Pozo de Verona (the House of the Wellhead of Verona). It grew so large that Phoebe confiscated it, then hired Julia to remodel it in 1903.

Among Julia's additions were a second-story bedroom for Phoebe, and a later swimming pool and separate residence for the Hearst grandsons. It is likely that Phoebe introduced Julia to W. R. at the Hacienda circa 1903.

telegraphed Phoebe earlier in the week to ask: "What's money limit for country house."[30]

Whatever arrangements W. R. had made with his mother, they were insufficient. When Phoebe arrived for a personal inspection, she was incensed to discover an elaborate fifty-room mansion under construction. Her reaction was swift. She moved into it herself, hiring Schweinfurth to continue the project and making the hacienda her principal residence. Schweinfurth wrote to explain the hybrid design concept he and W. R. had formulated:

"When we started out to build the house out there it was the intention to produce a restful, quiet country home entirely in keeping with the climate, the surroundings, and totally different in every way from the ordinary country house. The nearest neighbors of the hacienda are aborigines [the Ohlone are the local tribe to which Schweinfurth referred], the Mexican Indian settlement directly opposite the house, on the other side of the Creek, [which] would seem to indicate that the house as planned and built should have the accessories of a distinctly Spanish-Californian character. This was Mr. Hearst's original idea."[31]

Schweinfurth was still working on the project in 1900 when he died of pneumonia at the young age of thirty-seven. In 1903, Phoebe hired Julia to expand and complete her Pleasanton estate. Julia reportedly added a second story, which included a tower that housed

Julia commuted by ferry to her San Francisco office on Montgomery Street, which she opened in 1904 after becoming California's first licensed female architect.

Phoebe's bedroom; increased the size of the elegant music room; extended the verandas that stretched across the eastern side of the house; and constructed an entire wing for Phoebe's staff. In 1909, Julia returned to build two additional structures: an indoor swimming pool decorated in aqua-colored tiles; and Casa Bonita, an outbuilding also referred to as the "Boys' House," where all five of W. R.'s sons stayed when they visited their grandmother.[32]

Since Julia did not yet have her license, it was essential that she continue working under John Galen Howard's auspices. In the spring of 1904 Howard requested the university trustees' permission to relocate from Berkeley to San Francisco, where he maintained he would have better access to materials, contractors, and staff. It was a propitious time for such a move, because of recent transportation improvements. The newly established Key Route's electric streetcars (which stopped

near the Morgan home) traveled on a trestle that stretched 3 miles across the bay to Yerba Buena Island. There passengers boarded a steam-powered paddle-wheeled ferry for the final 2.85-mile journey to San Francisco's Ferry Building. With as many as ninety-seven daily runs, passengers seldom had to wait before boarding. They could make the journey from Berkeley to San Francisco in thirty-five minutes, for a ten-cent fare.[33]

Julia joined Howard when he relocated his ten-person office to San Francisco's Italian-American building at 456 Montgomery Street. While she continued working on his university projects, she also accepted independent commissions. Some came from her social connections with childhood friends and sorority sisters. Agnes Borland Hart hired her to design a modest wood-shingled cottage in Berkeley, and Elma Farnham commissioned a large and imposing home in nearby Piedmont. Phoebe Hearst also provided occasional introductions. This may have included recommending Julia as the architect for the North Star house, which combined the functions of a mining company headquarters and a manager's residence in Grass Valley, 60 miles northeast of Sacramento. Julia designed a striking 10,000-square-foot, two-story mansion in the Arts and Crafts style, using materials native to the site: cedar and redwood shingles for its upper story, and stone (taken from the tailings of the mine) for its large, open ground floor, which evoked a baronial hunting lodge in the forests of Northern Europe.[34]

The system of informal social connections on which Julia and her female contemporaries relied for referrals is often termed the "Women's Network." It flourished at the beginning of the twentieth century, when women had more leisure time, thanks to new labor-saving devices, including washing machines, vacuum cleaners, and refrigerators. Few women worked outside the home, but they nonetheless evinced increasing interest in improving themselves and their communities, due in part to the political momentum generated by the women's suffrage movement. Julia benefited from this network, but she also quickly built her professional reputation via the local press. Though she generally refused to give interviews, her business was undoubtedly aided by frequent newspaper articles that

referred to her by such terms as "one of the most successful architects on the coast."

This praise did not save Julia from having to contend with hostility, for instance, when she was under consideration to design a proposed residential wing for a Berkeley hospital in January 1904. A city council member objected: "Commissioner Elroy refused to vote on the resolution. He explained that he did not know Miss Morgan, who is the only woman architect in the city, and therefore did not care to sanction her appointment." He was overruled by the other council members, and Julia successfully submitted designs for the annex to Berkeley's Fabiola Hospital later that year.[35]

Among Julia's earliest commissions was her 1904 North Star House, which utilized the native redwood and stone near Grass Valley, northeast of Sacramento.

An early milestone in Julia's career placed her in the history books once more. On March 1, 1904, she became California's first female licensed architect, having passed the state board's evaluation. This allowed her to leave John Galen Howard's office and establish herself independently. She did not go far, relocating initially to another office in the same building. A friend of Julia's family claimed that she left Howard's firm after becoming aware that he had spoken of her as an excellent architect whom he "didn't have to pay . . . anything, because she is a woman." While this tale has not been definitively proven, it may well be accurate. Julia gave a public lecture a few years later in which she spoke about the miserably low wages a beginning female architect could expect. She may have been obliquely alluding to her own experiences. North felt that Julia likely viewed Howard as more of a businessman than an architect, and someone who delegated more tasks than he should have. These charges could never have been made about her.[36]

A common misconception is that Julia was one of the only female architects working in Northern California. In her volume *Early Women Architects of the San Francisco Bay Area*, architectural historian Inge Schaefer Horton documents fifty female architects who worked in the region from 1890 to 1951, some of whom preceded Julia. A few of these women became reasonably well-known: Lilian Bridgman, who designed houses in Berkeley; Ella Castelhun, who received her state certification license one year after Julia; and several of the women

who worked in Julia's office, including Dorothy Wormser Coblentz, Charlotte Knapp, and C. [Charlotte] Julian Mesic. Julia mentored many young women, in some cases even funding their continued education (as she did for Charlotte Knapp). There were always women working in Julia's office, but she was careful to maintain a balance between males and females. She didn't want her firm (which she titled Julia Morgan Architect) to become known as one that only employed women.[37]

Julia differed from her female contemporaries in having undergone a much more rigorous education. Most female architects and draftswomen began as apprentices and simply learned on the job. After the fall of 1903, women could enroll in the University of California's architecture department, which Howard opened that year. Between 1903 and 1912, eleven women graduated from the program. Of these, three married and never worked in the field, seven taught in local schools, and only one, Lilian Bridgman, became a practicing architect.[38] Though other Northern California women journeyed to Paris and sat in on architecture classes at the École des Beaux-Arts (including Fay Kellogg and Katherine Budd, both of whom preceded Julia by one year and became professional architects on their return to New York), no other woman successfully completed the École's challenging program. The number of American men who studied architecture at the Beaux-Arts before 1902 was 233; only forty of them successfully graduated with their *diplôme*.[39]

Even more singular was Julia's exceptional versatility. Instead of being confined to designing women's clubs and residential commissions, as were most of her female peers, she produced a wider variety of building types and a greater quantity of completed commissions than most of her American colleagues. Her work for William Randolph Hearst also placed her in rarefied company. Only two other American architects—both decades her senior—designed equivalently lavish estates. Richard Morris Hunt (1827–1895) created many elaborate mansions, including Alva Vanderbilt Belmont's Marble House, constructed in Newport, Rhode Island, in 1892, and George Washington Vanderbilt's Biltmore Estate in Asheville, North Carolina. Built in 1895, and containing 250 rooms, Biltmore is generally considered the largest private residence in America. Stanford White (1853–1906) also designed many palatial homes, including Louis Comfort Tiffany's French Gothic mansion on Madison Avenue and 72nd Street in New York (which was completed in 1882 and demolished in 1936). Another of White's major projects was Rosecliff, which he designed in 1902 for Hermann and Theresa Fair Oelrichs of Newport, Rhode Island. Dignified and formal, its columned exterior was patterned after the Grand Trianon at Versailles.[40]

Julia ran her office in a similar manner to Hunt's and White's, by imitating the organizational structure she had learned in the Paris ateliers. This time, however, she was the *patron*, and her staff were the *élèves*.

She gave them small sketches (similar to the *esquisses* initially required for a Beaux-Arts project), which she expected them to develop into fully detailed drawings (equivalent to the *projets rendus* that were judged at the École's competitions). Julia's longtime engineer and friend, Walter Steilberg, declared, "She probably had as efficient an office as I've ever been in." Though the hours could be long, many young architects, draftsmen, and draftswomen vied to work for her, since the experience was an education in itself: "The apprentices were paid ten dollars a week, and we lost money on them for a year.... Her criticisms were made in the form of quick but very definite sketches; to which she sometimes added this quotation from her friend and teacher Bernard Maybeck: 'If you strike a difficulty don't shy away from it; maybe it's an opportunity in disguise; and you can make a feature of it.'"[41]

Julia was soft-spoken, but she radiated "this wonderful quiet power," her client and friend Hattie Bell Marcus recalled. Ed Hussey, another one of Julia's longtime employees, mused: "She seemed rather modest, actually. There never was any sense of overbearing. She wanted to get the feeling of what the people wanted and to do everything correctly, but she in no sense gave you the feeling of superiority or that she was trying to impress people.... She got her ideas over, but she didn't have to do it in an obtrusive manner."[42]

Her attire was also modest, as architect Dorothy Wormser Coblentz recalled: "She always wore a kind of a gray-blue suit and a cape, her hair pulled up in a knot, and a

For work, Julia wore beautifully tailored silk blouses and woolen suits—as well as men's trousers underneath her skirts, so she could climb scaffolding.

rather largish hat, a white blouse with a high collar and white cuffs, always scrupulously white. I'm sure the shoes were very sensible. And she looked like a nobody. She couldn't have looked less distinguished."[43] Julia's white blouses were made in Paris and featured exquisite detailing. Like her architecture, they were quiet rather than bombastic, but they were beautifully made. The type of hand-tailored wool suit she wore—with its long fitted jacket and long matching skirt, pleated to allow for easy movement—was known as a "walking suit." In vogue in Paris in the 1890s, these outfits made sense in an era when women were becoming active outside the home. Julia continued to wear this eminently practical wardrobe throughout her career. She had her jackets equipped with large external pockets, allowing her to dispense with purses and keep her hands free. She wore men's trousers underneath her skirts so she could

climb scaffolding with complete confidence. She usually donned a bell-shaped hat, which provided partial protection from the sun. (She may also have found it useful as a means of elevating her height, since these high-crowned hats added an inch or two onto her just-over-5-foot-tall frame.)[44]

In the few short years since she had returned from Paris, Julia had accomplished a great deal: designed several major civic buildings, opened her own office, and hired her first employees. Then everything changed in an instant. On April 18, 1906, an immense earthquake (estimated at 7.9 on the Richter scale) struck San Francisco at 5:12 in the morning. Julia was almost certainly asleep at home in Oakland. One local resident recalled:

"I came out of a thick slumber with the con-
fused notion that I was on a bucking horse.

The plunging continued, followed by a deafening roar. I jumped out of bed .... but the swaying of the house flung me from one wall to the other, very much as a passenger aboard an ocean liner would be flung about by a heavy sea. Then, quite suddenly, the vibrations ceased. Fortunately it was daylight.... The family ran to the front windows and looked out. A fine dust from crumbling chimneys filled the air. But the frame houses of the quarter in which we lived were standing valiantly. We had all felt earthquakes before, and ordinarily before the shock was over we were disposed to joke about it. But this time we knew that we had passed through an earthquake that was no joking matter. Although, even at this point, we did not realize how serious matters were.... The streets were filled with people making ominous predictions. But we declined to share their pessimism. We felt that the worst was over, although disturbing plumes of black smoke began to appear on the horizon. But what was a fire or two? San Francisco had one of the most efficient fire departments in the country. The fires would be under control in half an hour."[45]

The federal government later estimated that the amount of damage caused by the quake itself was 3 to 10 percent of the total. The worst of these effects was the collapse of the municipal infrastructure, which began seconds after the first impact. Cast-iron water pipes broke all over the city—first, the 3-foot-diameter pipes that delivered water from the nearby reservoir; then the smaller pipes that routed it underneath the streets; and finally the thousands of street-corner hydrants, which immediately dried up. There was a pause between the first thirty seconds of shaking and the second thirty seconds. During this short respite, utility poles fell all over the city, sending arcing wires lashing and twisting into the streets to ignite anything they touched. The gas pipes that supplied the underground boiler units broke, and the escaping gas fanned and heightened the flames. Thousands of chimneys toppled, scattering glowing coals everywhere. Fuel tanks burst, causing rivers of kerosene, gasoline, and oil to pour through the houses and out into the street, heading straight for the flaming electrical wires.

Only seconds after the shaking stopped, twenty-five or thirty fires had broken out. With no water to fight the conflagration, the

The 7.9 earthquake that struck San Francisco on April 18, 1906, killed thousands, felled hundreds of buildings, and sparked fires that incinerated nearly 30,000 structures.

fire brigade was powerless to respond. The fires burned for three days throughout the northeastern portion of the city, blackening 2,600 acres (or 490 city blocks).[46] The exact number of casualties is unknown, but it is estimated at somewhere between five hundred and three thousand people (this wide range was due to the unknown number of residents in the city's densely populated Chinatown). While tragic, San Francisco's death toll would have been far worse if the quake had struck a few hours later, when the streets were full of people. In total, 28,188 buildings in the city were destroyed. Among its population of 400,000 residents, more than half were homeless.[47]

Oakland was largely spared. There were five deaths, and a number of damaged buildings, but the water system remained intact. One of the most affected structures was a block south of the Morgan home: the newly built Unitarian church, which collapsed in a pile of fallen masonry. Relief camps were set up around San Francisco, housing 50,000 people in the early days. At night, East Bay residents could look across the bay and see "a sky as bright as day along a forty-block front. Light filled the sky for miles around. . . . Observers saw great black clouds of smoke tinged with pink from the billowing flames. An occasional blast of explosive gave 'a suggestion of warfare,'" according to one writer.[48]

Few earthquakes of higher magnitude have ever been recorded in North America. The temblor's long-term effect on San Francisco was enormous; the cost of its destroyed property was $500 million (equivalent to $13 billion today), of which only half was insured. Almost every civic building in the city was damaged.[49] These were grim statistics, but for architects, they also held another meaning: Earthquakes represented not only tragedy but also opportunity.

CHAPTER SIX

RUNNING THE OFFICE

THIRTY-FIVE YEARS AFTER THE CITY'S DEVAS-
tation, Julia recalled: "I opened my own
office, where the earthquake found me."[1]
Her first independent operation had been
running for less than eighteen months when
it was destroyed in mere seconds. In a futile
attempt to create a firebreak on
the second day of the conflagration,
city officials set off dynamite
along Montgomery Street and the
rest of the business district. This
not only failed to stop the fire,
but also ensured that nothing
remained in its aftermath. Julia lost
her business records, as well as
many of her drawings and personal
files. She sent photos of the ruins
to Pierre, who replied: "What can
be more graphic, indeed, than your
pictures of vacant sites, displaced

foundations . . . and not sufficient water
to make mortar for bedding new footings!
Devastation could not be more complete. We
particularly regretted hearing of your own
losses of your plans, your sketches and notes
of travel & study abroad. . . . It must seem like

Julia's Montgomery Street office was destroyed by dynamite in a futile effort to halt the post-quake fires raging throughout the city.

a hideous nightmare to you."[2] It may well have seemed so, but it did not slow her down. One week after the quake, Julia placed an advertisement in the *Oakland Tribune*, listing her home address as her current office. Soon after, the newspaper reported: "Miss Morgan has built a temporary workshop in the yard of the Morgan home . . . where she is going on with her work."[3]

Both of Julia's reinforced-concrete buildings at Mills College survived the earthquake unscathed, as Susan Mills proclaimed in a letter that was excerpted in the press: ". . . because of the excellent work done by our architect Julia Morgan, her two buildings, the beautiful bell tower and the new library, suffered no damage."[4] (It may have given Julia some secret satisfaction to know that both the bell tower, on which Bernard Ransome had interfered, and the Margaret Carnegie Library, on which he had not, were equally unharmed.) There could be no better testament to her abilities, and this may have been the deciding factor in her selection as the architect to rebuild San Francisco's Fairmont Hotel.

Completed just a few weeks before the quake, this sparkling white six-story hostelry was a symbol of the city's increasing sophistication. In 1874, the cable car line was extended to the top of California Hill. This allowed the railroad magnates Charles Crocker, Leland Stanford, and Mark Hopkins—as well as James Flood, the silver king—to build splendid mansions atop what soon became known as Nob Hill. Another wealthy silver miner, James Fair, purchased property nearby, but he died in 1894 before beginning any construction. His two daughters (prominent East Coast socialites Theresa Fair Oelrichs and Virginia Fair Vanderbilt) felt San Francisco needed luxurious accommodations far more than it needed another Nob Hill mansion, so they commissioned architects James W. Reid and Merritt J. Reid to build a six-hundred-room hotel that resembled a Renaissance palazzo on the property instead. The Fairmont's reinforced-concrete exterior was sheathed in rusticated granite on the ground floor and covered in shining white terra-cotta tile on its five upper levels. The lobby was decorated in Louis XIV style, with immense marble columns supporting its elaborate white-and-gold ceiling. Construction began in 1903 and was completed in 1906, at which time the sisters sold the hotel to real estate investors Hubert and Hartland Law, just days before the quake.[5]

The city's firefighters fought hard to save the Fairmont, which was set back from the street, providing it some protection. "With a thin stream of water drawn from an old cistern, the firemen held the line for more than two hours. Eighteen hours of labor in killing heat had [already] left most of the men exhausted, but with little equipment and less water at their disposal, they continued the battle." The Stanford, Flood, and Crocker mansions had already succumbed to the fire—and then it was the hotel's turn: "The Fairmont, with its glacial beauty, was still untouched. But the same breeze which had helped hold back the fire from the south earlier, gently blew the searing heat off Sacramento Street until the windows could no longer resist. The flames entered a northwest corner room where paints and varnishes were stored. Before the morning [of April 19] was over, what had fittingly been called 'the most magnificent . . . [hotel] in the world' was gutted."[6]

The building remained standing, though it was little more than a hollow shell. The Law brothers initially hired Stanford White to rebuild it, but when he was killed in a tragic shooting just two months afterward, Julia took over the commission. The structure had shifted 7 feet from its massive concrete foundation, and many wondered if it was even salvageable. Julia worked for several weeks in a drafty construction shack behind the hotel—where she later recalled long nights spent reviewing her engineering calculations, while rats jumped over her feet—until she could stabilize the structure sufficiently to allow her to relocate her own office inside.[7]

The rebuilt Fairmont Hotel opened on the one-year anniversary of the earthquake: an extraordinary achievement, which Julia had accomplished on time and under budget. This triumph raised San Franciscans' morale and confirmed Julia's ascending reputation. The occasion also resulted in her being interviewed by an exasperating reporter, Jane Armstrong of the *San Francisco Call*. Knowing that Julia had studied architecture in Paris, Armstrong apparently expected to speak with a lively coquette, decked out in the latest French fashions. Instead, she described

The Fairmont Hotel had just opened when it was gutted by the 1906 fire. Julia was hired to re-engineer it—a task many thought impossible.

Julia as "a small, slender young woman with something so Quakerish about her, . . . dressed in drab and severely hairpinned." When Armstrong questioned her on how she had approached her role as the interior decorator, Julia calmly replied that her job had been to rebuild the hotel, not to decorate it. In later years, Julia became well-known for her reluctance to be interviewed. Armstrong's article (which also ran in the industry journal *Architect and Engineer of California*) may have contributed to her dislike of the process.[8]

Though she worked on the Fairmont Hotel commission by herself, there were so many jobs available that Julia took a junior partner for the only time in her career. She had met Ira Wilson Hoover when he joined Howard's San Francisco office in the spring of 1904, not long before her departure. Hoover was born in Ohio in 1871 and worked as a draftsman in various Cincinnati firms before studying

Julia's rebuilt Fairmont Hotel opened exactly one year after the quake, on time and under budget.

architecture at the University of Pennsylvania. He was known for his drawing ability, and was sufficiently talented to win a scholarship that allowed him to spend a year traveling through Europe, studying and sketching. Hoover apparently approached his work much as Julia did. A letter he wrote to his family during the scholarship competition could have been written by either of them: "Last week was the hardest one I ever experienced. I made one run of 64 hours, broken by only two hours of sleep. I began working Wednesday night at one o'clock (after sleeping two hours) and did not sleep again until Friday night at twelve. The men in the office were very kind to me, and made me take short walks, noons and evenings, and in other ways helped me through the week."[9]

In the summer of 1907, Julia and Hoover opened their office on the thirteenth floor of San Francisco's Merchants Exchange Building on California Street. Their move occurred only after Julia had completed the post-quake repairs she'd been hired to make on the building, which Chicago architect Daniel Burnham had designed in 1904 as a center for the city's maritime commerce. In collaboration with local architect Willis Polk, Julia also designed its skylighted lobby and commissioned talented marine painter William A. Coulter to create several cloud-filled scenes of sailing ships for its upper arches. Another former employee from Howard's office also joined them: Harriet Young (who became Harriet de Mari after her marriage), a draftswoman who worked for Julia for many years.[10]

In 1907, Julia moved her San Francisco office to the Merchants Exchange at 465 California Street.
She helped to design its skylighted hall, and commissioned its maritime murals by William A. Coulter.

Julia built many homes in the style now called First Bay Tradition, including the 1914 Bell house, which shows her characteristic blending of rustic elements and formal design.

Most of Julia and Hoover's collaborations date from 1907 and 1908. The majority were modest residences located in the region south of the university (including Elmwood Park and Claremont Court, areas now often referred to as the Brown Shingle neighborhoods). There was a tremendous demand for housing. In the weeks immediately after the earthquake, thousands of San Franciscans relocated to temporary outdoor camps scattered throughout Oakland, a sight one resident said reminded him of "Cripple Creek or Leadville in the days of a [mining] boom."[11] Many of these evacuees decided to remain in the East Bay, which had a much better climate than San Francisco's, as well as the considerable

advantage of functioning public utilities. The seven redwood-shingled houses commissioned by real estate investor Louise B. Goddard were typical examples of Julia and Hoover's work. These modest and comfortable homes had their entrance doors placed on the side rather than the street frontage, which made the best use of their rather narrow city lots. Furthermore, their central hallways and staircases allowed residents easy access to both the dining room and the living room, located on either side of the stairs.

Julia and Hoover also promoted their work by displaying it in local exhibitions, including one at the Home Club in East Oakland: "[The exhibit] will show work done by successful architects during their student days and the early periods of their development. Fellow exhibitors include Willis Polk, John Galen Howard, Bernard Maybeck, and others.... Among the many clever drawings to be noted are Miss Julia Morgan's sketch for the Friday Morning clubhouse in Los Angeles, and the composite by Miss Julia Morgan and Ira Wilson Hoover for [the Sunday school building of] St. John's Presbyterian Church at Berkeley."[12]

This modest Craftsman-style Sunday school building, completed in 1908, was the first of multiple structures commissioned by St. John's Presbyterian Church for its double lot on College Avenue in Berkeley. Though the exact date when Julia and Hoover dissolved their partnership is unknown, this project appears to have been one of their final collaborations. Hoover married in 1909 and relocated to Chicago, after which Julia never took another junior partner. Her former

employee Dorothy Wormser Coblentz mused: "I don't know how long that lasted, and I can't imagine it ever lasting because she certainly was not going to—I mean, wherever she was, she was boss."[13]

At this time Julia also worked on a few solo commissions that must have given her particular satisfaction: She prepared preliminary plans for the Oakland hospital known as the King's Daughters Home for Incurables (an institution with which she remained involved for many years); she designed a large redwood-shingled sorority house for Berkeley's Kappa Alpha Theta chapter, to which Julia belonged as a charter member; and she oversaw the post-earthquake repair of the Oakland First Baptist Church (where she was a member of the congregation).[14]

Julia's most important early project was her design for the sanctuary at St. John's Presbyterian Church (now known as the Berkeley Playhouse's Julia Morgan Theater),

Julia's masterful 1910 design for the sanctuary of St. John's Presbyterian Church in Berkeley (today's Julia Morgan Theater) relies principally on the interplay of wood and sunlight.

built two years after the Sunday school. Considered one of the finest examples of the East Bay's Arts and Crafts style, this worship hall celebrates the nobility of unadorned wood and the sanctity of daylight, both of which contribute to its numinous atmosphere. Julia turned the parishioners' economical building requirements into design advantages, particularly in her use of open roof beams and trusses that draw the eye down the central aisle to the altar. This simple space also strongly evokes a time-honored example of vernacular architecture: the humble American barn (so much so that when young Morgan North first saw it, he asked, "But Aunt Julia, where's the hay?").[15]

During the years immediately after the earthquake, Julia became a public advocate for San Francisco's careful redesign. In 1908 she gave a lecture at the California Club on the topic of civic architecture (disproving the conventional wisdom that she never gave public presentations). Her Beaux-Arts training was in evidence when she argued that "every public building—schools, libraries, and civic offices—should be distinguishable by certain features in the architecture," stressing the importance "of a building portraying upon its face, as it were, the purpose for which it was designed." This concept was known at the École as *caractère*.[16] She demonstrated this principle beautifully in her design for St. John's front façade. The building's role as a neighborhood church is gracefully established both by its residential scale and by the rhythmic symmetry of its clerestory windows and exterior gables.

In the post-quake era, Julia continued to champion causes large and small. In 1910, she led a group discussion about future plans for the King's Daughters Home. In 1912, she served as a judge for the Outdoor Art League's children's contest, titled "Merits of the Window Box." She openly supported women's suffrage and accepted a position as one of the patrons of the College Women's Suffrage League in 1912. (Some of Julia's clients opposed women's suffrage. Louise Goddard was strongly against it, and while Phoebe Hearst believed in the cause, her objections to the extreme actions of some of the suffragettes led her to repudiate the campaign. Nevertheless, Julia was not deterred from taking a public role to advocate votes for women.)[17]

Later in 1912, Julia presented a lecture titled "Women Choosing Architecture as a Career" for the university's Vocational Opportunities program. It is highly likely that Julia's exact words were quoted in a newspaper headline summarizing her speech: "Julia Morgan Says There Are Chances for Those of Her Sex Who Are Plodders." This final word was a surprising one, and perhaps a telling indicator of her opinion of her own work methods. Julia further elaborated:

"It is too soon to predict just how women will acquit themselves in a field so old, yet so new to them. A woman graduate will generally look for the largest immediate financial returns, while her brother will look for the largest future, and one of the first points to decide for the student seriously considering architecture as a profession is whether her interest and love for the work is strong enough to carry her through the student days, through the days of small earnings and through the vicissitudes of a business life. It might be a practical help to state that the salary of the college graduate on entering an office is usually about $10 to $12 dollars a week [equivalent to $265.00 to $315.00 today], or about what an office boy will earn who has been in the office for a year. If students could find work in offices even without salary, during part of the vacation period, they could not only gain insight into the way the actual work is done, but practical knowledge that would help them in obtaining a position on graduating."[18]

Thanks to Julia's colleague and friend Walter Steilberg, as well as several other members of her staff, excellent information exists to show how Julia's "actual work was done." Dozens of interviews with her family, friends, and employees were conducted in the 1970s by farsighted researchers at the University of California's Oral History Center of the Bancroft Library. A complex portrait emerges, one that especially illuminates Julia's management style.

Walter in particular never forgot his earliest encounters with her. He was looking for an engineering job in 1910, but had missed out on the post-quake rebuilding boom by a few years. At Arthur Brown Jr.'s firm, he was turned down, but told to try Julia Morgan's office instead. Walter recalled, "I guess he saw my look of dismay at the idea of going to work for a woman architect, and he said, 'Don't fool yourself, there is no man in the profession in this neighborhood who is any better as an architect.'" Julia did indeed need an engineer, and she promptly hired him.

"About the third morning I was there, I went in quite early. She was on the 13th floor of the Merchants Exchange Building. I went on into the library and there was a ladder going from the 13th floor clear out over California Street to a scaffold . . . and the scaffold was just a group of 2 x 12s with some 2 x 4s tacked to the edge and some chicken wire at the end. No such fancy scaffolding as you have today. Here was Miss Morgan coming down this ladder, and when she got down she just stepped off and said, 'Oh, you must go up and see what they are doing.' . . . Well, I was scared to death. I crawled up this ladder, and my only impulse was to lie down . . . and yell for help . . . . I think she was one of the most fearless people I have ever known."[19]

As the *patron* of her own atelier, Julia handed out the assignments to her employees, who numbered anywhere from six to ten people. Dorothy recalled:

"Her office was a real apprenticeship. To work with her was to work from the ground up, and it had certain drawbacks because you learned to be so thorough that you couldn't put your pencil down unless it meant something. . . . She had a little desk in the drafting room, a little work table . . . on which she had a few books; so when she was there she had a little privacy. . . . There

she would sit and concentrate and produce these funny little drawings in which the whole story was foreshadowed.... You saved those little scraps like jewels....
I remember on one occasion I was doing a house and when it came time to lay it out, it wouldn't go on the lot, and of course she came in ready to give me Hail Columbia. I fished out the little scrap, and she had made a mistake in copying down the figures.... So she said, 'Yes, it was her fault...' She was a delightful person, if you weren't being scolded."[20]

Walter remembered Julia becoming impatient when one of her draftsmen—who was particularly skilled at freehand drawing—departed from the sketch she had given him.

Instead he drew a beautiful staircase that was so low, it could only have been ascended on one's hands and knees. Julia tartly said, "Well, young man, I can't deal with fiction writers." Walter continued: "A lot of [inferior] architecture that we have is because people get themselves in a jam and then they twist themselves around ... to get out of the jam. She felt you ought to face the facts from the beginning."[21]

Julia was informal with her staff, whom she addressed by their first names. To them, she was always "Miss Morgan." When they discussed her in her absence, they often called her "J. M." Draftsman Ed Hussey recalled: "She never raised her voice or got angry, but she was very particular in her work. I know some big men used to quail in her presence, because

Julia was a generous but exacting boss. In 1921 her employees included (l. to r.) draftsman Louis Schalk, engineer Walter T. Steilberg, draftswoman Dorothy Wormser Coblentz, draftsman Thaddeus Joy, and painter Camille Solon.

she was very demanding and everything had to be right; but she did it in a very ladylike manner."[22] She respected the privacy of her clients, and expected her staff to do the same, but as Dorothy recalled:

"When the cat was away, the mice would play. When a job would go out for bids, we would have a pool and we would each put a dime in the pool guessing the amount of the contract. The one who got closest took the pool, which by then must have been all of eighty or ninety cents. We'd go out to the nearest bakery and buy a cake; then we would have a party and eat the cake. I remember one day when we were in the library with the cake on the table and she came in with a client. That wasn't very good [laughing]; her displeasure was manifest."[23]

While it is understandable that Julia wouldn't have wanted a client to witness her staff having such a celebration, there was an excellent reason for them to do so. In good years, Julia divided her excess profits among her employees, keeping only enough for the office overhead and her own living expenses. Money meant little to her, and neither did time, as author Elinor Richey recalled: "Since work filled her cup, she couldn't understand why it would not likewise suffice her staff ... who she seemed to have regarded somewhat as cousins once removed, taking interest in their children and sending presents at Christmas. But she also showed affinity by expecting them to like overtime as much as she." Dorothy recalled, "The pressure was terrible.... She didn't realize that people had private lives.... time meant nothing to her.... It was hard work but every minute was worthwhile."[24]

Julia kept long and unpredictable hours, visiting craftsmen in their studios as well as inspecting construction sites. She never learned to drive, North explained, because she liked to look around too much. But having a car and driver was essential to her work. For several years Julia was able to hire Avery for the job. She had tried employing him as a draftsman, but he was too unreliable. He might leave for lunch and then not return to the office for several days. Walter explained: "He was in frail health and he couldn't stand the tension of the drafting room.... So she took him out of the office again and he acted as her chauffeur for a long time. She had a Hudson, which was then a big car, and he drove her around to various jobs. If it was at all possible, she'd see a job at least a couple of times a week."[25] Perhaps while Avery

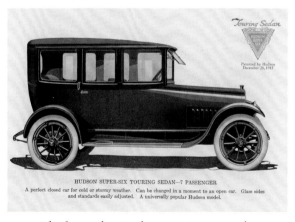

HUDSON SUPER-SIX TOURING SEDAN—7 PASSENGER
A perfect closed car for cold or stormy weather. Can be changed in a moment to an open car. Glass sides and standards easily adjusted. A universally popular Hudson model.

Julia frequently visited construction sites and artisans' workshops. When Avery's mental health began to deteriorate, he ceased working in her office and instead chauffeured her in a Hudson motorcar.

drove Julia throughout the Bay Area, the two of them reminisced about their many European adventures.

One of Julia's most dedicated employees, Thaddeus Joy (known as T. J.), was almost as close to her as a family member. He was twenty-three when she hired him four months after the 1906 earthquake, and he remained in her employ almost continuously for the rest of his career. Furthermore, T. J. and his wife, Anna, named their eldest daughter Julia.[26] He was a brilliant artist who excelled at producing full-size drawings (in an unmechanized era, when a draftsman's equipment consisted primarily of a straightedge and a T-square). His sister, two daughters, and son also worked in the office at various times. When T. J. traveled to Spain and met Arthur and Mildred Byne—American dealers in Spanish art who were old friends of Julia's—they shared with her their impressions of him: "We took a great fancy to your Mr. Joy though he was not as gay as the name might lead one to hope; but quiet, hesitant, and slowly revealing a very considerable supply of taste, sense, and ability. It was a pleasure to show good things to him, he understood at once; we felt it must give you satisfaction to [have] him on your staff."[27] Julia's Beaux-Arts philosophy was evident in T. J.'s drawings, in which he made a similarly adept use of architectural ornament, relying on the historic motifs he found in Julia's extensive architecture library.

The office was divided into four sections: a large drafting room for the engineers, draftsmen, and draftswomen (in which Julia kept her own drafting table at the back); a small

office for the secretary and office manager; Julia's own tiny private office; and the library, which was available to all her staff. Julia's first biographer, Sara Boutelle, described these areas in detail, calling the library the heart of the office:

"Bookcases lined the walls of the 12-by-14-foot room, at the center of which was a table where [architect and landscape architect] Charles Adams Platt's *Italian Gardens* [a favorite work of Julia's, published in 1894] or huge leather-bound French volumes on art might be open. At least five hundred books related to architecture were available for study, and everyone in the office was expected to consult them. The larger area of the main drafting room, with long, broad tables around which the designers worked (nine or ten of them in good times), had a massive drawing file topped by a bust of Dante. Here for reference were the drawings for earlier Morgan buildings. A prominent bulletin board featured different architectural photographs from Morgan's collection each week, and every member of her staff had to be familiar with these. Morgan had a high-backed desk in the drafting room, where she made many sketches and conferred at each step with those who drafted the working drawings."[28]

Julia emphasized the central goals of the École's curriculum: developing excellent drawing skills; becoming knowledgeable about historic architectural precedents; and learning how to creatively combine traditional motifs in order to arrive at a new design. She wrote to one of her former draftsmen, Bjarne Dahl:

"Your study idea is interesting, and probably will fix periods etc. in your mind. But I imagine what you need most is a freer design—a knowledge of the elements of various styles so that your hand rather than your mind will lead you into making more varied and interesting forms. You have a good sense of proportion and balance, but you lack fullness & richness of expression. I'd suggest you watercolor & freehand draw (doesn't that sound like familiar old advice?)—never mind, it's just as true and necessary—Why not try working in charcoal, making details of simple caps, ironwork, tile, large size on the wall [sic], of vases, anything to call for decorative invention—as though your days & nights were not full enough already! Even if you can't afford 'decoration,' the practice will free your eye & hand." [29]

A phrase Julia used often was "getting the feeling," which seems to have had two meanings for her. In the first case, she used it to convey her insistence that all finished work be of the same high quality that was produced by architects and builders centuries ago. Both the materials and the execution should successfully reinforce the unique theme of a building (another example of her focus on *caractère*). Julia's attention to detail caused some of her staff to grumble at times. Warren (known as Mac) McClure, one of her construction superintendents, wrote to a colleague: "Of course we hear much talk about 'Getting the feeling' and a lot of time and money-consuming antics are indulged in as usual." Julia was adamant about maintaining exacting standards, as Mac admitted on another occasion: "The lady visited us on Wednesday as you probably know. She was just 'so-so' and made us tear down one corner turret which was entirely up. The stones didn't have the 'right feeling.'" [30] Julia also used this phrase to mean that her designs should always address the feelings and desires of her clients. Elinor Richey wrote: "She had a knack of planning a house that suited her clients exactly. This came from genuine solicitousness of their needs and desires. Unlike the independent Maybeck, who started from an exterior design and sometimes cut short an objecting client with, 'But this is what I *see* for you,' Julia started her planning [by considering her client's] interior requirements and preferences." [31]

Sometimes a client's request was unusual; for instance, when one man told Julia that his wife hated right angles, she designed a house for them that contained none. Sometimes the request might seem trivial, like the man who told her he hated having to leave his warm bed in the morning. Julia rigged up a cable that allowed him to turn on the heater from underneath his bedcovers. Her focus on her clients meant that she met personally with all of them, rather than delegating this task to her staff. She generally saw them first in her small office, then led them into the library, where they could peruse engravings and photographs with her and discuss their ideas. At other times, however, she met with clients only off-site. This occasionally led to problems: Dorothy once designed a breakfast nook for a man she'd never seen, and it turned out he was so corpulent that it was impossible for him to fit into it.[32]

Julia was eager to train another female architect who would carry on her legacy, but this was a goal she never fulfilled. Dorothy referred to the women on the staff as "'Miss Morgan's female children' [who] all disappointed her, because they let things such as husband, children, easier jobs, etc., influence their staying there." Dorothy included herself on this list; she worked in Julia's office for only four years.[33] In 1915, Julia discussed the small number of female architects with a *Cal Alumni* newspaper reporter: "Few women persevere as architects though many of them take up the study. Many are impatient to reach the top of the ladder too soon, matrimony takes others, but the greatest lures are the teaching positions in the high schools. There is a large field for women there, and as the salaries are good one cannot blame them for accepting unless they are determined to become architects."[34]

Instead of training a single protégée, Julia supported many women's organizations and causes. These endeavors were often unprofitable; she frequently donated her services outright, or billed at a far lower rate than her usual 6 percent commission.[35] In 1912, she contributed the plans for U.C. Berkeley's Senior Women's Hall, to be built along Strawberry Creek. John Galen Howard had designed a hall for the male students (dubbed Golden Bear Lodge) in 1906, and by 1909, the

university's coeds were busily raising funds for their own retreat. Julia helped them select the exact site, a wooded hillside at the easternmost edge of the campus. The press reported that Julia would "aid the college women in every way. She will donate the plans for the structure and attend to the supervision of its building."[36] She designed a simple shed-roofed clubhouse with a clapboard exterior, clearly in the First Bay Tradition. A central fireplace occupied the main room's long wall, opposite which was an uninterrupted row of windows equipped with cozy seating. Girton Hall (the name they chose, in honor of Cambridge's Girton College, the first residential college for women) was initially intended only for the senior class, but it was soon opened to all female students. (In 2014, the building was carefully moved to the university's botanical garden, east of the campus. It is still in use and has been renamed Julia Morgan Hall.)[37]

In April 1912, Julia attended the university's spring pageant. Phoebe Hearst was also in the audience to witness *Parthenia: A Masque of Maidenhood*. Four hundred young women performed, all costumed as nymphs, sylphs, and dryads, in what the *Oakland Tribune* called "... a splendid pageant—one unique in the extreme."[38] Less than one week later, multiple newspapers announced that Phoebe had hired Julia to design a camp on her Pleasanton property, which would temporarily accommodate three hundred women for the YWCA's annual convention to be held the following month. (Phoebe generously offered her land because the Capitola hotel that usually hosted the conference was no longer considered adequate.)[39] This project—designing and constructing seventy-five platforms, each of which supported a four-person tent, as well as building a temporary auditorium and four large meeting tents—marked the beginning of Julia's involvement with the Young Women's Christian Association, for which she ultimately designed more than thirty projects over the next two decades.

The YWCA was founded in New York in 1858 as the Ladies Christian Home Association. By 1877, it had merged with a women's prayer group and renamed itself the Young Women's Christian Association. Chapters proliferated around the country as women grew increasingly independent. By the turn of the century, hundreds of YWCAs provided for the welfare of thousands of young women who had begun to leave their rural farms and move into cities to take jobs as stenographers, nurses, and teachers. Urban areas lacked suitable accommodations, and boarding houses—which relied on a transient male population—were particularly unsafe. Two separate divisions of the group handled these concerns: The Traveler's Aid Society assisted young women on their arrival, and the YWCA addressed their long-term needs by providing safe accommodations, recreational activities, educational classes, career counseling, and the vital opportunity to form social connections with other unmarried young women. Phoebe was very involved with both of these groups, and so were two of Julia's closest friends and former sorority sisters: Grace Fisher Richards, who was the first director of the Oakland YWCA, and Mary McLean Olney, who chaired

the building subcommittee for the YWCA's National Board.[40]

A few months after the summer conference in Pleasanton, Julia was in consultation with the Oakland YWCA staff about where to site its new building. The initial location under consideration was at Fourteenth and Castro Streets, very near the Morgan family home. The YWCA already had a small office on this property, but the proposed project was much larger: a three-story building with additional basement and mezzanine levels, the presence of which would have undoubtedly changed the character of the neighborhood. The press noted, "If another site is chosen, the plans will be changed to meet the requirements." Another site *was* chosen, on Fifteenth and Webster, six blocks east of Julia's home— though it isn't known what specific role she played in the decision.[41]

By December 1912, Julia was the de facto architect in charge of the YWCA's West Coast endeavors. Her first action was to take a cross-country trip to study YWCAs in Los Angeles, St. Louis, Pittsburgh, and New York. The press reported that she was "much impressed with the building at St. Louis, which is six months old. The lighting and general cheerfulness of this structure appealed to Miss Morgan, and they will be incorporated in the local building. . . . Miss Morgan made a special study of swimming pools while she was in the east, particularly those of the girls' schools, including Westover, Boston, and Greenwich."[42]

Construction on the Oakland YWCA was slated to begin in April 1913. Grace Fisher

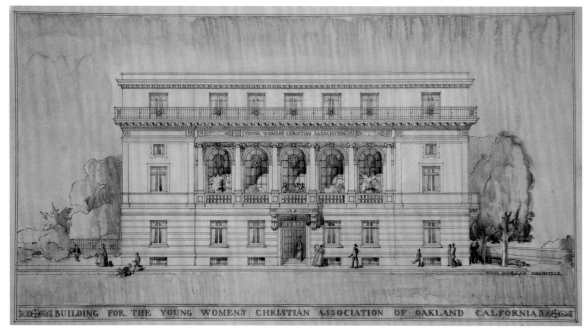

Julia's first major commission for the YWCA (Young Women's Christian Association)
was the palatial Oakland building at 1515 Webster Street, completed in 1913.

YWCAs were created to house young working women safely and economically, but Julia's
buildings also provided their residents with beautiful surroundings.

Richards had raised a sizable $200,000 (equivalent to $5.2 million today) in pledges for what she hoped would be "the finest Association building on the Pacific Coast."[43] Julia designed a magisterial structure, inspired by the Palazzo Medici in Florence (which was built for the banker Cosimo de' Medici by architect Michelozzo di Bartolomeo in 1460). It is interesting that Julia should have been inspired by a specific palazzo only seven years after completing the Fairmont Hotel, which was based on the general design of an Italian Renaissance palazzo. The precedent for the Oakland building's interior came from yet another Renaissance feature: a two-story arched courtyard created by Donato Bramante in 1504 for the Santa Maria della Pace Cloister in Rome. Julia had admired the use of light at the St. Louis YWCA; in Oakland she employed a glassed-in roof that bathed its interior with sunlight. The courtyard's walls were inscribed with a verse from Psalm 19:1–2: "The heavens declare the glory of God, and the firmament showeth his handiwork. Day unto day uttereth speech, and night unto night showeth knowledge," a reminder that the goal of the YWCA was to develop a young woman's spiritual—as well as moral, physical, and intellectual—growth.[44]

As usual, Julia was involved in every detail of construction. Administrator Mary Tusher remembered that "when Miss Morgan was building the Oakland YWCA, whose exterior design included fifty columns faced with small tiles, she sat down and lifted separately thousands of tiles, scrutinizing each. All imperfect tiles were returned."[45] Benjamin Ide Wheeler, U.C. Berkeley's president, spoke at the dedication ceremony: "Not the givers of money, though they are essential—but the makers—are those we should honor." He credited Julia, "whose rarely combined vision and practicality" made her the maker, and the "genius of the undertaking."[46]

In the spring of 1913, while the Oakland YWCA was underway, Julia was announced as the supervising architect for a permanent YWCA complex in Pacific Grove, a small oceanfront community south of Monterey. Phoebe was involved in its genesis, having urged the YWCA directors to construct a permanent site for the next year's summer conference. She donated the funds for its first building, the administration hall, and helped convince the Pacific Improvement Company (a consortium of realtors) to donate 30 acres of beachfront property to the YWCA (with the understanding that the conference camp would generate $30,000—equivalent to $800,000 today—in local investments within five years). Julia's first task was to move the platforms and tents from Pleasanton to Pacific Grove. This was Asilomar's modest beginning; Julia eventually designed more than a dozen buildings at the site over the ensuing twelve years, making it one of the largest Arts and Crafts–style compounds in the country.[47]

Pacific Grove was a site Julia had loved since childhood. Flora North recalled, "The whole family used to frequently come to Pacific Grove in the summer; they were old stomping grounds for her. She knew the area;

Asilomar—the YWCA's oceanside retreat in Pacific Grove—features more than a dozen of Julia's buildings, including the Stuck-Up Inn (the female staff's dormitory).

she could always out-hike me . . . she could do me in every time because you'd have to go to the next highest hill to see a certain view of the Bay."[48] The YWCA's conference center was first known as Guardamar ("Watch by the Sea"), then was more harmoniously named Asilomar ("Refuge by the Sea"), to celebrate the beauty of the local landscape. Julia used its regional materials—granite rocks, Carmel fieldstone, redwood beams, and cedar shingles—to construct buildings that deferred to the matchless setting. Though their exteriors remained simple, their interiors were carefully finished, with exposed beams, stone fireplaces, and generous windows that showcased the view.[49]

Julia designed nearly everything at Asilomar: its stone entrance pillars; its social and dining halls; its chapel and its eight-hundred-seat auditorium; and even its lodges and employee residences (including the "Stuck-Up Inn" for the women and the "Pirate's Den"—a pun on the dessert-loving "Pie-Rats"—for the men). Asilomar is still in operation, and little altered; its new additions have been sensitively done. It is possible to stay there and experience what thousands of young women encountered when they attended their leadership conferences from 1913 on.

It is perhaps less easy to comprehend how meaningful it was for these young working women to make the trip, after having spent an entire year staging bake sales, bazaars, wagon rides, and variety shows to pay for it. One attendee reminisced in 1920:

"The morning hours [were] filled with conference classes, so full of inspiration and help. Afternoons for pleasure, hikes, drives.... Supper time all gathered together in the beautiful dining hall. The college girls who had charge of the dining hall had taken the name 'the Stuck Ups.' When things seemed a little quiet, these girls would gather, [and] march around the room, singing 'We Are the Stuck Up Girls'.... Then came chapel, a marshmallow roast, and a quiet gathering and prayer in one's own group circle. The ten days go by so quickly. When we say goodbye, we begin to hope and plan for next year."[50]

During the spring of 1913 (when in addition to the Oakland YWCA and Asilomar, Julia was completing the Spanish-style Miss Ransom and Miss Bridges' School for Girls in Piedmont), the press announced she would be designing the downtown headquarters and printing plant for W. R.'s *Los Angeles Examiner*. This was not her first project for Hearst: In 1910 she designed a large Mediterranean estate in Sausalito (which remained unbuilt, due to his lack of funds). Two years later, she constructed a small bungalow on land he owned along the south rim of the Grand Canyon. (This modest cottage was demolished in 1942, when the property was added to Grand Canyon National Park.) It was quite a leap on W. R.'s part to hire Julia to design a modest bungalow, then almost

From 1913 to 1915, Julia designed her first large commission for W. R. Hearst: his Los Angeles Examiner *building, at Broadway and Eleventh avenues.*

immediately afterward entrust her with producing a five-story 100,000-square-foot concrete structure occupying the entire block of Broadway between 11th and 12th Streets in Los Angeles. His faith in her was absolute, however. Built entirely in the Mission style, the *Los Angeles Examiner* building was surrounded by an open arcade at street level, and topped by a 35-foot-high dome covered with yellow and blue ceramic tiles. A central arched entrance opened into an extravagantly decorated lobby, where wrought-iron grilles, gold-leafed columns, and molded plaster ornaments mingled in profusion.[51] This two-year project represented the first time Julia had worked closely with W. R., who was eager to participate in every design decision.

This was the busiest Julia had been since she opened her office nine years before. It is unlikely that her clients realized the strength and courage she needed to keep working throughout this time. On March 17, 1913, her youngest brother, Sam, was on his way to a fire in the station's roadster. He had been promoted from fireman to fire chief the previous year, so he was being driven by J. Schiflett, his subordinate. Without warning, Schiflett crossed directly in front of a streetcar. The press reported that Schiflett "either did not see the approaching streetcar or did not realize the speed at which the trolley was going. When the Automobile was halfway across the tracks it was struck by the streetcar and turned over several times." Both men were thrown into the street, and Sam sustained by far the worst injuries, having "a fracture of the jawbone, [and] possible internal

In 1913, Sam—Julia's youngest brother—died at only thirty-three, when the automobile in which he was riding was struck by a streetcar.

injuries, and . . . a large portion of his scalp torn away." He was taken to the hospital in "a precarious condition."[52]

Sam was the sunniest member of the family, blessed with more self-confidence than the other Morgan men. The Norths recalled that he and Julia shared a special bond, and could talk about anything together.[53] He had many friends and was described in the press as one of Oakland's "choicest bits of masculinity," who served as an active board member of the irreverent Anti-Osculation Society (Society Against Kissing), "declaring that not only is it an aid to microbes, but a trap by which innocent young bachelors are lured to matrimony."[54] Eliza worried about Sam's safety, writing Julia on one occasion how relieved she was to encounter a fire that she knew Sam had missed, since he was on his way to San Francisco at the time. Then Eliza looked up and saw a familiar figure standing high atop the burning building: It was Sam, who had learned of the fire just before boarding the ferry and had rushed back to fight it. Sam knew his profession was dangerous, writing to Julia about a cross-country trip he was taking: "I hold that a person had better see all that he can when he gets a chance. I have got the chance so I am going to take the trip. Of course it will cost me a few dollars, but then I am liable to get killed any hour; and I might as well see a little of this world as well as the next."[55]

Sam's accident was followed by six months of the family's anxious watching and waiting while he lingered at nearby Providence Hospital. He was young and vigorous, and for awhile he seemed to be recovering. Instead, Sam died of pneumonia on September 3, 1913, at the age of thirty-three. Two days later, they held his quiet funeral at home, in the living room where Emma and Hart had married thirteen years before. Sam was buried in the family plot at Oakland's Mountain View Cemetery.[56] The youngest member of the family had died first—the one Morgan male who at an early age had discovered a career at which he excelled. Their heartbreak at his loss—the emptiness they felt when Sam did not bounce through the door each evening—must have been severe.

Julia had been the architect for the Oakland hospital known since 1908 as the King's Daughters Home. (It was officially named the King's Daughters Home for the Incurables, but Julia preferred to leave off "the Incurables," to make it sound less bleak.)[57] After Sam's death, the hospital became a cause for all three Morgan women. Both Eliza and Emma served for decades on its board, and Julia remained involved in the hospital's expansion plans. Eliza asked Julia to design a decorative wrought-iron entrance arch, which she donated to the hospital in memory of Sam.[58] Each time they passed beneath that archway, they must have been thinking of him.

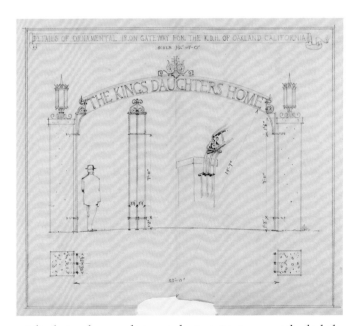

Julia designed a wrought-iron archway as Sam's memorial, which the family donated to the King's Daughters Home, an Oakland hospital.

CHAPTER SEVEN

A LITTLE SOMETHING

JULIA WORKED STEADILY FROM 1913 THROUGH 1916, completing the *Los Angeles Examiner* building and continuing her numerous designs for the YWCA. Asilomar, where eleven of her original buildings survive, occupied much of her time. Julia's 1913 Social Hall (known today as the Phoebe Apperson Hearst Social Hall) was the compound's first major project. It possessed many of Asilomar's characteristic design features: a single-story reinforced-concrete structure, surfaced with river rock and crowned by a redwood frieze beneath a sloping roofline. The interior was one large room with exposed trusses and a welcoming stone fireplace. In 1915, Julia completed the Grace A. Dodge Chapel. For a dozen years, it was used for assemblies as well as church services (until Julia built Asilomar's large auditorium, Merrill Hall, in 1928). The back wall of the chapel—behind its combination altar and stage—consisted entirely of west-facing windows, an eloquent reminder that Pacific Grove's ocean view was the best scenic backdrop.

When the YWCA held its 1915 national conference in the new Oakland building, Julia was praised for more than its beauty. Her impressive urban palazzo honored and inspired its users, thereby redefining the entire concept of YWCA architecture: "[Its] success has implanted the idea of giving travelling girls and women more than merely convenient surroundings[;] . . . Throughout the US, associations are planning more gracious architecture for their coming buildings."[1]

In 1914, a unique YWCA project was on the horizon: Julia's design for a three-story exhibition hall for the San Francisco World's

RIGHT: *Asilomar's 1915 Grace Dodge Chapel shows Julia's skill in using local materials that defer to their natural setting.*

Julia built Merrill Hall, which seated 800, in 1928; despite its large size, it retains the Arts and Crafts feeling of Julia's other Asilomar buildings.

Fair, known formally as the Panama-Pacific International Exposition (or PPIE).[2] Hosting this elaborate festival was a gesture of defiant optimism for a city so recently devastated by earthquake and fire. In her capacity as the PPIE's honorary women's chair, Phoebe Hearst lobbied for a YWCA building and even helped subsidize it, but she did not have the authority to select its architect. In spite of Julia's design having already been approved by the YWCA board, the fair's architecture committee awarded the commission to the Beaux-Arts-trained architect Édouard Frère Champney.[3] Likely at Phoebe's insistence, Julia was hired to design its interior, a welcoming space with a central information desk, a large circular staircase, an open mezzanine for restaurant seating, and pleasant meeting rooms on its second floor. Julia also designed two simple board-and-batten resting cottages located in the carnival-like Joy Zone. These small, quiet

havens gave women a place to retreat from the noise (and the occasional racy exhibit) featured in this amusement section of the fair.

As political tensions increased in Europe, San Francisco's fair administrators considered canceling the event altogether. Instead, they proceeded, making sure to point out to potential European exhibitors that sending their art for display in Bernard Maybeck's masterful Palace of Fine Arts (the only structure from the fair that survives today) would protect it from potential wartime damage.[4] Since war was declared in Europe on July 28, 1914—five months before the fair opened—the PPIE came to symbolize a more idyllic time. Many Californians, including W. R., regarded it as the New World's decisive architectural triumph over Old-World Europe. After the fair closed in December, he wrote, "No other exposition here or abroad has ever displayed so much artistic and architectural loveliness."[5]

The Lombard House, at 62 Farragut Place in Piedmont, typifies Julia's dedication to her clients; she designed it to resemble an English watercolor in Lombard's collection.

While Julia worked on the PPIE, she also designed some of her most luxurious homes, several of which were in Piedmont, the small hill town located between Berkeley and Oakland. Noted primarily in the nineteenth century for its spa hotel, Piedmont Springs, this city of seven thousand became a luxury enclave in the post-quake years. Two of Julia's notable commissions are located across the street from one another. The Ayer house, at 246 Sea View Avenue, was designed to emulate the medieval houses of Saxony, featuring brick on its ground floor and half-timbering above. Richard Bartlett Ayer was a wine merchant, and Julia designed painted plaster reliefs of grape vines over its entrance door. The

J. L. Lombard house opposite, at 62 Farragut Avenue, also featured exposed framing, but in an English Tudor style, and based on a specific precedent. Lombard showed Julia a nineteenth-century watercolor of a house in Croydon, England, and asked her if she could pattern her design on it. Julia's response was characteristic: She'd never attempted such a thing, but she would see what she could do. She created a 10,000-square-foot home that echoed the painting in many aspects, including its gables, oriel windows, and decorative stonework. This pair of large brick-and-stucco homes reflects Julia's second design phase, which coincided with a general evolution in architectural styles throughout the East Bay. After 1910, wood-shingled bungalows mostly went out of fashion, succeeded by more elegant—and often larger—stucco-clad buildings.[6]

Julia's projects for the YWCA continually increased, a circumstance she regarded as conclusive proof of one of her design philosophies: "Don't ever turn down a job because it's beneath you, [or] because you think you want to do something larger." Around 1910 she had produced a two-room cottage in Monterey for her old friend Grace Fisher, who later became the first director of the Oakland YWCA. Julia modestly attributed all her succeeding YWCA commissions to that two-room building; of course, they were actually generated by her own outstanding talent.[7] Each of her YWCAs addressed the needs of its specific residents. In rural Fresno, she inaugurated "Pullman kitchenettes," explaining, "Many of the girls come in from the country and can bring supplies from home each week. . . . Most . . . preferred to do their own cooking. . . . so a little series of kitchens each complete with a sink, work table, gas stove, and individual food locker sprang into being."[8] In San Francisco's eight-story YWCA, known as The Residence, Julia included small individual dining rooms and kitchens in her design, so the girls would be able to entertain their friends privately. When she was asked, "These are minimum wage girls; why spoil them?" she replied, "That's just the reason."[9]

After America joined the war in April 1917, Julia devoted much of her time to designing YWCA hostess houses in San Diego, San Pedro, and Palo Alto. These homelike buildings, constructed near military training camps, provided visiting families with comfortable accommodations, including sleeping quarters, reception rooms, a cafeteria, a nursery, and occasionally even athletic facilities. The

In her 1922 Fresno YWCA at 1600 M Street, Julia included several small kitchens, so the girls could prepare the food they received from their families' farms.

San Francisco Examiner reported: "Miss Julia Morgan ... has offered to design any or all of the hostess buildings at the camps. This was to be her bit, she said, toward the war work of the YWCA."[10] In a national effort, Julia collaborated with two women with whom she had studied architecture in Paris: Fay Kellogg, who designed hostess houses in the Southeast, and Katherine Budd, who designed them in the Midwest.[11] Julia was also put in charge of overseeing all YWCA construction, requiring her to "superintend the plans for hundreds of buildings in this country and overseas. Doubtless her own ideas will be incorporated.... as [her buildings] are models of utility, comfort, and good taste."[12]

While the YWCA concentrated primarily on the needs of young women aged eighteen through twenty-five, thousands of independent clubs across the country provided similar benefits for adult women. In the nineteenth century, many of these societies focused primarily on self-improvement; by the 1920s their purpose had expanded to include community improvements. When the California Federation of Women's Clubs was founded in 1900, it represented forty organizations with a combined membership of 6,000; by 1920 it represented 531 organizations with a combined membership of 55,000.[13] Julia designed two women's clubs early in her career—San Francisco's Century Club in 1905 and Los Angeles's Friday Morning Club in 1907—and several more over the next two decades. She herself attended the founding meeting of the San Francisco Professional Women's Club in 1916—an organization

At The Residence, her eight-story San Francisco YWCA at 940 Powell Street, Julia designed private eating areas, so young women could entertain their friends away from the crowded dining room.

Julia also designed many independent clubs for adult women, including the Foothill Women's Club in Saratoga, 50 miles south of San Francisco.

that promoted networking and potential career advancement.[14]

Two excellent examples of Julia's women's clubs are the Saratoga Foothill Club and the Sausalito Woman's Club, both built between 1914 and 1918 in the First Bay Tradition. On the Saratoga lot, which was located at the base of a hill, Julia stressed horizontality, designing a single large room with an aisle on one side for the kitchen and other services. Its interior was bathed in light from two walls of windows and an additional rose window, while its redwood-shingled exterior was softened by pergolas that helped it blend into the residential neighborhood. For Sausalito's hillside site overlooking the bay, Julia designed what appears to be a simple redwood-shingled rectangle. In fact, the building has eighteen corners, in order to take advantage of its angular lot and dramatic ocean views.[15]

Walter Steilberg was working in Julia's office during this time, when they had what may have been their only disagreement. She sent him to shoot dozens of her buildings for a photo essay that ran in the November 1918 issue of *Architect and Engineer of California*. Walter surprised her by writing an accompanying article that included these breezy lines: "Gone are the good old days when domestic architectural design was simply a matter of crowning a hilltop with a picturesque pile that would keep out most of the rain and all of the neighbors." He recalled years later that this phrase "didn't delight Miss Morgan. She thought [it] was so trivial. . . . She was

displeased with it. I think her only comment was 'The building should speak for itself.'"[16]

In the midst of Julia's increasing workload came another family tragedy: On March 22, 1918, her older brother Parmelee died in a Pasadena sanitarium at the age of forty-eight. The presiding doctor listed his cause of death as "Cerebro-Spinal Lues," another term for neurosyphilis. Incurable until the advent of antibiotics in the 1940s, this form of syphilis was particularly severe, causing nerve damage that led to mood swings, loss of language, weakened muscles, and eventual death. This cruel disease was both agonizing and scandalous; its victims and their families often kept the diagnosis a secret, fearing social censure.[17]

While Parmelee found professional success elusive, he was more fortunate in his private life. In 1911, at the age of forty-one, he had married twenty-three-year-old Sarah Moon of St. Louis. Their daughter, Judith Avery Morgan, was only seven when Parmelee died. The name of the family member listed on his death certificate is Julia's; it appears she shouldered much of the responsibility during his long illness. Walter recalled that around this time, Julia "would go [by train] . . . to work in Pasadena; she would be away from the office for several days. The capacity of that little lady for work was just incredible."[18] This was likely truer than he realized. Parmelee's letters to Julia during her Paris years reveal his gentle sense of humor and sincere brotherly affection. Surely his death, five years after Sam's, afflicted the Morgans severely.

LEFT: *Saratoga's Foothill Club and the Sausalito Woman's Club were both built from 1915 to 1918 in the First Bay Tradition. Julia flooded Saratoga's club with light; she positioned Sausalito's to take advantage of its view of San Francisco Bay.*

— 119 —

W. R. frequently changed his mind and was often slow in his payments, but Julia felt these difficulties were recompensed by the design opportunities his projects provided.

They held a private funeral for Parmelee in their home, then buried him at Mountain View Cemetery in Oakland. Their stress and sorrow at his loss took a toll on Eliza's health. North reported that she had a stroke the following year and spent the last decade of her life largely incapacitated.[19]

Parmelee had only been dead a year when W. R. approached Julia in the spring of 1919, asking her to design a little something at San Simeon because he was getting too old for camping in tents. She could certainly have turned him down. Her YWCA work involved frequent travel, and her office was a financial success. Dorothy explained: "She didn't need publicity. She always had word-of-mouth references. People kept coming to her. Every job she did was satisfactory to its clients."[20] In addition to her work obligations, her family responsibilities were also increasing. Emma and Hart had moved to a nearby house in Berkeley, but Julia still lived at home with Avery, her parents, and a domestic servant.

Nevertheless, she enthusiastically consented to begin W. R.'s San Simeon project, just as she would unhesitatingly undertake many more of his commissions over the next twenty-seven years. Julia became in effect Hearst's "architect royal," in charge of all his building schemes. While they never had a romance, their connection could best be described as professionally intimate. Walter said, "There was this strange comradeship with [Julia and] Mr. Hearst and it was really genuine comradeship.... They were both long-distance dreamers.... People who belong to that breed don't think of anything but their work. It's not a virtue. It's just that they're made that way, that's all."[21] Dorothy explained, "She was the only person in the world who'd never tried to take advantage of him; he had complete faith in her and she was utterly loyal to him. It was a very nice relationship."[22]

The most important link between them was Julia's love for Phoebe. Julia was aware that W. R.'s seventy-six-year-old mother had spent the 1918 Christmas season with him and Millicent in New York, where she caught a chill. It turned into the deadly Spanish influenza that killed an estimated 50 million people worldwide from 1918 through 1920. In what was effectively her farewell letter, Julia wrote to Phoebe in the spring of 1919: "And so through it all is the thread of your kindness since those Paris days when you were so beautifully kind to a painfully shy and home sick girl. My mother's and yours are the greatest 'faiths' put in me, and I hope you both know how I love and thank you for it."[23]

When Phoebe died on April 13, 1919, at her Pleasanton hacienda, she was widely mourned. California's courts were closed, and all federal buildings flew their flags at half-mast—the first time a woman had received this national recognition. During the preceding twenty years, Phoebe had donated $20 million (equivalent to $300 million today) to many organizations that are still flourishing, including the California missions; the Sempervirens Fund (which became the Save the Redwoods League); the Parent-Teachers Association (PTA); the National Cathedral Girls School in Washington, D.C.; and the University of California. Phoebe's memorial service at San Francisco's Grace Cathedral included

California Governor William Stephens and U.S. Senator James Phelan among her pallbearers.

W. R. inherited an estimated $8.5 million from Phoebe's estate (equivalent to $128 million today). He was fifty-six at the time (which was older than it sounds, because the average life span of an American male in 1919 was 53.6 years).[24] For at least a decade before his mother's death, Julia had known that W. R. hoped to hire her to design an elaborate residence, once he received his inheritance.[25] While he could be a challenging client, he also presented Julia with unparalleled opportunities, Flora explained: "She got plenty of work, but it wasn't the kind of work that she had undoubtedly dreamed of doing. Hearst was probably a windfall in a sense, because she had the training for what he had in mind, and the imagination and the ability."[26]

One indicator that W. R. was in a hurry to begin the project lies hidden within Julia's

On this drawing—one of 10,000 created for San Simeon— Julia and W. R. discussed the proper siting of the three cottages that encircle twin-towered Casa Grande.

Casa Grande's design was inspired by Spanish Renaissance architecture, but it was sturdily constructed of steel-reinforced concrete covered by a limestone veneer.

records. Although Phoebe died on April 13, Julia's first visit to San Simeon occurred on April 8.[27] This was likely the day when W. R. rode his horse up the mountaintop while Julia remained in her taxi, being pulled over the difficult portions of the trail by cowboys riding alongside. While Phoebe remained the owner of San Simeon, W. R. was not allowed to build there. She had evidently not forgiven him for being overly extravagant in 1895, when she took possession of his Pleasanton estate to punish him for overspending on its construction. Phoebe's will even stipulated that the hacienda must be sold and the money distributed among her five grandsons, ensuring that W. R. would never own the Pleasanton property.[28]

San Simeon was his favorite spot in any case; he had been dreaming about building there for decades. Though W. R. began his

discussion with Julia by proposing that she construct a single bungalow, his plans quickly escalated. Walter recalled: "I don't think it was a month before we were going on the grand scale."[29] Since W. R. did not live at San Simeon year-round, he and Julia relied on letters and telegrams, which provide an incomparable chronicle of their collaboration. From the beginning, W. R. deferred to Julia's authority, writing, "I make a lot of suggestions and if any of them are impracticable or imperfect from an architectural point of view, please discard them and substitute whatever you think is better."[30]

Soon the scheme had evolved to include a large main building encircled by three cottages at a slightly lower elevation. In discussing potential architectural styles with Julia, W. R. dismissed California's missions as "very crude and rude examples" of regional buildings, identifying Santa Barbara's mission as the best one, but still calling it "almost clumsy to my mind." Next they considered emulating the Spanish-Colonial style of the 1915 Panama-California Exposition, a relatively modest world's fair in San Diego that was staged alongside San Francisco's much larger celebration. (San Diego's fairgrounds survive today as Balboa Park.) Julia pointed out that its buildings were too large to emulate, "because while the Exposition covers acres with their buildings, we have a comparatively small group, and it would seem to me that they should charm by their detail rather than overwhelm by more or less clumsy exuberance." W. R. agreed, asking her, "But after all, would it not be better to do something a little different than other people are doing out in California as long as we do not do anything incongruous?"[31]

They decided instead to look to the sixteenth-century architecture of the Spanish Renaissance. San Simeon's twin-towered main building, which they named Casa Grande, was inspired by the single-towered cathedral Santa María la Mayor, in the town of Ronda in Southern Spain. Its front entrance was modeled on a sixteenth-century cathedral doorway in Seville. Photographs of both appeared in American architect Austin Whittlesey's 1917 book, *The Minor Ecclesiastical, Domestic, and Garden Architecture of Southern Spain*, one of many volumes they consulted, in true Beaux-Arts style. Employing the architectural language of the past was a creative act, in Julia's mind; it had nothing to do with copying. She explained the concept to another client, who wrote to inquire if she had based her 1920 design for Berkeley's Baptist Divinity School on the nineteenth-century red-brick Oxford Town Hall, of which he had shown her a photograph. Julia replied, "Your memory as to the architectural history is correct. We both know that it is not a copy of the Oxford Hall Tower, but the type of that Tudor Gothic is *embodied* [my emphasis] in your building."[32]

The first structures completed were the three cottages that encircled the front façade of Casa Grande, in much the same way that Mediterranean residences encircle the plaza of an ancient cathedral. Julia's inspiration for the cottages came from the Renaissance villas and farmhouses of Southern Spain, where surfaces were left largely unadorned except for ornamentation around the windows and doorways. Though W. R. wanted to start with the main building, transportation delays convinced him of the wisdom of beginning with the simpler cottages. They commenced construction on all three simultaneously in February 1920. Though at first W. R. and Julia referred to these cottages by the alphabet letters A, B, and C (nicknames that endured), Hearst also eventually gave each one a formal Spanish name that described its view: Casa del Monte faced north to the Santa Lucia mountains; Casa del Sol, in the center, faced the setting sun; and the southernmost Casa del Mar faced the ocean.[33]

From the beginning, the project was overrun with difficulties. Labor unrest was common after the war, leading to a scarcity of construction materials. In addition, shipments were often delayed, whether they arrived by train or by the coastal steamers that docked at San Simeon Bay. Julia reported to W. R.: "The mills are all shut down, the men out on strikes, and it looks doubtful if they will be operating again in time.... The shortage of every kind of material and of workmen out here is incredible." She usually dictated her letters to her secretary, Harriet de Mari, but occasionally wrote in longhand, including this letter, whose draft she sarcastically

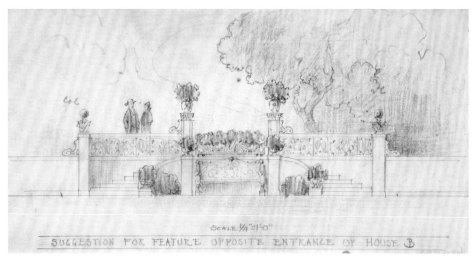

SCALE ¼"=1'-0"

SUGGESTION FOR FEATURE OPPOSITE ENTRANCE OF HOUSE B

Julia was San Simeon's sole architect, interior designer, and landscape architect. It was Job Number 503 among her 700 projects. Her drawing shows two figures who resemble herself and Hearst.

Construction began in 1920 with the three cottages, which were named for their dramatic views. This central one was Casa del Sol, flanked by Casa del Mar and Casa del Monte.

ended with the phrase, "Great life these days." This comment was eliminated from Hearst's final copy.[34]

Julia also had her own hiring problems, as she explained to Hearst. She sent some of her usual San Francisco crew of construction workers to San Simeon, but they refused to stay: "The San Francisco men sent down on the 'bonus' plan have nearly all come back: one turned back at San Simeon, some got to the top of the hill and did not unpack, and some stayed a week or more. They all agreed that the living conditions, money, and food were all right, but they 'didn't like feeling so far away from things.' I am hiring country men as fast as I can."[35]

Another of her early challenges involved excavating the 6-mile road that stretched from the ocean to the 1,600-foot-elevation hilltop. The laborers initially relied on mules and wagons for the work, but once a rough pathway was completed, they used slow-moving Mack trucks with chain-driven motors to transport materials. Everything but the region's native oaks had to be hauled up the hill, including the topsoil and mature trees for the gardens. Julia declared, "I look now at all the old medieval hill-top castles with a sense of fellow understanding and sympathy with their builders. . . ."[36]

Transporting herself to this remote location (which she generally visited at least twice a month) was also a complicated undertaking, since California's famed Highway 1 did not span the entire distance between San Simeon and San Francisco until 1937. Julia's office

records indicate that she made an astonishing 568 separate journeys to San Simeon—an eight-hour train trip in each direction, plus a two-hour car ride from the station to the hilltop. She managed it most efficiently by almost never staying overnight. On one occasion, her draftsman, Bjarne Dahl, accompanied her. He recalled that they worked a half day in the office on Saturday, then caught the ferry from San Francisco to Oakland, where they boarded the night train for San Simeon. It arrived at the San Luis Obispo station as early as 3:00 in the morning, when they ate an early breakfast and waited for taxi driver Steve Zegar, who drove them to the hilltop: "When we got up there, she'd work with the contractor *all day long*. . . . Then it was time to go home. We'd get home the next morning, and I'd be pooped—all tired out—and she'd go right to the [office] door and go to work. . . . She was never tired."[37]

Another trial for Julia involved having to contend with W. R.'s rapidly accumulating purchases, as Walter explained: "Miss Morgan had to deal not only with the visible client across the table from her, but also these other clients who were peddling antiques to Mr. Hearst from all over the world." A lifelong art collector with widely eclectic interests, W. R. described himself as "like a dipsomaniac [drunkard] with a bottle." When art dealers showed him things, he had to buy, and his timing was opportune.[38] In 1909, American export duties were lifted on art that was more than a century old. What began as a trickle of fine objects leaving Europe became a flood after 1918, when war-torn countries needed funds to rebuild, and long-held British fortunes were devoured by inheritance taxes. W. R. haunted New York's art galleries and auction houses, maintaining the same high level of involvement in every art-buying decision that he displayed in every building decision. His possessions fitted so seamlessly into San Simeon's architecture that it is easy to assume he had purchased everything prior to construction. In fact, he owned less than 5 percent of the hilltop's approximately twenty thousand objects before 1919. Julia incorporated Hearst's expanding collections into her constantly evolving design, while simultaneously maintaining the estate's atmosphere of symmetry and balance. Her Beaux-Arts training proved the perfect preparation for this difficult endeavor.

Unlike most prominent American art collectors—including financier J. P. Morgan and industrialist Henry Clay Frick—W. R. specialized in the decorative arts (furniture, metalwork, pottery, and textiles) rather than concentrating on the fine arts of painting and sculpture. Hearst's collections ranged widely in quality as well as in age, origin, and category, since he bought whatever appealed to him. He was particularly interested in antique ceilings, buying dozens of Spanish examples from the American art dealer Arthur Byne. Julia had known Arthur's wife, Mildred, during her years in Paris, and her letters to the Bynes (who became permanent residents of Spain) were remarkable for the frankness with which she expressed her opinions. Julia clearly felt that W. R. was on the losing side

in many of his transactions: "I think you will find you will have a very appreciative and interested client. He has been so thoroughly the victim of some of his dealers that he will, on his side, greatly appreciate real knowledge and fair treatment."[39]

Julia provided the Bynes with a candid description of San Simeon:

"We are building for him a sort of village on a mountain-top, miles from any railway, and housing . . . his collections as well as his family. Having different buildings allows the use of varied treatments. . . . So far we have received from him, to incorporate in the new buildings, some twelve or thirteen [train] carloads of antiques, brought from the ends of the earth and from Prehistoric down to late Empire in period, the majority however, being of Spanish origin. They comprise vast quantities of tables, beds, armoires, secretaries, all kinds of cabinets, church statuary, columns, door frames, carved doors in all states of repair and disrepair, overaltars, reliquaries, lanterns, iron grille doors, window grilles, votive candlesticks, torcheres, all kinds of chairs in quantity, six or seven well heads. . . . I don't see myself where we are ever going to use half suitably, but I find that the idea is to try things out and if they are not satisfactory, discard them for the next thing that comes that promises better. There is interest and charm coming gradually into play."

On another occasion she sent them a similarly lengthy list of diverse objects, all located

Casa Grande's Refectory was lined with Gothic choir stalls and topped with an Italian Renaissance ceiling. Julia extended or trimmed Hearst's collected objects as necessary, to fit them into the buildings.

in the Assembly Room (Casa Grande's largest sitting room, with dimensions of 83 by 31 feet), and staunchly concluded, "Now, I know it sounds frightful, but *it is not!*"[40]

Julia was San Simeon's sole interior decorator, a responsibility she preferred to keep for herself. Walter recalled, "She had a horror of decorators coming in and spoiling a house...."[41] Hearst's most recent acquisitions were sent to the four warehouses they built along the coast, where staff members photographed each item and noted its dimensions. After examining these photos and corresponding with Hearst, Julia incorporated the selected article into her design scheme,

even though the object was seldom the proper size. She wrote to W. R. about his third-floor bedroom suite: "The Gothic Sitting Room ceiling is in and Gyorgy [a woodcarver] is finishing it.... It took some real good nature on the part of the 'wormers' [craftsmen who were antiquing the modern portions] to match up new with old work." Sometimes this complicated process of amalgamation surprised even Julia, who confessed to the Bynes: "I have developed an absorptive capacity that seems ungodly when I stop to reflect."[42]

It is possible to glimpse Julia at work on the hilltop, because she uncharacteristically consented to appear in a home movie that

Hearst shot in 1921. Titled *The Lighthouse Keeper's Daughters: A Romance of the Ranchos*, it was a silent melodrama that W. R. wrote, directed, and starred in—as John Jenkins, the dashing hero—with Millicent costarring as his damsel in distress. In Julia's scene, she stands with them both in front of Casa del Sol—the center cottage, clearly under construction—and unrolls a drawing that they peruse. She is smiling and relaxed, wearing what might be a calla lily tucked into her hatband. W. R. penned this affectionate title card to explain Julia's role in the story: "You now detect/The architect/With patient gaze/She views the plans/That are no man's/Hers is the guilt/For what she built/And hers the praise."[43]

In addition to being the sole architect and interior decorator, Julia was also San Simeon's presiding landscape architect. She and W. R. determined every aspect of the estate, including positioning the buildings, selecting the plants, and hiring the gardeners. They even had four enormous two-hundred-year-old live oaks (*Quercus agrifolia*) moved, in order to ensure that the trees were located in the most picturesque spots. This unprecedented effort involved encasing each tree's massive root system inside a huge concrete basin, which they were then able to move with winches. All four trees survived their relocation. W. R. and Julia both revered these majestic native oaks. When a grass fire threatened the buildings, his first telegram to her read, "Think fire very serious; would rather have building burn than trees."[44] Their other priority was showcasing the hilltop's unparalleled vistas, which stretched for more than 100 miles in nearly all directions. W. R. declared at the beginning of construction: "The main thing at the ranch is the view." Creating spacious patios on the precipitous slopes was difficult, as Julia explained to the Bynes: "... all garden work is on steep hillsides, requiring endless steps and terracing."[45]

Julia had largely completed the initial garden design in 1922, when she suggested that W. R. should hire the Bay Area artist Bruce Porter as a landscape consultant. He was a polymath who had designed the stained-glass windows for San Francisco's Swedenborgian Church and the gardens at Filoli, William Bowers Bourn II's bucolic Woodside estate 30 miles south of San Francisco. When Porter visited San Simeon in 1922, he was dazzled by its scope and beauty. Julia revealed: "Am just back from San Simeon with Mr. Porter—that is, what is left of him.... As [I] thought probable, he grasped the place as a whole and from the painter—as well as planter—viewpoint."[46] Porter produced an enthusiastic report early in 1923, writing: "Even now, with but three of the buildings completed—they strangely magnify themselves into the bulk and importance of a city." W. R. was delighted with Porter's observations: "Very wonderfully good report many artists could have spent a lifetime on the property and not have made as good a one." Porter's summary also mentioned a location below the cottages where W. R. and Julia had already decided to build a water feature. Hearst noted in the margin: "This should be a very romantic spot, a place for young lovers—and maybe old ones."[47]

It proved a prophetic description, because on this site Julia eventually designed the unforgettable Neptune Pool. It features a classical temple façade, made from six ancient Roman columns that support a seventeenth-century statue of the site's namesake, Neptune, the Roman god of the sea. The pool's 104-foot-long oval basin—located in front of the temple—is 3 to 10 feet deep. It holds 345,000 gallons of shimmering water, filtered and heated for year-round use. No evidence exists to prove that Julia even knew how to swim, but she brilliantly understood how to transform a utilitarian swimming pool into a stunning garden feature.

Built over fourteen years, in three different versions, the Neptune Pool provides one of the best examples of Julia's ability to blend disparate elements into a seamless whole.

The Neptune Pool was rebuilt twice, yet it remains unfinished. Here Julia tried out the idea of adding larger columns to flank the temple—which they did not pursue.

Julia's spectacular Neptune Pool—named for the seventeenth-century statue atop its temple— features ancient Roman columns and 1930s marble nymphs. Its 104-foot-long basin ranges from 3 to 10 feet deep and was heated for year-round swimming.

Hearst acquired the columns (which combine ancient and modern elements) from a Roman art gallery in 1922. Later that year, he wrote to Julia with the news that he had purchased three freestanding statues of Neptune and two sea nymphs: "This Neptune fountain though not beautiful is quaint, and although the nymphs are not over attired the dominant figure is an elderly gentleman with whiskers who lends respectability to the landscape—for those at least who don't know his record."[48] They sunk these figures into concrete so they would resemble a carved relief in the temple's pediment. W. R. also commissioned Parisian sculptor Charles-Georges Cassou to carve four marble statues of nymphs caressing swans, as well as the *Birth of Venus* sculpture group located in the alcove opposite the temple. By day the pool's curved marble colonnades frame far-reaching views of the ocean and mountains; by night, they form spectacular floodlit reflections in the still water. It's no wonder that in the 1990s the distinguished architect Charles Moore referred to the Neptune Pool as "a grand liquid ballroom, for the gods and goddesses of the silver screen."[49]

Many Hollywood movie stars visited San Simeon, often at the invitation of W. R.'s longtime companion, actress Marion Davies. The two met in New York in 1915, when nineteen-year-old Marion was dancing in the chorus of the Ziegfeld Follies. The fifty-two-year-old Hearst was entranced by her beauty, warmth, and insouciance. For several years they tried to keep their relationship a secret, while W. R. attempted to obtain a divorce from Millicent (who was Catholic). When

After 1925, Hearst lived openly with actress Marion Davies, the young and vivacious hostess at San Simeon. They never married because Hearst was unable to obtain a divorce.

this effort failed, he separated from Millicent and began to live openly with Marion in California. Between 1917 and 1936, she starred in forty-five films (all but one produced by Hearst). Critics consider her roles in three late-1920s comedies directed by King Vidor to be among her best: *The Patsy*, *Show People*, and *Not So Dumb*.[50] Marion was funny, kind, and unpretentious, in spite of being the perpetual recipient of Hearst's excessive generosity. It's no wonder that many of her glamorous friends (whom she laughingly referred to as "the Younger Degeneration") soon made San Simeon their home away from Hollywood, including Charlie Chaplin, Carole Lombard, Clark Gable, Jean Harlow, Greta Garbo, Cary

Grant, and Harpo Marx. Hearst also invited prominent people from other professions: statesmen Winston Churchill and Calvin Coolidge; financiers Bernard Baruch and A. P. Giannini; screenwriters Anita Loos and Frances Marion; tennis champs Alice Marble and Bill Tilden; and authors George Bernard Shaw and Aldous Huxley, among many others. W. R. maintained a somewhat cordial friendship with Millicent, who continued to reside in their five-story, thirty-room apartment on New York's Riverside Drive. But Millicent visited San Simeon only rarely, and the two women never officially met.[51]

After hosting a particularly large weekend party, W. R. wrote to Julia: "All those wild movie people prevented me from talking to you as much as I wanted to. Next time I shall go up alone and we can discuss *everything*. Nevertheless, the movie folk were immensely appreciative. They said it was the most wonderful place in the world and that the most extravagant dream of a moving picture set fell far short of this reality." Julia replied, "I liked and enjoyed very much the movey [*sic*] people. They are artists, and alive. It was a pleasure also to see the way those who did not go swimming went around absorbedly taking in detail. To tell the truth, I was quite thrilled myself."[52]

Guests generally arrived by train from Los Angeles, in groups of no more than twenty. Tennis and horseback riding were popular afternoon activities, since W. R. excelled at both. He and Marion were also animal lovers, and in 1925 he impulsively decided to build an elaborate private zoo. Julia wrote: "The lions are beauties—about the size of St Bernards and as well kept and groomed as human babies. It seems incredible that any

Hearst—an animal lover—built an extensive zoo at San Simeon. Julia designed its bear pits, giraffe house, open-air shelters, and special quarters for Marianne, the elephant.

living creature could contain the resentment felt by those wild cats. They have not [been] 'tamed' in the slightest."[53] Hearst's menagerie grew rapidly. Within a few years, Julia had designed separate enclosures for his big cats and primates, as well as pits for the bears, a comfortable house for the elephant, and tall shelters for the giraffes. Hundreds of exotic grazing animals—including various species of antelopes, zebras, moose, llamas, emus, Barbary sheep, and sambar deer—roamed 2,000 acres of fenced-in pasture. Julia designed several open-fronted log shelters alongside the road, so the animals would congregate where guests could see them. She wrote to W. R.: "The animals arrived in beautiful shape. I had to rub my eyes last night when out of the semi-darkness staring at the lights were grouped three ostriches, five zebras, five white deer two with big horns, a llama, and some speckled deer. All in a group!"[54]

The zoo animals were new additions, but W. R and his parents had raised cattle at San Simeon since the 1860s. (Today, 85,000 acres of the original property comprise the Hearst family's cattle ranch.) In the 1920s, the ranch contained 250,000 acres. Though she had no previous experience designing farm structures, Julia created many ranch buildings that are still in daily use, including the cowboy bunk-house, poultry headquarters, and dairy barn, as well as the airplane hangar and airstrip. She also built San Simeon's estate village, a group of comfortable Spanish-style homes

In 1930, Julia created this Mission-style concrete warehouse, one of five in which Hearst stored his many art acquisitions.

Julia also designed the Spanish-style estate village along San Simeon's shoreline, where Hearst Ranch employees still reside.

along the shoreline (where Hearst Ranch employees still reside). Sixty miles north of San Simeon, Julia designed an inland ranch compound known as the Milpitas Hacienda, featuring a bunkhouse for cowboys and an elegant apartment for Hearst.[55]

In her correspondence with W. R., Julia was unflappable, cheerful, and unfailingly detail-oriented. One word that almost never appeared in their letters was "can't." They both believed that anything was possible, once the proper expedient was found. Julia wrote to one of her engineers, Walter Huber, after he had suggested that they should reduce the height of a room by lowering its antique ceiling beams: "That is *not a solution*. The ceiling has in the main to stay where it is, and some way of accomplishing it be found—anything else is [a] waste of time."[56]

Julia's generally calm demeanor did not indicate weakness. W. R.'s second son,

William Randolph Hearst Jr. (known as Bill Jr.), watched them work together for decades and recalled:

"Julia was about five feet two inches tall and weighed no more than a hundred pounds. She wore horn-rimmed glasses and usually dressed in tailor-made suits with handmade Parisian blouses. Always prim and proper, she topped her understated yet distinctive garb with a trim, dark hat affectionately called the Queen Mary style. Underneath that impeccable attire and highly professional air was a steel-trap mind and a will of iron. I used to listen to her and the old man go at it in her small office at the top of the hill. She and Pop had some real squawks, let me tell you, but both were so formal and low-keyed that an outsider would hardly have noticed. Indeed, through all the years she always called him 'Mr. Hearst' and he referred to her as 'Miss Morgan.' At the end of most discussions she deferred to him as the client. But not without forcing my father to consider all the questions in her mind, the cost, and the new architectural problems created.... She managed to cajole, plead, demand, and warn Pop in the most courteous, professional language. But, if one read carefully between the lines, she caught the old man up short many a time and indicated she would not retreat on her view unless he had a darn good answer.... Pop loved to go round and round with her because he was at heart an amateur architect.... Julia and Pop referred to one another as 'fellow architects' and both got a great laugh out of that."[57]

Another astute observer of W. R. and Julia at work was Adela Rogers St. Johns, one of Hearst's top newspaper reporters, who visited San Simeon frequently. She recalled that "*Miss* [*sic*] Morgan ... could say nothing [in] more ways than my Great Aunt Betsy Bogart.... Mr. Hearst understood and obeyed what Miss Morgan didn't say...."[58] Julia would "steer" Hearst by asking a clarifying question or showing him a better alternative. North explained: "She wasn't going to put in a horizontal line when she knew that a vertical line would be the only thing that would be right. She would work him over by showing him sketches of his way, and showing him how it would not look as well as another way. She understood what he was groping for."[59]

W. R. tested Julia's patience only occasionally. In 1923, he concluded that he would save money by bringing in his own manager, who would have "the right to hire and fire as occasion requires," as he explained. Hearst was oblivious to the real reason for San Simeon's cost overruns: his frequent changes of mind. Julia rebelled, writing, "I do not now see just how the new scheme will work out.... to do the work with your approval (and mine, incidentally) requires artists ... and the handling of more or less temperamental people. If these people are chosen by someone else ... there is every chance for friction and misunderstanding.... Please do not think I am not willing to fit in with your new plans or to resign, if you prefer, entirely. Thanking you always for the pleasure the work has been to me."[60] Julia made her point. Hearst's manager never appeared, and she remained the final authority on the hilltop.

San Simeon brought Julia more rewards than frustrations, Flora explained: "[They shared] ... a genuine love of antiquity and of accomplishments of the past, and I think she appreciated his knowledge and understanding of history and art and horticulture. She also recognized the need he had for those things because she too had the kind of a mind that could use up subjects so much more quickly than people with smaller minds and [they] needed more materials to chew on."[61] Walter remembered watching them sitting together at dinner in the 72-foot-long Refectory: "She sat directly across from Hearst and they were talking back and forth and gesturing and he was drawing things and she was drawing things. The rest of us could have been a hundred miles away; they didn't pay any attention to anybody. It wouldn't have surprised me at all to see a spark traveling from one skull to the other, back and forth, because these two very different people just clicked."[62]

It is unlikely, however, that Hearst was aware of the personal challenges Julia experienced during the early years of San Simeon's construction. On February 14, 1924, her father, Charles, died at home at age eighty-two. His final year had been terrible, North explained: "My grandfather had a stroke in the lower hall and the doctor came in and gave him a massive injection of something that kept his heart beating but he was otherwise a total vegetable and Avery insisted on nursing him for almost a year; he wouldn't let anybody else near him. When Grandpa died, Avery had a total nervous collapse and it was several years before he could do anything at all again."[63]

Charles had never attained the professional success he fervently desired, though he received public acclaim on a few occasions. As a member of the Oakland school board, Charles gave a speech and presented the high school diplomas to Julia's graduating class. In 1896, he was selected for a three-person commission tasked with analyzing the feasibility of adopting voting machines, but this honor concluded with the press charging him and his son-in-law Hart with corruption.[64] Nevertheless, there was dignity in Charles's continued efforts, for instance when he wrote to Julia in 1901: "Again I am working upon my [Mount Shasta] 'Inn' proposition and with more definite grounds for hope than I have ever had before. It may be another disappointment, but I shall continue to try as long as life lasts."[65]

Julia likely inherited her persistence from Charles, as well as her pragmatism and intelligence from Eliza. She would need all three traits during the second half of the 1920s, when her projects started to multiply and her health began to deteriorate.

CHAPTER EIGHT

A WIDENING SCOPE

BILL HEARST JR. WAS ELEVEN IN 1919 WHEN his father began to build San Simeon, and for the next twenty years, he had a front-row seat as the estate continued to grow:

"If my father was crazy to undertake the project, so was Julia . . . who was bold enough to agree with his vision. . . . Julia herself hired, oversaw, and paid the many artisans and laborers who worked at San Simeon— sometimes as many as 150. She dealt with stone casters, ornamental plasterers, wood-carvers, tile designers, tapestry workers, and others. In effect, she worked as the architect and contractor. Pop authorized her to pay premium wages despite the Depression. I often saw her tiny figure bent over some part of the work, then nimbly climbing over barricades or other obstacles to inspect another job. She was like a rabbit, hopping hither and yon; but as she straightened up in her suit, a regal lady arose. The two had an extraordinary adventure together. . . . But Julia never forgot how it all began. In her correspondence and conversations with Pop she constantly referred to the project as 'the ranch.'"[1]

Though the public began to call the property Hearst Castle while it was still under construction, W. R. did not generally use that name. In 1925 he formally christened the estate *La Cuesta Encantada* (The Enchanted Hill), likely because its high elevation usually ensured that the hilltop remained in sunshine, sitting just above the summer fog that often shrouded the coast. Hearst seldom used this poetic term, however; he, too, nearly always called it "the ranch," which had been his lifelong habit.[2]

In addition to her work at San Simeon, Julia designed hundreds of other projects, each identified in her records by an inventory number. Though the highest of these was 794, this figure is not an accurate tally of her work. With only a few exceptions, Julia began assigning numbers at 201, perhaps because she didn't want to reveal her relative inexperience early in her career. If her numbering system increases our estimate of her total output, San Simeon provides an effective counterbalance. The entire project was given one number—503—even though the hilltop buildings alone measure 110,000 square feet, excluding her numerous designs for other ranch structures and staff residences.[3]

Apparently Julia wasn't particularly interested in coming up with a cumulative total. Her secretary Lilian Forney, who worked for her from 1923 to 1957, explained, "... we never counted. I've been asked to give a list ... I said, 'No, she didn't want one.' When she finished a job, she gave them [her clients] their plans and that was it."[4] Walter affirmed that Julia recoiled from any sort of self-aggrandizement: "She just didn't have any patience with that sort of going around and patting yourself on the back." He pointed out, "[I]f people can't take it on any other basis except arithmetically, ... the square footage of other things that she did was quite as great as what she did at San Simeon." He also stressed that each job received her maximum effort, and Julia was careful not to favor one project over another. "Her thought, which she might even have expressed, was 'Some people might have said that I am a shrewd businesswoman. I don't

think I am, but I am smart enough to know that it's very poor policy to say that one child is better than another child. It's not decent.'"[5]

Various church commissions she undertook in the early 1920s demonstrate Julia's meticulous attention to every aspect of construction. A parishioner from the First Presbyterian Church of San Rafael commissioned her to create two war-memorial windows, incorporating a few fragments of medieval stained glass that he had salvaged from the bombed French cathedrals at Rheims and Verdun.[6] Julia imitated a fleur-de-lis painted on a shard of the original glass and used it as the border motif, but she altered the design by splitting its stem in two so that it resembled a human figure, to better

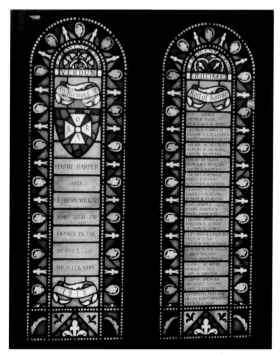

Julia designed these stained-glass windows—incorporating fragments of medieval glass—as a war memorial for the San Rafael Presbyterian Church.

memorialize the fallen soldiers. In the spring of 1921, she completed the Berkeley Baptist Divinity School, a four-story reinforced-concrete structure lined with Tudor brick. The school's director, Dr. Claiborne Hill, recalled that Julia arranged for an inactive kiln to be reopened in order to manufacture the brick, and she persuaded the owners of a defunct slate quarry in the Sierras to resume operations in order to obtain the roof shingles. Hill continued, "We would have liked very much to have the inside woodwork all of oak, but our funds would not permit that. Here Miss Morgan became our good angel. She told me one day that she was going to finish the first floor woodwork in oak, and that the expense would be her contribution to the building fund."[7]

Julia was also hired that year to build San Francisco's Emanu-El Sisterhood, a Jewish residence for women, located on a sloping lot at 300 Page Street (the San Francisco Zen Center has occupied the building since 1962). Objections were raised because Julia wasn't Jewish, so she asked Dorothy Wormser Coblentz to be her collaborator. Together they designed a U-shaped brick building with Italian embellishments, including Corinthian columns supporting its arched entry. They also incorporated Jewish imagery, using the Star of David in the wrought-iron balconies and mounting cast-plaster *mezuzahs* (sacred scroll cases that held Hebrew verses) beside the interior doors. Dorothy relished this unprecedented opportunity to work as Julia's equal: "I knew what they [the clients] had asked for, and when I couldn't solve what

she suggested . . . I could go ahead on some other tack. But that was the only time in her office that I ever met a client."[8]

Julia continued her work on several YWCA commissions, sailing to Hawaii in 1920 to inspect the site for an administration building she would later design for their Honolulu branch.[9] In addition, she completed a Mediterranean-style YWCA in downtown Pasadena in 1923. That same year, Pasadena's city administrators decided to include it within their newly designated Civic Center District. Though Julia's budget-conscious project preceded this plan (which was intended to showcase Pasadena's domed city hall and its environs), her YWCA's Southern European details—including Mission-style terra-cotta roof tiles and plentiful decorative wrought iron—coordinated well with the scheme. Walter engineered the building and regarded it as one of Julia's finest examples of "aesthetic concrete," where "the structure was in effect the architecture of the interior."[10]

From 1925 to 1926, Julia worked on the Hollywood Studio Club, which the YWCA built to house some of the throngs of young women inundating the movie lots, determined to become the next great film star. Mary Pickford and former actress Constance Adams (who married director Cecil B. DeMille) rallied a number of studio executives' wives and successfully raised $150,000 (equivalent to $2.2 million today) toward a residence that would keep these girls safely housed at 1215 Lodi Place, a mile from the emblematic intersection of Hollywood and Vine. Julia's elegant three-story building resembled a

In 1925, Julia built the Mediterranean-style Hollywood Studio Club, a YWCA dormitory for aspiring actresses.

villa from the Italian Renaissance; its central portion featured an arched entrance, flanked by two slightly higher towers. Sunny courtyards and spacious reception rooms graced the first floor (the only level that men were allowed to enter), and there were accommodations for one hundred upstairs. For $15 a month (equivalent to $230 today), a girl received two meals a day and the opportunity to reside there for as long as three years. During its fifty years of operation, an estimated ten thousand actresses stayed at the Hollywood Studio Club, including Marilyn Monroe, Kim Novak, Rita Moreno, and Donna Reed.[11]

Julia also designed Santa Barbara's Margaret Baylor Inn, a Spanish-style residence hotel for young women, which she arrived to personally inspect on the morning of June 29, 1925. She was standing outside the train station at 6:42 a.m. when a 6.8-magnitude earthquake struck the city, destroying many

downtown buildings and killing thirteen people. Thaddeus Joy anxiously telegraphed Hearst: "Miss Morgan arrived Santa Barbara six this morning. Can you help me get word of her."[12] The following week Julia wrote to the Bynes: "Monday last I stood in the street in Santa Barbara while the town literally went down—quite an experience."[13] She watched shop windows roll like waves before they shattered, and the quake's impact threw her into the street amid a cloud of dust. She grabbed a gunny sack from a nearby ice wagon to protect her head (which earned her a shout of protest from the wagon's owner), then felt her way back to the sidewalk by following the streetcar tracks. She later spoke of how instructive it had been for her to watch "buildings in motion," but it could have been fatal. Bjarne Dahl explained, "She was standing there talking to a fellow on the corner, and the shock was so great that it threw her to the middle of the street. She crawled [back]

Julia was outside Santa Barbara's train station at 6:42 a.m. on June 29, 1925, when a 6.8 earthquake struck the city. She was thrown into the street but was otherwise uninjured.

on her hands and knees, and when she turned around, the man was gone. They found him under a ton of bricks later."[14]

Mrs. Forney, who witnessed Julia's nearly constant travel throughout California, overseeing various projects, explained, "She worked *all* the time.... I wouldn't call her a loner at all, but ... she's like any professional person who gave her whole life to her profession. She had no home life, really. She'd come home, take a train somewhere...."[15] Julia may have welcomed the distraction, because living at home grew more difficult after Charles's death in 1924. Eliza's health had deteriorated, and Avery's emotional collapse was long-lasting.

Therefore, at the age of fifty-one, Julia embarked on new plans for the future. The Morgan home on Fourteenth Street was showing its age, and their Oakland neighborhood was becoming slightly run-down, but Eliza was adamant that she didn't want anything changed. Julia had installed electricity in her own quarters upstairs (and likely in

Avery's as well), but Eliza wanted to retain the gas fixtures, even though their pipes had formed coatings on the inside that impeded the gas flow. Julia's farsighted response was to purchase a Victorian house for herself in San Francisco—a typical Italianate two-story home, built in 1877—located at 2229 Divisadero Street.[16] This provided her with a convenient pied-à-terre if she was working late, since it was less than 2 miles from her office.

Next she addressed the problem of Eliza needing more care, by formulating an ingenious and thoughtful solution. In 1909, Emma and Hart had moved into a new house that Julia designed for them at 2414 Prospect Street in Berkeley. The family owned the vacant lot next door at 2404 Prospect, and on this site, unbeknownst to Eliza, Julia built another house in 1924. North explained:

"She made a room exactly the same— proportions and fireplace and everything—as her [mother's] room in the old house was. We brought Grandma out on Thanksgiving Day for dinner to our house, which was the usual thing, and then after dinner was over we had the usual conversation in the living room. They took Grandmother and walked her across the path into the new house. She looked at the downstairs [which contained living quarters for a nurse]; she didn't recognize it. But the minute she got upstairs, the bed and dressers and all the things were in exactly the same place, and there was a fire in the fireplace. She made no comment whatever ... about the switch."[17]

By 1925, the Morgans' Oakland neighborhood was declining, but eighty-year-old Eliza didn't want to relocate. Next door to Emma's Berkeley home, Julia built a house that exactly duplicated Eliza's bedroom, and their mother never realized that she had moved.

Julia continued to live with Avery in their big house on Fourteenth Street. She and Emma engaged a nurse for Eliza, and Julia visited her mother in Berkeley as often as she could. She wrote to Walter, "My mother is stronger in body and mind, quite herself as to keenness, but is confined to bed—or at most a small voyage around her room."[18] North explained:

"[They] had the closest of all [the] family relationships . . . [Julia] used to come and spend hours and hours. . . . [she] would take the last ferry over (at about 2 a.m.), and she'd sit by her mother's bedside. . . . They'd talk for three or four hours till six o'clock in the morning . . . and [she'd] go back to the office." Flora added, "So she missed one night . . . she'd sleep maybe four or five hours the next night and make up for it . . . She had the constitution of an ox."[19]

Besides these responsibilities and her continuing work at San Simeon, Julia undertook several additional projects for Hearst. When Maybeck's wooden Hearst Hall at the University of California burned to the ground on June 20, 1922, W. R. immediately expressed his desire to replace and improve it, suggesting that Ben should once again provide the design. Maybeck obliged with a series of stunning chalk drawings on brown paper, depicting an enormous compound of gymnasiums and museums, including a domed auditorium that evoked his Palace of Fine Arts in San Francisco. Julia was enlisted to supply the practical underpinnings of the project—the only campus building on which they collaborated. Elinor Richey wrote, "The pair had in common a Beaux-Arts education, mastery of detail, a preference for principle over style, [and] a prodigious output. . . . There the similarity ends. . . . [Julia] was brisk, businesslike, systematic, [and] possessed of executive ability.... he had a purely artistic nature, was erratic, temperamental, unconcerned with money, worked mostly alone, preferring his drawing board set up under an oak tree.... In sum, she was an arch conservative, he, the Bay Area's best known eccentric."[20]

Nevertheless, Julia and Ben had great respect for one another, and the project was a success. Their reinforced-concrete Phoebe Apperson Hearst Memorial Gymnasium was sited west of the former Hearst Hall, and contained a large swimming pool lined in the same marble and using the same filtration system as San Simeon's Neptune Pool. It similarly featured a temple-like pavilion at its center, flanked by large square urns ornamented with classical maidens (resembling those that topped the colonnades of Maybeck's Palace of Fine Arts). Two smaller pools and three skylighted gymnasiums made up the rest of the compound, along with locker rooms and offices. Dorothy explained,

"[It] was supposed to be Maybeck's job, but it was done in Julia Morgan's office and if it works, if you can get from here to there, it's because it went through ... [her], not because of Maybeck."[21] Ben did appear more focused on aesthetics than practicalities, as draftsman Ed Hussey explained: "When they had the grand opening of the Hearst Gymnasium, Mr. Hearst was there and he wanted to know where the men's room was. Mr. Maybeck, the architect, couldn't tell him; he had to get somebody else to find out where it was."[22]

The Hearst Memorial Gymnasium has been described as a "fragmented temple," since it was the only portion of the commemorative complex ever built. Soon after its dedication in April 1927, W. R. wrote Julia that he had changed his mind about funding the auditorium and art gallery, explaining, "I find that I am not in a position to begin work on the University museum at present. I have just bought some papers in Pittsburgh and it has left me pretty well exhausted for ready money."[23]

When Maybeck's wooden Hearst Hall on Berkeley's campus burned in 1922, Hearst hired Maybeck and Julia to replace it with the classically inspired, reinforced-concrete Phoebe Apperson Hearst Memorial Gymnasium. Completed in 1927, the gymnasium is Julia and Maybeck's only architectural collaboration on campus. Hearst intended to augment it with an art museum and amphitheater, but these were never built.

Julia was very familiar with the phenomenon of W. R. suddenly withdrawing funds that he had previously promised to furnish. He viewed money as a means, not an end, and regularly exceeded his income. Bill Jr. explained: "Despite his wealth, my father had little interest in money as such. It was only a blank space to be filled in on a check to accomplish a specific aim."[24] The consequences of Hearst's overspending fell mostly on Julia, since he supplied her office with a fixed sum each month (usually between $30,000 and $50,000, equivalent to $390,000 and $650,000 today), from which she was expected to pay all expenses. He would then barrage her with new ideas and additional requests, and as a result she frequently fell into arrears and therefore postponed paying herself, often for months at a time. When Arthur Byne complained about how long it took W. R. to pay for his purchases, Julia stuck up for him loyally, writing: "I am most sorry to learn of your treatment by Mr. Hearst as I certainly would not have expected or foreseen it. Our own relationships with him have been satisfactory. Payment usually late, but always sure, the greatest trouble being his changeableness of mind—but in return, he compensates to some extent by allowing me to change mine now and then."[25] Hearst's indebtedness actually took quite a toll on her, as North explained: "She suffered the tortures of the damned in staving people off to whom he owed money that she'd made the commitments for and then he would be very slow coming through on them. There

were many phases of that thing that weren't too pleasant."[26]

One of Hearst's most extravagant purchases around this time was an entire Spanish monastery, consecrated in 1144 and named for St. Bernard of Clairvaux, a twelfth-century French abbot credited with founding the Cistercian order.[27] Julia had informed Byne that W. R. was in search of a medieval cloister, writing: "Mr. Hearst said jokingly the other day, after a walk over the Hill, that he had laid out five years of work ahead for me.... He is very anxious to get a cloister, a big well—mantels ... the bigger, more architectural things. You must wonder what we do with it all!"[28]

Spain was experiencing political unrest throughout the 1920s (the period that preceded the Spanish Civil War), and its existing antiquities laws were vague and not rigorously enforced. Byne found an abandoned cloister—in ruins and being used as a farm and stable—approximately 120 miles from Madrid:

"The monastery is located in one of the most desolate corners of Spain.... On the whole it is surprisingly well preserved.... For years past the monastery in question has served as headquarters for a huge wheat farm. For this reason the cloister openings have been walled up and the once sequestered walks turned into stables. However[,] this walling up has served to protect the capitals from inclement weather.... You must take into consideration that ... the complications involved in buying a thing of this sort are without end; that I have to smooth innumerable paths with money, and last but not least, the demolition and packing must be carefully superintended by myself...."[29]

No sooner had Byne discovered this cloister (which they referred to by its location, as "Sacramenia") and quoted Hearst the price of $35,000 for its purchase (plus another $50,000 for its demolition and shipment—equivalent to $520,000 and $750,000, respectively, today), than W. R. instructed Julia to ask Byne if he could obtain another medieval cloister as well. At that time Hearst was intending to use Sacramenia for his planned art museum on the Berkeley campus, and to erect the other cloister either at San Simeon or in Southern California. Julia was aware of the absurdity of her inquiry: "Mr. Hearst ... does want for himself something really very fine, gothique [sic], transitional, or Renaissance and I am sure if you would find the something the question of expense would not enter. I imagine you are laughing—you and Mildred—when you get this preposterous request, but Mr. Hearst announced last night, 'You know we sent Mr. Byne a perfectly good list of pictures of possible looking patios and cloisters and surely some of these Signors, Dukes, etc. are hard up enough to part with one of them.'" Julia's description of any request of W. R.'s as "preposterous" was unprecedented, even when she was writing to the Bynes. This word was thoroughly blacked out in the office's carbon copy of her letter.[30]

Throughout 1925 and 1926, Julia received numerous letters from Byne detailing the complexities of disassembling and transporting the ornamental portions of an entire monastery. Byne oversaw the whole operation, which involved hiring a crew; carefully dismantling the buildings; marking every stone to allow for its future reassembly; buying a sawmill to manufacture the wooden cases for shipment; packing the medieval stones into 10,751 straw-filled crates; and constructing a 20-mile road to transport the crates from Sacramenia to Peñafield, and then to Madrid for shipment to New York. Upon their arrival, Hearst's warehouse employees took over, unpacking the crates and arranging for the cumbersome necessity of replacing all the packing straw with excelsior (due to quarantine restrictions caused by a recent Spanish outbreak of hoof-and-mouth disease). The crates were then stored in one of Hearst's New York warehouses, pending their future shipment to California.[31] Julia was fascinated by these logistical details. Since her family and business obligations prevented her from traveling to Spain, Byne's letters were as close as she could come to observing these procedures firsthand. She was also particularly drawn to the sincerity and strength of early medieval architecture. Walter explained, "She loved structure, you know, and so did I."[32]

While she was following this saga, Julia received the commission to design a new chapel and columbarium (a mausoleum intended to store crematory urns) outside the gates of Mountain View Cemetery, where

her two brothers and her father were already buried. It became known as the Chapel of the Chimes, a modern concrete building into which Julia incorporated extensive ornamentation in cast stone. Using beach sand for its aggregate, this high grade of molded concrete was poured into plaster forms to dry, then removed and cured in water for additional strengthening, until it resembled carved stone. Julia's cast-stone designs for the columbarium's delicate tracery panels and medieval arches resembled the architecture of the Sacramenia monastery, which she had seen only in photographs. The new building was meant to be earthquake-resistant, the press explained: "Excavation of over 8,500 cubic feet has been made into the hillside in order to have the new chapel and Columbarium unit accessible directly from Piedmont Avenue. . . . The whole structure is of solid concrete construction of scientific earthquake-proof character. In part it is based on studies at Santa Barbara, where the architect, Miss Morgan, was during the shake [*sic*]. The building will be late Romanesque and early Gothic in expression."[33]

To execute the tracery work, Julia almost certainly hired the Belgian craftsmen Theo and John Van der Loo, a father and son whom she also employed as the cast-plaster and cast-stone masons for San Simeon. Their studio was located on Berkeley's nearby Piedmont Avenue, making it easy for her to check in with them during the week. Construction manager Lawrence F. Moore explained: "The Gothic tracery of the interior of our new chapel and tower is fascinating as it develops under the hands of the skilled workmen.

In 1927, Julia began constructing one of her most lyrical and reverent buildings: Oakland's Chapel of the Chimes, a columbarium (a mausoleum containing funerary urns) at 4499 Piedmont Avenue. Its design inspiration was a twelfth-century Cistercian monastery that Hearst had purchased in Spain in 1925.

In the late 1920s, Julia built a Venetian swimming pool—spanned by a marble bridge—in front of Marion Davies's Santa Monica Beach House, a Georgian-style building designed by architect William Flannery.

These men are Old-World trained craftsmen; men who have lived among buildings of the character of the one that is being constructed here, and who have worshipped in churches such as this."[34]

While the columbarium was under way, Hearst began two major construction projects in Southern California, with Julia as architect. Early in 1926, he wrote her to say that Marion wanted to expand her Beverly Hills home at 1700 Lexington Avenue. Julia was soon overseeing the mounting of antique beams in Marion's Georgian-style hall, as well as replacing its modern fireplaces with numerous eighteenth-century mantelpieces.[35] Evidently, W. R. felt that this remodel was

insufficient, as Marion's biographer, Fred Lawrence Guiles, recounted:

"One evening in May 1926 Hearst picked up Marion at her house on Lexington Road and drove her to the beach at Santa Monica. In those days before air conditioning, it used to get torrid in the flatlands of Beverly Hills where Marion lived, and they often would go to one particular spot along Ocean Front Road and sit on the sand, holding hands. . . . 'Do you like it [here]?' he asked her. 'It's fine,' she told him. And as simply as that it was agreed that she would move out of Beverly Hills to the beach at Santa Monica."[36]

W. R. purchased two existing buildings next to one another and hired architect William Flannery to tear down the walls between them and create a large Georgian structure (which they christened the Beach House), containing ten bedrooms, a dining room that seated twenty-five, a library with its own projection equipment, an art gallery for Marion's growing painting collection, and a total of thirty-seven antique mantelpieces.

Hearst hired Julia to design the charming two-story Colonial-style guesthouse on the north side of the Beach House, as well as a tile-lined swimming pool—spanned by a Venetian-style bridge of white marble—located between the two buildings. (Significantly, Julia's structures both survived the cataclysmic 6.7-magnitude Northridge earthquake of 1994, though Flannery's edifice was completely destroyed. It has been replaced by a modern building known as the Wallis

Annenberg Community Beach House.)[37] In spite of Flannery's position as architect, W. R. still looked to Julia, writing: "When we come to the decoration of the interior of the Beach House, in order to prevent too much similarity in the ten bedrooms, I think it might be well to have [on] the top floor for instance, one Dutch bedroom, one French bedroom, etc. Of course the majority of the bedrooms would be straight Colonial, and I suggest on the second floor we use interesting [wall]papers with white wainscoting..."[38] His funds were insufficient to cover these new projects, as Julia found it necessary to remind him: "We have spent a goodly sum on the two southern houses, and would appreciate a payment on account when convenient to you."[39]

Meanwhile, Julia's wide-ranging duties at San Simeon continued, at a rate sufficient to monopolize a less energetic architect's career. Hearst confessed that though he hadn't initially intended to become so attached to the estate, he now "saw no reason why the ranch should not be a museum of the best things I can secure."[40] Therefore, Julia spent much of the second half of the 1920s enlarging many of the hilltop features she had previously completed: expanding the first version of the Neptune Pool; modifying the east-facing tennis courts so a pool could be installed beneath them; designing two more cottages (which remained unbuilt); enlarging the garden terraces and walkways to take better advantage of their views; completing Casa Grande's first-floor public rooms, including the Assembly Room, the Refectory, and the Morning Room; pouring a south wing to house its kitchen, pantries, and staff quarters; and enlarging its third story as well as heightening the bell towers.[41]

The more San Simeon grew, the more creative and enthusiastic W. R.'s suggestions became. He proposed several schemes that

Julia also created the neoclassical guest house north of Marion's Beach House. Its understated architecture contrasts with its colorfully tiled bathrooms.

they didn't pursue, but which were nevertheless delightful to contemplate. In 1926 he wrote: "How about a maze in connection with the zoo. I think getting lost in a maze and coming unexpectedly upon lions, tigers, pumas, panthers, wild cats, monkeys, macaws and cockatoos, etc. etc., would be a thrill even for the most blasé. If the space is big enough—and we will make it big enough by cutting off more hill if necessary—we could have a great maze with all these 'animiles' [sic] and birds and with a pretty pool in the middle, with cranes and flamingos, etc., and a fountain and EVERYTHING."[42] The following spring he suggested:

"I have an idea for a winter pool. We could put a big hot-house down where we were going to build the Persian Garden, and in the middle of this hot-house we could have a big pool. . . . In the hot-house . . . we would have palms, ferns, and a whole lot of orchids. . . . The temperature of the hot-house, and of the pool too, would be warm on the coldest, bleakest winter day. We would have the South Sea Islands on the Hill. . . . Here we could serve tea, or poi, or whatever the situation called for. The pool, of course, would be the main attraction, and we might put a turtle and a couple of sharks in to lend verisimilitude. This, except for the sharks, is not as impractical a proposition as it might seem. It is merely making a hot-house useful, and making a pool beautiful."

Julia responded just as fancifully, "I like your idea for the combination indoor pool and orchid green house. . . . There could be a plate glass partition in the pool and the alligators, sharks, etc., could disport on one side of it and visitors could unsuspectingly dive toward it. This [is] the other architect's contribution to your idea."[43]

W. R.'s expansion plans came about because he and Marion had begun to entertain at San Simeon more frequently. They invited parties of guests from Los Angeles for the weekend, and occasionally stayed on the hilltop for several weeks in a row. This made Hearst less available to Julia, who wrote him after one such gathering: "There are many details to go over, that do not seem fair to bring up when people all want you. It was a beautiful party."[44] Adela Rogers St. Johns once again turned her penetrating reporter's eye on Julia, whom she observed at dinner in the Refectory, calling her a

"double-take of unexpectedness. For she was a small, skinny, self-effacing lady whose iron will was *fem incognito* and *sotto voce*. Her graying hair was held in a small knob at the back of her head by bone pins, her gray tweed tailored suit was inches too long, and she used no make-up at all. At dinner, with the Queen of Rumania [sic], the Duchess of Sutherland, our ranking novelist Gertrude Atherton, the Marquise de la Falaise de la Coudray (Gloria Swanson), Mrs. Tom Mix in all her diamonds, First Lady Grace Coolidge, Cissy Patterson of Dupont Circle, Washington, Mary Pickford, who really queened it in Hollywood, the governor's lady, and Mrs. Flo Ziegfeld (Billie Burke) present, Miss Morgan, in a blue foulard dress with white daisies, was like a small neat bantam hen among birds of paradise. Except that she always sat on Mr. Hearst's right."[45]

Julia chose to maintain her punishing schedule, in part because of her real affection and admiration for Hearst. Mrs. Forney remarked: "She was a very brilliant woman, as Mr. Hearst was brilliant. *He* was so interested in architecture, too. As she says, 'He could have done it himself, if he'd been left to it.' She gave him much credit."[46] Though Julia relied on her exceptional reserves of stamina and energy, she often failed to take proper care of herself. Bjarne recalled: "When we were working at night she'd have a soda cracker and chew on that, with maybe a glass of water. I often wondered why she didn't eat more." Mrs. Forney reported: "She had her little round Lifesavers and little hard candies, and that kept her going. She never bothered to eat very much, you know. Burned everything she cooked."[47]

In the fall of 1926, Julia's health broke down. T. J. wrote to W. R.: "Miss Morgan was stricken with a serious intestinal illness which necessitated an immediate operation. She was in a dangerous condition until yesterday ... [when] she showed her renewed interest in life by asking ... [about] San Simeon."[48] Hearst was concerned at this news (though perhaps not sufficiently aware of the possibility that his increasing number of projects may have contributed to Julia's illness). He telegraphed: "Glad to hear you are better; please don't attempt too much too

soon; remember your reserve vitality has been exhausted and you must rest and let reserve accumulate; you should organize your office and do less detail yourself." Julia wrote back quite meekly: "Thank you very much for the kind telegram. I will try to heed its admonitions. It is a great pleasure to be able to play at work again."[49]

Julia returned to work as soon as possible, even though—as she later confessed to Walter—she was not yet entirely well: "If I have not written, it is not that I have not followed you in [my] mind. Days have been oftener than not just barely gotten by with. But an accident, by good luck, made me go back to [the doctor]. ... So [I] am on the real mend, & gaining in energy if not in weight."[50]

Throughout the 1920s, in addition to her design work for Hearst and for numerous institutions, Julia completed many residential commissions. Clients frequently hired her multiple times, Dorothy explained: "She must have known the means of her clients, what they expected. ... I think she fitted her job to the client. She certainly didn't economize on workmanship; there's no question of that. ... If there wasn't much money, it was a smaller house. ... Every client ended up a friend and was very grateful."[51] For the wealthy dried-fruit exporter Abraham Rosenberg, Julia designed a large English manor house at 3630 Jackson Street in San Francisco's Presidio Heights. She also produced a four-story brick apartment building (now demolished) at 353 California Street, near the Merchants Exchange Building, and an unbuilt funerary monument that honored all three

Rosenberg brothers.[52] Helen Eels Livermore, the second wife of Bay Area lumber magnate Horatio P. Livermore, commissioned Julia to build a retreat at Montesol, the family ranch in Calistoga. Made entirely of Douglas fir, this cabin had a long breezeway to capture the cool winds and a sheltered porch that overlooked a cliffside view. Julia also designed Helen Eels Livermore's San Francisco home, a beautifully sited redwood-shingled house at 1023 Vallejo Street on Russian Hill. Initially Julia created a simple pied-à-terre with a bedroom and living room on the main floor, and the kitchen and dining room below. She remodeled it twice—in 1927 and 1930—adding a second terraced suite that took further advantage of the city views.[53]

Julia's work for the Glide family provides one of the best examples of her multiple commissions. Lizzie Snider was born in Louisiana in 1852 and relocated to Sacramento with her family in 1869, where she met and married rancher Joseph Glide in 1871. After his death in 1906, Lizzie managed the family estate, which grew substantially when oil was discovered on their cattle ranch. Lizzie moved to Berkeley in 1916 and commissioned Julia to build her home: an L-shaped, half-timbered Elizabethan residence at 160 The Uplands. In 1919, Lizzie hired Julia to construct an elegant Georgian house for her daughter Eula and son-in-law Roy H. Elliott at 1 Eucalyptus Road, also in Berkeley, and in 1921 she commissioned her to build a fourteen-room Mediterranean residence for her daughter Mary and son-in-law Charles Goethe at 3731 T Street in Sacramento. (Known today as the Julia Morgan House, it is currently owned by Sacramento State University.) In 1923, as a gift to her hometown, Lizzie hired Julia to create the

Julia's clients often rehired her. In 1919, philanthropist Lizzie Glide commissioned this Federal-style house at 1 Eucalyptus Drive, Berkeley, for her daughter Eula and son-in-law Roy Elliott.

In 1921, Lizzie Glide also commissioned this Mediterranean house at 3731 T Street in Sacramento for her daughter Mary and son-in-law Charles Goethe.

Sacramento Public Market, a classic English-style two-storied covered marketplace at 13th and J Streets. (This reinforced-concrete building, faced in brick, housed government offices beginning in the 1970s; since 2001, it has served as the entrance façade for Sacramento's Sheraton Hotel.)[54]

The grandest of the Glide commissions was the dramatic palazzo Julia built in 1928 for Lizzie's daughter Elizabeth and her son-in-law Selden Williams, at 2821 Claremont Avenue in Berkeley. With 6,200 square feet and many dramatic features—including Gothic stone tracery windows and a delicate Venetian-marble arcade—this elegant home was intended to accommodate many social events. It had a tragic history, however. Selden

Williams died within two years of its completion, and though Elizabeth continued to occupy the house, she soon became a recluse. North was only twelve years old when the Williams house was under construction, and he recalled that Julia gave him his first job when she hired him to photograph it weekly. He also remembered that it had distressed his aunt to know that this beautiful and lively mansion should be relegated to decades of silence and solitude. (Though the University of California purchased it in 1971 for use as their vice president's home, it has been in private ownership since the 1990s.)[55]

As the Williams house neared completion, Julia was anxious to travel to Honolulu to inspect the large YWCA she had recently

In 1928, Julia designed a lavish Italian-style villa for Elizabeth, the third Glide sister, and her husband Selden Williams, at 2821 Claremont Avenue in Berkeley.

designed across from the Iolani Palace, the 1882 residence of Hawaii's last monarchs. She had to postpone her trip for several months, as she explained to Bjarne: "I had expected to surely have been in Honolulu before this, but the serious illness of my brother . . . and my mother's condition, make it impossible to leave here. . . . Work generally has slacked up considerably. . . . I have been grateful for the lull, as you can imagine."[56] Some months later, she admitted that Avery's health—likely both physical and mental—was not improving: "I miss his companionship—after so many years—it looks as though he would not be about for some time yet."[57]

She was also feeling some ambivalence about San Simeon during its expansion. Julia confessed to Walter: "The hill work still goes on. Please go up soon after your return and tell us if it is worth anything or not before your eyes tire. It seems sometimes quite lovely these days, & then again, very discouraging.

We are covering it [Casa Grande] entirely with stone to the tower tops—& it has a more serious air."[58]

She continued to push herself in order to maintain her heavy workload. In 1928, after a long day spent with W. R. on the hilltop, Julia collapsed from the heat, writing him afterward, "I regretted more than I can say upsetting things so on your last Sunday, and the loss of the time with you. It was a true sun stroke—nothing organic—hereafter I shall wear large flopping thick headgear, and promise in any case never to repeat it."[59] The incident alarmed Hearst, who responded:

"Miss Morgan you <u>must</u> stop working so hard. All your friends will be really angry with you if you don't. You haven't any right to <u>destroy</u> yourself and that is exactly what you are doing. You wouldn't treat an <u>engine</u> the way you treat yourself. It isn't <u>good practice</u>. You don't get the best work or the most work that way. You can't <u>race</u> all the time. You must <u>rest</u> some time. Please take the boat and come abroad for a couple of months. We will see a lot of things and get a lot of ideas—and we will have a good time."[60]

He was unable to convince her to travel abroad with him and Marion (an activity many society architects engaged in with their wealthy clients), but perhaps W. R.'s exhortation had some effect, because Julia took another step toward simplifying her life in the future.

In April 1929 she purchased the house next door to her San Francisco residence on Divisadero Street, and connected the two buildings. After removing the top story from the southernmost one, she turned this one-story house into her private dwelling, shifting the orientation of her living room so it overlooked the garden rather than the street. She converted the two-story house into three sunny apartments that she rented to tenants (often young female employees). She also added a garage and a front entrance that connected both houses, and removed the backyard fence to create a spacious garden.

This expansion made her holiday entertaining easier, as Julia explained to Bjarne: "These larger rooms made it possible to get 36 [of her employees and their families] to dinner,—I had all guests [aged] from 4 years to 16—in my rooms, & it certainly was a gay, if nothing else, affair."[61] She was proud to hire a chef and host these Christmas dinners for her employees, which she had done even before buying the second house: "I never would have thought without trying that 2211 could have 32—or more to dinner, but this is the 2nd experiment, and it seems to be a success, judging from <u>sounds</u>. I love to have the children as well as the elders, and they have been wonderfully good—even little 'Danny,' Jack Wagenet's boy of 2½."[62]

Julia was very fond of children and treated her employees' offspring like her own nephews and nieces. She sent them postcards during her trips and frequently brought them presents—not only at Christmas, but

In 1925, Julia bought a San Francisco Victorian at 2229 Divisadero Street, removing its upper story. Years later she purchased the house next door, converting it into rental apartments. Julia lived in the single-story house for nearly thirty years.

also as consolation for trials such as tonsillectomies.[63] Mrs. Forney recalled, "It showed how really personally she felt about her employees, because whenever we wanted to collect for a present for her at Christmas, she'd warn me, 'Please, no gifts for me. . . . Some of these families may not be able to afford it.'"[64]

Immediately after celebrating Christmas in 1929, Julia decided to pay a solo last-minute visit to her New York relatives, sensing that Eliza's declining condition would soon preclude such a trip. She wrote Bjarne: "Just now on the impulse, I hastily packed two grips in the office, went home & told my mother I'd decided to accept an invitation to my relatives in New York, & here I am as far as Nebraska! . . . It's the 1st real vacation in years."[65] She continued in another letter: "I wanted so much to see again some very dear faces, in very frail bodys [sic]—and do the few things possible now, & perhaps not later."[66]

It may have seemed an opportune time to make the trip, because one of Julia's most important projects—the Berkeley Women's City Club, at 2315 Durant Avenue—was nearing completion. She had been hired in 1928 to build this massive reinforced-concrete structure, which served as the gathering place for numerous independent clubs in the area. With six stories, forty-two guest rooms, and 46,105 square feet, it presented an engineering challenge, as Walter recalled: "Miss Morgan had confidence in me to solve the engineering problems. . . . I couldn't have done it, if I hadn't had her collaboration. . . . I had to support all that weight of . . . [the second floor] columns

The six-story Berkeley Women's City Club at 2315 Durant Avenue was opened in November 1930, only eleven months after construction began.

on the arches for the [first floor] swimming pool. . . . I think it is probably the most complicated concrete structure that there is in this part of the country."[67]

Aptly nicknamed "the Little Castle" and located near two of her former haunts—the University of California campus and the Kappa Alpha Theta sorority—this monumental building remained a favorite of Julia's. Her design for the club's serene tile-lined swimming pool presaged her conception for San Simeon's indoor Roman pool, built two years later; and the club's rounded arches, delicate capitals, and groined vaulting evoked the medieval architecture of the monastery at Sacramenia. Julia designed every aspect of the project with considerable care—its light fixtures, ceiling panels, china, cast-stone lions—even its bookplate. Mrs. Forney

RIGHT: *Julia designed every detail of this 46,000-square-foot, reinforced-concrete building—including the floral chandeliers in the second-floor Members' Lounge.*

The Berkeley City Club demonstrates Julia's genius at building swimming pools; her prowess in using modern materials to evoke the past; and her skill at creating fanciful ornament, including this cast-stone nature sprite in the Drawing Room fireplace.

recalled, "Miss Morgan used to slip into the building when she thought nobody would see her, and go right through . . . [it] to make sure that *her* building was being cared for properly. . . . [The] City Club looks like Miss Morgan [in] everything that was chosen."[68] C. Julian Mesic, Julia's model maker, wrote in the *Architect and Engineer of California*: ". . . after many weeks of concentration at the job, the architect suddenly appeared relieved and radiant—satisfied that the craftsman had caught the spirit of the design due in a large measure to patient cooperation, display of models, and the loan of helpful books to the workmen."[69]

Julia was pleased not only with the success of the Berkeley Women's City Club, but also with a prestigious award she received around this time. In May 1929, the University of California presented her with an honorary doctor of laws degree. Her acceptance of this tribute was unusual; she typically refused any public acknowledgment, particularly interviews. Mrs. Forney recalled: ". . . [One day] I saw a note on her daily calendar: 'Reader's Digest. Nope . . .' Meaning she hadn't given [them] an interview and didn't intend to." Bjarne said, "She would never have her picture taken. She was always so afraid that somebody was going to take her picture when we [office staff] were all together."[70] On this occasion, however, Julia consented to being photographed in a cap and gown as part of the ceremony. Thirty-five years after graduating with a civil-engineering degree, Julia heard the university's president, William Wallace Campbell, read this encomium: ". . . Designer of simple dwellings and of stately homes, of great buildings nobly planned to further the centralized activities of her fellow citizens; Architect in whose works harmony and admirable proportions bring pleasure to the eye and peace to the mind."[71]

It is to be hoped that Eliza was aware of her daughter's honorary doctorate, since it would have made her immensely proud. Eliza died the following year, on June 13, 1930, at the age of eighty-five. Julia wrote to Bjarne and his wife Eve: "... my mother was very ill & ... One reason I have not written was because of that illness—She did not get better, but died in June—We knew we could not keep her always but she was so dear, & had conquered so many ills,—it seemed very hard to part with her—Since then I have moved to the San Francisco house Bj [Bjarne] knows of—Have annexed some more rooms & will make that my abiding place—for the present at any rate."[72]

Julia was fifty-eight when she and Avery moved out of their Oakland home, which they continued to own and likely rented out. Julia relocated to Divisadero Street, where she lived for the rest of her life. One of her tenants next door recalled her homecoming routine:

"We would hear the front door close very quietly, and soon the fragrance of coffee would assail our nostrils and we knew that Miss Morgan was safely in—and ready for bed after two or three cups of strong, black coffee! [Her] interests in life did not include food.... If left to her own devices, Miss Morgan would open a can. To leave something cooking on the stove, was fatal for her—as her mind would be on something

In 1929, at age fifty-seven, Julia received an honorary doctorate from her alma mater, the University of California.

and she ... would be recalled by the aroma of burning toast, or something scorching in a pan."[73]

Avery did not accompany Julia. His illness—which was almost certainly early-onset Alzheimer's—had not improved, and he moved instead into a care facility in nearby Los Altos, south of San Francisco. Bjarne recalled that Julia "was always looking out for her brother," just as she had done since their Paris days. For three years, this seemed an acceptable housing solution, until Julia received distressing news: Avery had suddenly vanished.[74]

CHAPTER NINE

DESCENDING FORTUNES

IN THE SPRING OF 1931, THE PRESS COVERED Avery's disappearance: "Deputy sheriffs and police of San Mateo and Santa Clara Counties were engaged in an intensive search today for Avery Morgan, a prominent architect of Los Altos, after Miss Julia Morgan, his sister, reported to Los Altos police that he had been absent for a week. Miss Morgan believes he may have been a victim of amnesia and expressed fears for his safety." Avery was found the following week, living in "a hermit's cabin … after a resident had reported seeing a strange figure on a lonely road [on] Sunday."[1] This tendency to withdraw into nature was a lifelong trait of his; Eliza's letters to Julia in Paris mentioned several times when Avery had wandered off on their family camping trips.[2] The difference in this case was not only the duration of his disappearance, but also the growing instability that caused it. Avery spent the rest of his life in small residential care facilities where he was doubtless visited frequently by his sister. From this time on, his name appears rarely in Julia's papers, with one exception: When she traveled, she mentioned him more frequently ("Card for Avery") than anyone else on her correspondence and gift lists.[3]

Avery had disappeared during the second year of the Great Depression, by which time it was apparent that the economy would not soon recover. Julia encouraged Bjarne and Eve not to despair about the hard times: "The turn of the tide may be on us now—in any case, it cannot be far off, probably will come very slowly over next winter and spring. What is needed is young courage, and a realization that money in itself is but a small part of living, a means, not an end. I think the simpler living and a return to simpler pleasures is a healthful and worthwhile result, if the high level of wage and income is never reached again."[4]

Julia's life changed little, despite these worsening conditions. Her workload remained heavy before and after the 1929 stock market crash, and she concluded the decade by designing several more women's clubs. In 1928 she completed the four-story Spanish-style "Home" at 555 Baker Street in San

Julia built her 1929 Riverside YWCA (today's Riverside Art Museum) in a Mediterranean style that complemented the nearby Mission Inn without imitating it.

Francisco, which served as the statewide headquarters for the Native Daughters of the Golden West, to which she belonged. In 1929 she built the Riverside YWCA at 3425 Mission Inn Avenue, one block from the sprawling 1903 landmark Mission Inn. Frank Miller, the inn's founder, had lobbied for the YWCA to be built in the same florid Mission style as his two-hundred-room hostelry. Instead, Julia chose a style described in the press as "Californian, with a mixture of Spanish and Italian in its lines," that blended well with the inn but retained its own identity. (In 1967, the Riverside Arts Center purchased the structure, which today houses the Riverside Art Museum.)[5]

At the start of the 1930s, Julia began working on some of her most distinctive projects, including the Japanese YWCA at 1830 Sutter Street in San Francisco's Japantown. At this time, Japanese girls were not allowed to join San Francisco's segregated YWCA, and

the 1913 Alien Land Law prevented Japanese citizens from owning private property. The Japanese community nevertheless raised funds for the building's construction, an effort Julia aided by donating her services. Her design was modest but graceful: a simple stuccoed-concrete structure incorporating many features of Japanese architecture, including a cross-gabled roof and a second story that slightly overhung the first. Inside, a small dark lobby was connected via an enclosed corridor to a large light-filled auditorium. The stage along its north wall was surmounted by a *ranma*, a carved wooden screen depicting mountains and water. On the east side of the stage, an open circular portal led into the *tokonoma*, a large alcove used for tea ceremonies, which contained *chigaidama*, staggered shelves for storing small items.[6] (Known today as the Nihonmachi Little Friends Building, it still plays a vital role in its Japantown neighborhood.)[7]

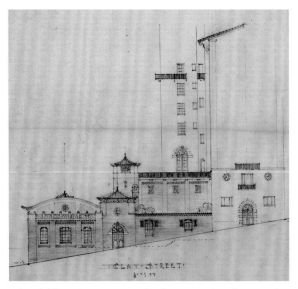

Julia's lifelong fascination with Chinese art found its zenith in her 1930 design for San Francisco's Chinese YWCA at 965 Clay Street (today's Chinese Historical Society Museum). Julia carefully researched its architectural ornament and even began studying Chinese calligraphy.

In 1930 Julia was hired to design San Francisco's Chinese YWCA, which replaced the original 1916 building at 897 Sacramento Street. The need for these hostelries was urgent, as YWCA administrators explained, due to "constant demands . . . for the housing of the traveling Oriental girl who cannot go to the high-priced hotel and who is not admitted into the less expensive rooming houses."[8] The new Chinese YWCA was located on a steeply sloping lot at 965 Clay Street. It adjoined the large site at 940 Powell Street where Julia was simultaneously rebuilding The Residence, the YWCA's eight-story women's hotel. Though the Chinese YWCA's planning committee asked The Residence's administrative board to include separate living quarters for Chinese women in its new design, this request was refused. Julia suggested various solutions,

even indicating her willingness to design two completely separate entrances, but The Residence committee decided there should be no connection between these buildings or their occupants.[9] (In 1953, The Residence's central committee voted to lift all restrictions and welcome everyone into its facility, which has been used for senior housing since 1980.)[10]

Julia built both structures from the same materials—reinforced concrete faced with brick—even though they stylistically honor different architectural traditions. The Residence resembles a Renaissance palazzo, to which Julia added visual interest by contrasting its structural concrete with the brick. A rusticated concrete façade marks its street level; two vertical rows of concrete quoins divide the structure into thirds; and its concrete top story features a triple-arched window framed by a projecting wooden cornice. Its public rooms include an elegant paneled library that contains a French fireplace, and a central dining room that at Julia's instigation was augmented by several smaller rooms where girls could entertain their friends privately.

The Chinese YWCA was Julia's third project for members of this community. She was careful to avoid the stereotypical Chinese imagery (including pressed-tin, multitiered pagodas, and imitation curled eaves) that ornamented many structures in Chinatown. Her Methodist Chinese Mission School at 940 Washington Street—known today as the Gum Moon Residence Hall—was dedicated in 1912. Its brick façade features understated Chinese references, including

Chinese tiles ornament the upper façade of Julia's 1924 Ming Quong School for Girls (today the Julia Morgan School for Girls) at 5000 MacArthur Boulevard in Oakland.

the colorful tiles that line its upper soffit as well as the distinctive Chinese keystone tile, decorated with peonies, that surmounts its entrance. In 1924 she designed the Ming Quong Home for Chinese Girls at 5000 MacArthur Boulevard in Oakland (known today as the Julia Morgan School for Girls). Though it appears Mediterranean at first, its stuccoed-concrete walls are decorated with Chinese tiles, and some of its entrances feature pairs of *shishi* (guardian lions, known informally as foo dogs). For the Chinese YWCA, Julia worked closely with the organization's Chinese American committee and successfully incorporated many characteristic features, including three exterior towers topped with

green Chinese roof tiles; a circular moon gate that led into an enclosed courtyard with a koi pond; and a large painted dragon that covered the floor of the long corridor leading to the gymnasium. In the late 1930s, this latter room was packed on weekend nights with young Chinese couples dancing to the music of the Cathayans and the Chinatown Knights, popular local big bands.[11] (In 1996, the building was sold to the Chinese Historical Society of America, which operates a small museum about the Chinese immigrant experience.)[12] As with the Japanese YWCA, Julia donated her services for this building, saying, "I would like to give it as a tribute to the contributions of those two countries to architecture."[13]

Julia had special empathy for immigrants and the hardships they experienced. After the 1906 quake, she rebuilt the reinforced clinker-brick Donaldina Cameron House (known at that time as the Culbertson House) at 920 Sacramento Street, which since 1874 had served as a refuge for Chinese girls forced into prostitution. (It is still in operation as a social-service center.)[14] In 1909, Julia also completed several structures at the U.S. Immigration Station located on Angel Island, the largest island in San Francisco Bay. Her brother-in-law Hart Hyatt North was its chief immigration officer. He had presumably approved the initial architect, Walter J. Mathews of Oakland, who was hired in 1907. Inspired by the immigration station at Ellis Island, Mathews conceived a central administration building supplemented by cottages where medical and administrative staff determined immigrants' eligibility for admission—an anxiety-inducing process that could drag on for months, often concluding with a denial.[15] When Mathews abruptly departed in July 1909, six months before the station's January opening, Julia stepped in to complete the unfinished hospital, disinfectant annex, two cottages, and the U.S. Appraiser's office.[16] In 1919, she was hired to design San Francisco's Potrero Hill Neighborhood House at 953 De Haro Street. This organization was founded chiefly to serve Eastern European immigrants, particularly the Molokans from the Kars region of the Transcaucasus, who fled Tsarist Russia in 1905. (Known today as The Nabe, it remains a community resource center.)[17]

Julia particularly enjoyed designing the Chinese YWCA, since it provided an opportunity to learn more about Chinese art. Walter recalled that she often wandered around Chinatown, which was less than a mile from her office. She also sent a young employee, Polly Lawrence McNaught, to search the Chinatown shops, as Polly explained: "I was always on the lookout for very fine embroideries. I think she just liked to collect . . . nice old things."[18] Julia even began to study Chinese

In 1919 Julia designed San Francisco's Potrero Hill Neighborhood House at 653 De Haro Street,
which primarily assisted refugees who had fled Tsarist Russia.

calligraphy in the 1930s. Walter reminisced, "I came into the office one night . . . and she was bending over [her desk] and working with a little brush. . . . She said, 'Oh, you startled me. I was just copying some of these characters. They're so beautiful, even if you don't know what they mean.' And she had a booklet there, *Introduction to Colloquial Cantonese*."[19]

In 1931, despite her heavy workload, Julia agreed to take over Maybeck's commission for the women's dormitories at Principia College, a Christian Science university located 30 miles north of St. Louis in Elsah, Illinois. Ben was hired in 1923 to design the entire compound, his single largest commission. He produced thirteen Elizabethan-style buildings (eleven of which survive) for what was then a 300-acre campus (which now comprises 1,200 acres). The job continued through 1938 due to site changes and labor unrest. It was proving too much for Ben, as Julia confessed to Bjarne: "We are busy here, but chiefly on Mr. Maybeck's work at Principia—Am leaving today for St. Louis to see the work & try to get closer co-operation between all elements. . . . we may drop out soon, if Mr. Maybeck has strength to carry fully. He is not strong— cannot apparently stand the pushing strain of construction."[20]

Ben was sixty-nine at this time, and his architecture firm had closed decades earlier. Around 1914 he had begun routinely using Julia's office space and equipment to design his major projects, including his Palace of Fine Arts. On smaller jobs, Ben worked from home, preferably on a large drafting table outside.[21]

Ben and Julia joined forces again in January 1930, when Maybeck's Wyntoon— the seven-story stone castle he had designed for Phoebe Hearst in 1902—burned to the ground. The cause was likely an electrical short triggered by animals chewing on the power lines. W. R. loved Wyntoon for its mountain air (at 3,000 feet elevation) and its spectacular forest setting, but he did not inherit it when his mother died in 1919. Phoebe left it to his cousin, Anne Apperson, from whom he had purchased it in 1924.[22]

As he had done when Maybeck's Hearst Hall on the university campus burned in 1922, W. R. asked Ben to design a new Wyntoon, in collaboration with Julia. She knew the site well, since Hearst had recently hired her to build its stables, tennis courts, and swimming pool. At the time of the fire, they were discussing some major alterations, including joining Maybeck's medieval guesthouse (which Phoebe had christened The Gables) to the original stone castle located 150 feet away.[23] This conflagration provided Hearst with new construction opportunities. One of his recent purchases would also provide wonderful building materials, since Arthur Byne had found Hearst another Spanish monastery.[24]

In 1930, Byne wrote Julia:

"This is the famous old Cistercian monastery . . . in the mountains of Cuenca. . . . To begin with it is an isolated mountain property far from any village. Next, the owner is the sub-director of the Bank of Spain, an old friend and one of vast influence . . . the owner will be an assistance instead of an obstacle. The owner's reason for selling is that the buildings are in danger of collapse.... Mountolive consists of a magnificently vaulted church out of which you can produce a great salle [room] and several smaller ones besides; next, the Chapter House is in itself a splendidly vaulted chamber one of the finest I have ever seen; then there is the Refectory, severe in Cistercian manner but very imposing."[25]

The monastery of Santa Maria de Óvila (its actual name, though Byne referred to it by the code word "Mountolive") was located on the banks of the Tagus River, 90 miles northeast of Madrid. Though consecrated in 1181, its Gothic buildings were constructed primarily during the thirteenth century in the austere but elegant Cistercian style. Today the wholesale removal and relocation of such an ancient building would be unthinkable. In 1931, Spanish laws that prohibited the export of cultural monuments were sporadically enforced, and Byne often bribed officials to circumvent them. Spanish monasteries (including Sacramenia and Mountolive) had been secularized by the government in 1820, then sold to private owners.[26]

When Byne first saw Mountolive, it was in ruins. Trees and bushes grew from its vaulting, and the roof tiles and stone sculptures had been removed.[27] Nevertheless, its columns, capitals, ridged vaulting, and carved doorframes remained, as well as thousands of blocks of beautifully cut limestone. Julia sent

In 1931, Hearst purchased Santa Maria de Óvila, another twelfth-century Spanish monastery, then being used as a stable and wheat farm. Today's cultural patrimony laws would prevent purchasing and exporting such an ancient building.

Walter to Spain to assist with the dismantling, and he later reminisced, "Perhaps this was one of the most ambitious house-moving jobs in history." He also recalled, "At that time [1931] the monastery had been abandoned for nearly a hundred years ... the pressure of the rain-soaked earth covering the vaults had become very great, causing the collapse of some and the rupture of others." He wrote to Julia about the carved limestone: "It is impossible to give an idea of its beauty."[28]

Excited by this project's potential, Ben and Julia presented W. R. with a plan for an even larger Wyntoon: a Teutonic castle faced in Mountolive's limestone, featuring sixty-one bedrooms and a circular study on its eighth floor.[29] This plan was too impractical and expensive for even Hearst to pursue. Maybeck withdrew from the project, but Julia presented W. R. with various design proposals for a rebuilt Wyntoon that would somehow incorporate the medieval stones. Surely her most remarkable idea was for the swimming pool they planned to locate inside Mountolive's reconstructed chapel, which was 150 feet long and 50 feet high. It was never built, but the historian Robert M. Clements Jr. described its proposed features: ". . . changing rooms and lounges in the old side chapels, shallow water for wading in the apse, 11-foot-deep water in the central plunge, and a diving board where the altar had been."[30] Perhaps it would have been in shockingly bad taste, as this description implies; perhaps not, since Julia was at the height of her genius when she designed swimming pools.

By 1931, W. R. was feeling the financial impact of the Depression. He wrote Julia about San Simeon, where construction was continuing, "We have got to make some economies on account of the dull times."[31] They proceeded with several relatively low-cost tasks: completing the residential quarters for his northernmost cattle ranch, the Milpitas Hacienda; constructing several Mission-style bungalows for staff residences in the estate village near San Simeon Bay;

and pouring concrete for the upper portion of Casa Grande's four-story north wing, where they had already completed the first-floor movie theater.

An appealing project, however, tended to banish Hearst's intentions to economize. Throughout 1931 and 1932, Julia designed one of the hilltop's most enthralling spaces: the Roman Plunge, an indoor swimming pool located beneath the east-facing tennis courts. Its basin, walls, and floor are lined with 1-inch squares of Venetian glass tiles, most in a deep lapis blue or 22-karat gold, the latter sandwiched between clear glass. These tiles form mosaics depicting mermaids, mermen, and sea creatures cavorting, in a whimsical Art Deco style. W. R. was a fine swimmer, a necessity since this pool is 10 feet deep. The only shallow portion is a narrow 3-foot-deep alcove located behind the central diving platform. The pool is tranquil and still, its basin's 205,000 gallons of water acting like a mirror. In the daytime, sunlight streams through its tall windows and illuminates its sparkling tiles. At night, the alabaster globes that crown its marble lamp standards glow like reflected moons on the water.

As the pool neared completion, a rare employee problem arose. Julia seldom experienced personnel difficulties, because she championed the hilltop staff whenever W. R. raised any objections. She also earned the construction crew's respect because of her highly technical knowledge of building techniques. She didn't always remember the workers' names, but she would occasionally

LEFT: *Julia's design for the indoor Roman Plunge references both fifth-century Ravenna and Art Deco Hollywood. Its ten-foot-deep basin, diving platform, shallow alcove, walls, and floor are covered in fanciful mosaics of Venetian glass.*

say when instructing one of them, "Do it this way, friend." She insisted that any inferior workmanship be ripped out and redone, and occasionally she even lent her bare-handed assistance to the process.[32]

The only staff member who proved difficult to manage was construction superintendent Camille Rossi, an engineer whom Julia had sent down from her office in 1922. He soon began to flout her authority, and also to quarrel with other employees. After Rossi caused a particularly unpleasant incident early in 1932, Hearst fired him. Rossi responded so emotionally that W. R. wrote to Julia, "Mr. Rossi seems to be in such desperate straits that I am repenting letting him go. What do you say, Shall we try him for another year?" Though she may have been appalled by this suggestion, Julia replied calmly, "Any decision you come to in regard to Mr. Rossi I will of course fall in with cheerfully, but I believe that not carrying through will make him doubly hard to work with—he is so unbelievably revengeful and finds so many ingenious ways for indirect expression of his sentiments. I may be unreasonably tired of operating with a constant sense of contrary purpose, and not see conditions fairly or fully as your fresh eye can."[33] She then deftly exposed Rossi's hypocrisy by enclosing the happy letter she had just received from him in response to her having arranged for him to work at Principia College: "Going to St. Louis may be fine. . . . Well let us hope that everything is for the best."[34] As a result, Rossi departed, surely to Julia's satisfaction.

When she hired George Loorz as his replacement, Julia made sure to select someone who was both an affable manager and a talented engineer. In 1924 Loorz had graduated from the University of California with degrees in mathematics and civil engineering. He had previously worked on the university's Hearst Memorial Gymnasium, Marion's Beach House swimming pool, and Wyntoon's tennis courts and swimming pool, so Julia knew he was exceptionally competent and conscientious.[35] When George arrived at San Simeon, he began tackling a wide range of projects: mounting the thirty-six bells in Casa Grande's twin towers; completing its duplexes—four two-story guest suites that featured a loft bedroom on each upper level and a bathroom and sitting room below; finishing W. R.'s elaborate third-floor Gothic study; and building roads and bridges throughout the ranch's backcountry.[36]

George's hiring coincided with W. R.'s acceptance of Julia's new and comparatively modest plan for Wyntoon, which involved no monastery stones.[37] Among its earliest components were three Bavarian-style cottages, set on an oval green alongside the rushing McCloud River below Angel Creek. The term "cottages" is misleading, since each stuccoed half-timbered house had multiple stories and many rooms. The one closest to the creek—which was also the largest—remained unfinished inside. It was known at various times as Sleeping Beauty House or Fairy House, but its geographical location ultimately determined its name, Angel House. In the

RIGHT: *When Maybeck's Wyntoon burned in 1930, Julia built several replacement structures, including a charming Bavarian village. Hearst and Marion stayed in Brown Bear House, decorated with fairy-tale scenes by the Hungarian artist Willy Pogány.*

The Bavarian village contained the unfinished Angel House and the completed Cinderella House, also decorated with Pogány's paintings. Under the strain of simultaneously constructing Wyntoon and San Simeon, Hearst fell deeper into debt and Julia's health deteriorated.

center was the three-story triple-turreted Cinderella House, and slightly removed from the other two was W. R.'s own two-and-a-half-story residence, Brown Bear House.

These buildings were delightfully picturesque from the front and absolutely thrilling from the back, where their balconies literally overhung the rushing current. The exteriors of both finished cottages were covered with charming murals painted by renowned Hungarian illustrator Willy Pogány.[38] Cinderella House featured scenes from the familiar story, including a painted clock above its entrance door, permanently stopped at five minutes to midnight. Brown Bear was decorated with depictions from a lesser-known Brothers Grimm fairy tale, "Bearskin," in which a man is turned into a bear for seven years. Midway through his ordeal he becomes engaged to an unwilling princess, then disappears. Once the spell is broken, he returns—handsome, young, and rich—to marry her at last.[39]

In addition to the Bavarian cottages, a few other structures stood nearby: River House, a Colonial-style guesthouse from Phoebe's era; and the office, a modest wood-shingled bungalow that served as Hearst's communication center. Across the river Julia built Bridge House, with a wood-shingled square tower that evoked Maybeck's original Wyntoon. Here guests joined W. R. and Marion to play cards and watch movies in the evening. On this side of the river Julia also constructed a Swiss chalet to house the female staff, as well as a charming little teahouse made of half-timbering and stone.

Less than half a mile downstream was a second compound, which included the previously constructed stables on one side of the riverbank, and tennis courts and a swimming pool on the other. Nearby stood The Gables—the second building Maybeck designed for Phoebe—about which little is known, since one of Julia's first tasks was to remodel and enlarge it in 1932. Its dining room held sixty, and all meals were served there until the building burned down in 1944.[40]

After that time, meals were taken in the third residence, located farther downriver where the water made its tightest turn—a phenomenon that inspired the building's name, The Bend. This was Charles Stetson Wheeler's original hideaway, built by Willis Polk in 1899. Here Phoebe fell in love with the region and decided to build her own Rhineland castle nearby. W. R. purchased The Bend in the spring of 1934, at which time Julia began to enlarge and remodel it, transforming the rustic hunting lodge into a Gothic-Revival mansion as dramatic as its matchless setting.[41]

These three groups of buildings were located within a mile of each other, alongside the river. In 1935, *Fortune* magazine described Wyntoon's incomparable scenery: "... along the edge of the McCloud River, which twists and writhes in its headlong tumble to the lowlands, its buildings are like doll's houses tucked unimportantly beneath towering pine and fir and cedar. The majesty of those trees is indescribable. From 6-foot bases they shoot straight to heaven and smack the blue, cloudless sky. And everywhere the roar of the McCloud, and the pine-in-sunshine smell."[42] (Today Wyntoon is privately owned and still used by members of the Hearst family and Hearst Corporation employees; it is inaccessible to the general public.)

Both San Simeon and Wyntoon required a construction superintendent on-site. George remained at San Simeon, while Julia sent her longtime employee Mac McClure to head operations at Wyntoon. He had previously been living on the hilltop and supplying Hearst with spur-of-the-moment drawings in the intervals between Julia's frequent visits. Mac and George became great friends, and their letters provide an unparalleled account of events at each location. Both men soon noticed that starting a big job at one estate often triggered an interval of belt-tightening at the other, since Hearst continued to overspend.[43]

Julia was sixty when she began construction at Wyntoon. In addition to maintaining her San Francisco office, she was now designing two enormous estates in two of California's most remote locations. By August 1932, her chronic ear problems had worsened, as she explained to client Grace Barneburg of San Luis Obispo's Monday Club, a women's club for which Julia had promised to design a clubhouse gratis. Julia reluctantly informed her of the need for a brief delay: "... the ear trouble developed into an acute stage, necessitating a radical mastoid operation and while all went well, the aftermath is a bit slower than usual, and even as a beturbaned Turk, [my] traveling is not yet in order."[44] The mastoid process is a bone located directly behind each ear. Its principal function is to provide

Julia donated her services in designing The Monday Club at 1815 Monterey Street in San Luis Obispo, 45 miles south of San Simeon. Despite her health problems and Avery's worsening dementia, she didn't withdraw from the project.

attachment support for many head and neck muscles. Today the bacterial infection known as mastoiditis is easily treated with antibiotics, but in the 1930s the condition was much more serious.[45]

Julia, impatient to be well, wrote W. R. the following month: "May I ask a grand favor? Next time your plane goes from here [San Francisco] to the ranch, may I have a passage? . . . The doctors have no objection . . . as am rested and quite well again, although a head dress will have to be a costume note for some time to come. It will be mighty good to see San Simeon again."[46] Hearst readily acquiesced, but it soon became apparent that Julia had not recovered. She wrote George explaining that she ". . . had to go back to the hospital for a 2nd siege of the nature of the 1st only deeper in—If it had to happen, it's as convenient as any time—The 1st one was a chance anyway, & this is another. You are a great comfort George, for I know you will keep the needed balance."[47] W. R. telegraphed her concernedly: "Dear Miss Morgan I think if you drank a bottle of English or rather Irish stout every day it would do you a lot of good stop you eat so little the porter would give you strength stop may I send you some Dublin stout?"[48]

At the bottom of this telegram Julia drafted a few lines of a humorous poem, likely intending to send it to W. R., who frequently wrote amusing verses. Julia was not equally skilled in this area, and it is not known whether she ever completed her composition, which included these phrases: "The kindly doctors probe & drain/& cannot develope [sic] a single pain. . . . But the kindly doctors suggest/that a simple dropping on the/floor might/keep them hospitalized for, ever more."[49]

Her second surgery unfortunately made things worse. Julia lost her equilibrium—a calamity, since she regarded climbing scaffolding as essential to her work. Her balance never completely returned. She continued to inspect construction sites nevertheless, requesting that George (or someone else whom she knew well) walk directly in front of her so she could follow behind him while placing her hand in his coat pocket.[50] Hattie Bell Marcus, Julia's client and friend, recalled: "She used to walk a little bit bent. I've seen her downtown . . . walk near the buildings and sometimes touch the buildings as she came along. . . . But it was never mentioned."[51]

North explained the terrible damage caused by the second procedure: "They had to operate again and remove the whole inner ear, and in so doing they severed the facial muscle on one side." In consequence, Julia's face was twisted into a distorted grimace, with the left side of her mouth turning upward toward her left eye. The doctor so regretted his mistake that he never sent her a bill. Flora recalled that Julia "realized that in some respects he was more hurt than she was. She used to send a present to him every year at Christmastime. . . . an armload of orchids, because he had said his wife loved orchids."[52]

Julia also endured a third operation in a failed attempt to correct her facial deformity, the appearance of which bothered her greatly, as Mrs. Forney confirmed: "She said, 'Oh, I don't think I'll ever work again.' She didn't want to go out looking any different than she had before."[53] North explained, "She kept the office going, but she didn't like to see people. . . . she had a little cubby hole . . . across the hall where she hid away. She

Julia's surgeon botched an operation on her inner ear, severing a facial muscle, which disfigured her face and destroyed her equilibrium. Nevertheless, she continued her work at San Simeon and Wyntoon.

could be there all day and all night and no one would know the difference except her staff." He added, "She went to San Simeon . . . on sneak trips, but she didn't appear in the dining room or anything of that sort."[54]

Julia kept on working through it all, as George reported to Mac in December 1932:

"She was quite strong, that is she lifted heavy chairs etc. but Oh the equilibrium. I think she staggered more than ever. While we [were] going thru one of the tapestry boxes in the [basement] Vault she simply fell into it. She said, 'I certainly have a jag on tonight.' Again she was sketching something leaning on her elbow on a table and went flop down with her face on that. Each time I merely put my arms around her, pick her up bodily and set her in the nearest handy spot and we go right on with the business. It is really pathetic."[55]

Julia regretted that her health problems delayed their progress, as she confessed to George in March 1933:

"As you see, I'm emerging, still too slowly—If the next few days go well, the ear is closing, apparently the last gap, why it will not be but a few days & I can move around, circulate etc., again—Unfortunately it may be some months before my looks are normal, which I much regret as it will perhaps look as though I was not as well & able as I will be. Am most sorry to have 'fallen down' for your sake, & am very appreciative of your way of handling it—Unfortunately, still for a few days cannot do more than for a few consecutive (2) minutes—I will probably come up early in week & stay over a day or so if a party is not on. . . ."[56]

One week later, W. R. requested that all construction at San Simeon be shut down for the immediate future, perhaps in a vain attempt to encourage Julia to stay home and rest.[57]

If so, Hearst's efforts were unsuccessful. Mac told George later that month:

"Here is a little item which you are to keep to yourself or I am to be shot at sunrise. Two weeks ago when Miss M. was here and she told me she was going for a short walk by the flume and not to bother about her, 3 hours later she returned covered with mud, blood, and bruises to such a degree that I had to take her to the hospital. She had fallen off the flume down the wet and rocky bank about 20'—cutting her head open and severely bruising herself. Fortunately and miraculously she was not badly hurt and was out again in two days. Can you beat it?"[58]

George replied, "Yes Mac the first thing she told . . . [me] was about that fall etc. She is firmly convinced that it helped her equilibrium and facial paralysis. Said she told her doctors about it and they said, 'Quite possible but a little too rough treatment to recommend to a patient.'"[59]

Julia's failure to fully recover prompted her to do something unprecedented: invest in a private retreat where she could rest and heal. In the spring of 1934 she bought a small home in Monterey, one of her favorite places since childhood. Julia's work on Asilomar between 1913 and 1928 meant that she knew the area well. She chose a stuccoed cottage—with an ocean view—near Franklin Street, behind a larger house in Monterey Heights. This spot was also ideal because it was roughly halfway between San Francisco and San Simeon. Julia's frequent Sunday visits to the hilltop remained the same, but instead of leaving San Francisco on Saturday night, she left on Friday night.

In 1934 Julia purchased a Monterey cottage where she could rest on her way to San Simeon. She added the upstairs studio (now a private apartment), which retains its fireplace and its elaborate ceiling. The only surviving photo from Julia's time shows a few of the Chinese frescoes she collected.

She'd disembark at Monterey, rest for twenty-four hours in her little hideaway, then catch the southbound train for San Simeon on Saturday evening.[60]

The cottage was set back from the street, North and Flora recalled: "The house was surrounded by very tall trees, so it was rather dark. Some of the interiors were kind of a faded apricot stucco. . . . She played around with the color down there, and was interested in the reflections of the green from the outside . . . counteracting that, I guess, with some warmer color."[61] There were two small bedrooms and one bath upstairs, and a large living room and kitchen downstairs. Julia purchased the house as well as two adjacent lots, and eventually bought several more, to ensure that she had privacy and room for fruit trees and a garden.[62] She didn't spend all her time resting and relaxing, as Mrs. Forney recalled: "And just to unwind, she'd go down to Monterey and *really* do some heavy work, cleaning up and everything. . . ."[63]

The only room Julia added on to the building was her personal studio, where she spent much of her time seated at her drawing board at one end of the room. She furnished it with family pieces, creating a diagram that identified "Pa's chair," "Grandpa's chair," and "Avery's bureau" in their respective locations.[64] Its decorations were unpretentious, Flora recalled: "She would have pictures on the walls that were just cut out of magazines that appealed to her. . . . There was no reason she couldn't have had good paintings, or whatever she wanted. . . . In certain rooms there were,

say, ten pictures pasted one on top of the other—not behind the glass, just on top of the glass. . . . Her tastes were catholic as far as art was concerned."[65]

Julia equipped her retreat with three luxuries, all showcased in her studio. She built a brick fireplace, in front of which she placed a large couch with lots of cushions. "She loved a big burning fire," North explained.[66] She constructed a striking wooden ceiling with geometric coffering that resembled Hearst's antique Spanish ceilings at San Simeon. And along the upper walls she displayed ten 3-foot-high Chinese frescoes of painted goddesses clad in swirling robes and holding their attributes, including trays and baskets laden with fish.[67]

The cottage was the only building Julia bought solely for herself. She was very happy there, for instance writing at Christmas to one of the artists who worked at San Simeon: "Thank you very much for all the quaint & pretty devices to make my house & garden so dear—&,—like a story book house, without one bit of worry or concern as to its Keep-up—or Keep-down!"[68] She entertained frequently, often inviting Flora or Bjarne and his wife for the weekend. These guests drove her down, allowing her to bypass the train. Julia's friend Hattie Bell Marcus reminisced about her weekend visit: "Behind this big mansion was a smaller home that she owned. . . . [Upon our arrival] she went right to work. I read and walked in the woods. We'd stop for meals and go find some nice place to eat, and she'd go back to her work. We went back to town on Monday and she said, 'I just wanted you near me.'"[69] The Monterey cottage also gave Julia an introduction to Sachi Oka, a young Japanese girl who became her housekeeper. Sachi was working for the owners of the large house when Julia hired her sight unseen. Within a few years, they had become devoted friends.[70]

Even spending time at her tranquil cottage did not bring about Julia's recovery. Therefore in October 1934, W. R. intervened, convincing her to take a trip to Europe—which he described as a research expedition, doubtless to make it sound more like work—and insisting on taking care of all the arrangements. He wrote:

"The member of the family [her sister Emma] is a fine idea, and the lady is apparently just the one you should have with you. If you pardon me for butting in a little bit, I am going to see that you get a comfortable cabin on the boat so the trip will really do you some good. Then when you land, please land at Naples, and I will have our correspondent get a nice automobile for you and your relative to take you down to Pompeii and Sorrento and Amalfi and to the temples at Paestun [sic]; then back to Naples and then up to Rome. When you have satisfied yourself with Rome, the automobile will take you to Perugia and Assisi and Siena and Florence, and via Bologna to Venice."

He then sketched an itinerary of twenty-five additional cities throughout Western Europe, ending with London and Southampton, and concluded: "The automobile is going to be my automobile, as I have some stored in England, and I am naturally going to attend to everything in connection with it; and all you have to do is just sit in it and be a good girl, which I know is very hard for you to do. Please let me try to help make the trip agreeable."[71]

Julia consented, and the only change in Hearst's initial plan was that he sent their car and driver along with them on the boat, perhaps to prevent Julia from declining these services once they arrived in Europe. She carefully kept a newspaper's society column that described their luxurious departure: "Off to Naples for the three-month tour of the continent sailed MISS JULIA MORGAN, famed San Francisco architect, together with her sister, MRS. EMMA M. NORTH, an automobile, and a chauffeur. Her cabin was alive with flowers and goodbye bundles, baskets, and packages, and it seemed as though half of San Francisco were down to see her off. She was glad to get off, too, for she told us that she wants a rest, but our bet is that she'll sneak in a sly look-see at Europe's new architectural developments."[72] Julia had last seen Europe thirty-three years before and longed to return. A few years earlier she had written to Walter, who was vacationing in Switzerland: "I loved Vevey and all the lovely lake towns—My, but I'd like to resee it all with these eyes."[73]

Though their travels were beset by rain, the trip was still a success, and midway through it Julia revealed how dire her condition had been when they departed. Her office manager, James LeFeaver, wrote George in January 1935: "Miss Morgan ... said that ... she already felt well repaid for the trip. We could not gather definitely as to the state of her health, but she does say that she is becoming enthusiastic about doing things, and to us that is a very good sign."[74] Julia and Emma returned home a month sooner than Hearst had hoped, as Mac reported to George: "I think she looks very much better and am sure the trip helped her. However her improvement will prompt her to become very active again, I'm afraid, and will undue [sic] a lot of good the trip will have done."[75]

Mac was correct. Three months after Julia's return she was working harder than ever at Wyntoon, and he confessed to George that he was fed up:

"This last week has been one of the worst I have ever put in. Personally I do not think it is worth such an awful effort. We have worked until midnight for five nights running—and now as I write this I can see J. M. tugging and lugging porch and lawn chairs herself, but I am too tired and calloused [sic] to go out and either stop her or help her. All of the rooms have been furnished and refurnished about four times—curtains changed and rugs rolled out and rolled up again until we were cockeyed—So let the Chief come soon, says I—at least it will put a stop to this, whatever else may be in store for us."[76]

Later that year, when Wyntoon was closing down for the winter, Julia confessed her struggles to her longtime Parisian mentor, François-Benjamin Chaussemiche:

"Your letters have been a great pleasure & inspiration these months during which it has taken all I have had of reserve energy to carry through work undertaken. This partly due to the long distances to be traveled each week, partly due to some setbacks in general recovery. . . . work on this project has been very difficult—physically and because of the difficulty of keeping men working happily under such conditions."[77]

Throughout 1936, Julia continued to oversee various Hearst projects: remodeling Marion's Santa Monica Beach House; completing the final version of San Simeon's Neptune Pool, as well as installing a beauty parlor in Casa Grande's north wing; refurbishing Hearst's *San Francisco Examiner* building, including designing a tall and dramatic wrought-iron grille for its front façade; finalizing Bridge House and continuing her work on The Bend at Wyntoon; and even flying to Arizona to confer with Hearst about designing a large hotel—never built—at Grandview Point, where he owned land on the south rim of the Grand Canyon.[78]

Still there was a feeling of uncertainty in the air. Hearst's finances remained precarious, and in September Julia told George and Mac that construction at both Wyntoon and San Simeon was to be shut down for the remainder of 1936.[79] Furthermore, George told his business partner, Fred Stolte, that Julia "has definitely decided to close her present office soon after the first of the year when she has completed what they have on hand. . . . Mr. Hearst has not yet discussed his plans

RIGHT: *In 1936, Julia remodeled the Hearst building at 5 Third Street in San Francisco, but as W. R.'s funds dwindled, she began to travel. Her family explained, "She only traveled when she couldn't build."*

with her and she is not going to call him. If he doesn't send his program by Thanksgiving she intends to go back [to New York] and get it all settled definitely. . . . I don't think she's mentioned this to anyone but [her office manager] Jimmie LeFeaver and ourselves, in case something should cause her to change her mind."[80]

Julia was approaching sixty-five late in 1936 when she followed through with her intention, reducing her staff and moving her office to a smaller space on the eighth floor of the Merchants Exchange Building. She explained to Bjarne and Eve: "I intend to do only work that has something of special appeal hereafter—& do it with even more care. . ."[81] Construction at San Simeon continued, with Julia putting the final touches on three guest bedrooms in the north wing, but in May of 1937 W. R. wrote somewhat ominously: "I have suddenly been called to New York."[82]

This was the day of reckoning. Hearst's years of overspending had finally caught up with him. He was approximately $87 million in debt (equivalent to $1.5 billion today) and facing complete financial ruin. All building projects stopped while W. R. and his advisers struggled to avoid bankruptcy. George wrote to Julia:

"From Randy [Apperson, Hearst's cousin, whom he employed as the ranch manager] I learn that Mr. Hearst is a pathetic, broken man. . . . Apparently his creditors are quite anxious to hurt him if they can. Furthermore a government tax investigation seems

imminently possible. . . . I am glad to hear that Randy reports Miss Davies to be very considerate of him, to be his only real comfort. They are here on the hilltop alone. She stole him away from New York as he seemed so worried and confined there that she feared he might not stand it."[83]

Julia, who also knew how to comfort W. R., wrote to him immediately, saying: "I am sorry my voice was so husky last night. This is just to say that Wyntoon is at its best, the tiger lilies coming out and the wild roses and all the foliage beautifully clean and fresh from the late rains. The houses too are cheerfully crisp and fresh. I do hope you will have the pleasure of it while this fine weather holds." She concluded her letter with a meaningful phrase: "As always, with appreciation for all you have given me of interest and pleasure."[84] Julia confessed to George, "I wrote today, telling him . . . how I hoped he would come [to Wyntoon] before the heat & dust took toll of its beauty—It would do him good I am sure— there is enough activity and much he has not seen at all—It is all I can think of doing."[85] In fact, there was a great more for Julia to do. The years ahead would prove that her collaboration with Hearst was far from over.

CHAPTER TEN

OUT FROM THE SHADOWS

IN MAY 1937, ON THE BRINK OF FINANCIAL ruin, W. R. officially halted all his building projects. Unofficially, however, construction continued—though on a greatly reduced scale. Mac recalled: "The crew was reduced by three-quarters or more, but work went on under something called a budget allowance, which irked Mr. H. He usually got the budget padded. My little [construction] shack was in the east court and W. R. H. spent hours in it every day. I recall Miss Davies popping in at times with the question, 'What are you kids cooking up now?' The 'cooking up' was usually something akin to the Vatican or Windsor Castle, to the later disconcerting of Miss Morgan and the treasury."[1] Julia still traveled to San Simeon two or three times a month, and also regularly visited Wyntoon and Hearst's Southern California properties.

However, much of the work she supervised involved relatively minor improvements.[2] She explained to a former employee: "[We] are still holding on—mostly on very reduced Hearst work widely spread out—It may finish with this year—although S.S. will not be,—never will be,—completed."[3]

With no major projects on the horizon, at the age of sixty-six, Julia began to travel. North explained: "She only traveled when she couldn't build."[4] She wrote W. R. in August 1938: "The lure of the ocean wave is always strong, and conditions in the office such that it seems a good time to yield to it. I have a reservation on the only suitable craft going from San Francisco through the canal direct to Europe before [it becomes] too late in the year to think pleasant. It is on a fruit boat as it is to be an ocean vagabondage from port to port in the general direction of Sicily as boats are available." Hearst replied gloomily: "I hope you have a grand time. I am sure you will. Certainly I would like to make such a trip myself, but I guess I will have to stay here and try to make enough money to put up another house—or to finish those already begun."[5]

From this time on Julia made frequent journeys, almost always by freighter. Cargo vessels—which seldom took more than a dozen passengers—were less expensive than ocean liners and docked at many more ports. While their freight was being unloaded, Julia could explore neighboring towns by foot or by taxi, returning to the familiarity of the ship each evening. She planned her route as she went along, exiting one boat and booking passage on another almost as if she were catching buses. As usual, she brought along a diary—in this case, a blank book labeled Recipes—in which she could sketch and make notes on art and architecture. On this first solo trip, however, her routine changed. After finishing her customary descriptions, she kept on writing, probably in order to be doing something besides staring at the local inhabitants. What began as her typical *aide memoire* gradually transformed into a repository for Julia's private musings. Discovered around 2005 in a private archive, this journal provides the single most revealing record of her inner thoughts.[6]

Julia's diary entries were often laced with humor. After viewing a small cemetery in Amalfi, she wrote: "The dead would have no difficulty in rising, for they are not exactly buried."[7] In Torcello—an island in the Venetian lagoon—she described an eager young boy and a local cat, both interested in a handout:

"Alfredo is 10—mostly eyes, out of a very passé black service suit—thin as a rail—He runs the elevator, the errands, the excess baggage—Eyed me appraisingly coming up, ran for the key—rushed down the crooked hall & its ups & downs of steps—threw open my window, drew back the white curtain—I.E. believed he had put himself on record. . . . The 'Alameda' spotted cat at the restuarant [sic] is like Alfredo. . . . She is stream-lined, her orange black & white wattles making a sort of hood over her eyes & between the ears, ending in wide black bands around her green black eyes, [and] all pure white thence down—She eyes you speculatively [sic], & you relent—Then feel a touch on your knee—next a very gentle touch on your arm—all in the eyes, not a word—The children were never content with what you gave them, either."[8]

Her sympathies were invariably with the downtrodden:

"It is pathetic the efforts of [the] very poor to have for their children <u>clothes in</u> the [accepted] <u>style</u>—. . . . [even when it's] impossible to tell [the] original Material, so many the patches—<u>but no holes</u>. And how the mothers manage to have those immaculately clean & clothed babys [sic] under the living conditions . . . makes one very humble—such white little capes & coats & booties, & such pale little faces—true courage that, & devotion. Another lession [sic] in the necessity of pulling together all elements of a design, if any great result is to be obtained."[9]

She respected religious faith, even when she did not share it:

"The other day in Venice in a neighborhood Church I saw a young man—white faced, in a strain of outpouring before a lovely Madonna—her arms out, dainty, light with flowers & candles,—the poor thing on his knees, just trying to make her understand his devotion & his plea—Perhaps she [is] the one lovely sure thing in his life . . . [with] poor hard living, anxious political lives, uncertainty everywhere—but that this beautiful lady is, will be there—will listen to & understand & be willing to be adored—and to accept devotion. . . . The necklace one loves, she shall have—the lace collar, his mother's work, the earrings, her first & only—I would not want to take it from them, because to them it is truth . . . & that we know is a wide thing—of various interpretations."[10]

The damage from her mastoid operation still plagued her. At Ancona—a town on the Adriatic, northeast of Rome—she wrote: "Ancona has a grey clay path a goat would have work on . . . but a respectful little girl sees our trouble & asks if she could help, & her little brother one could cry over, his head all done up in a way so known, mastoids, white, thin—I never could have made it [without them]."[11] When she returned to a Palermo restaurant she had visited with Emma a few years before, Julia received a shocking reply to her friendly overture: "The old waiter, when I remarked he must have been here many years, replied—'Yes, I remember you by your crooked face!' No use trying to fool yourself when there are children or 'foreigners' around."[12]

Though Julia generally avoided speaking about her physical difficulties, Mrs. Forney's daughter Lynn recalled hearing of one occasion when she joked about them. Julia described encountering a weaving drunk heading toward her, and the comical dance that ensued as they both lurched around, trying to avoid each other.[13] Her usual habit was to ignore impediments and focus only on her goals. When she returned from Europe in the spring of 1939, she wrote George: "I find I must keep busy—have too much strength & too many ideas to drop out of an active life—just how and what it will result in is not yet clear—Mr. Hearst looks better than I had reason to expect & will, [I] am sure, make the grade and surprise everyone. However, I think only repairs & minor things will be done anywhere this year. . . ."[14]

Julia instead designed a small Berkeley shopping center at 2580 Bancroft Way—directly across from the campus—for her longtime client, Oakland entrepreneur Fred C. Turner. Thirty-two years earlier, she had constructed the Turner family's wood-shingled

*Julia designed several projects for the Turner family, including the Fred C. Turner stores,
built in 1916 at Piedmont Avenue and 40th Street in Oakland.*

Berkeley home at 255 Ridgeway Avenue.
In 1917, Fred's wife, Elsie Lee Turner, had
commissioned Julia to design a brick-fronted
two-story shopping center at 40th Street and
Piedmont Avenue in Oakland. Known today
as the Fred C. Turner Stores, this Italianate
structure still features the colorful terra-cotta
roundels—known as della Robbia wreaths—
that Julia mounted on its exterior. In the
early 1930s, she built a Berkeley apartment
complex for the Turners at 66 Panoramic Way.
Julia's 1939 Turner shopping center—done
in a simplified French Regency style—was
occupied for many years by a well-known
Berkeley restaurant, The Black Sheep. (An

eight-story housing complex recently replaced
it, but the Turner building's front entrance
has been preserved.)[15]

In 1939 she also began a project for the
spice heiress Else Schilling, with whom
Julia had become close friends seven years
before. They were both hospitalized at the
time—Julia for her mastoid operation, Else
after a riding accident. Though Else was
fourteen years younger, she too had grown
up in Oakland, and their paths frequently
crossed at YWCA functions and other social
events. In the early 1930s, Julia had designed
a cottage for Else's father in rural Woodside,
and redecorated two apartments—for father

and daughter—in San Francisco.[16] This latest commission was more substantial: Else hired Julia to design Bow Bay, her large summer house on the southwestern edge of Lake Tahoe. Constructed of stone and cedar, and inspired by Austrian hunting lodges, its interior featured exuberant wood carving, including an open ceiling composed of dramatic arched trusses. Though Else's summer home was imposing—with eight bedrooms and 4,000 square feet—she often traveled to Monterey to stay in Julia's modest cottage, according to housekeeper Sachi Oka.[17]

Sachi was seventeen when she began working for Julia, whom she described as "like a mother, a friend, not [like] an employer at all." One of Sachi's jobs was to fetch Julia from the Monterey train station on Friday night and make her dinner. She recalled:

Sachi also remembered three occasions when she drove to San Francisco to make Thanksgiving dinner at Julia's Divisadero home. "At that time I was driving an old 'tin can' Ford, and she said, 'Your car is old. What kind of car would you like? I'll get one for you.' My mother, I knew, would love a Pontiac.... [Julia] bought me a ... brand-new Pontiac."[19]

This level of generosity was customary with Julia. Flora recalled, "How she used her money is somewhat of a mystery. We know she helped a good many people." North added, "The idea of making money bored her, aside from [earning] enough to get by.... I don't believe anybody who worked for her got much less than she took out for herself.... her top people had better homes than she did." Flora concluded: "She never said 'I' anyway in her whole life that I can remember. It was always 'we.'"[20]

"The next morning I would go and fix her breakfast.... I'd ask her, and she'd say, 'Oh, just toast is okay.' But then I would make scrambled eggs and bacon.... She was upstairs and she was in bed, and I would take her breakfast to her. She'd say, 'Okay, pull a chair out and sit and talk to me.' For two hours we would talk.... we just got along so good and ... she was as young as me ... that's how I felt, you know. [Julia was in her late sixties.] She was a lot of fun. A sweet person.... She never got mad."[18]

At a family gathering in the 1940s, Julia sits at left, with her nephew's wife Flora North above her. Julia's employee and close friend Sachi Oka stands nearby.

However charitable, Julia expected W. R. to meet his obligations and pay her for her efforts. In June 1939 she made one of her periodic requests for funds, typically including Mac's interests along with her own:

"...there is with me in my small way as with you in your large one, a necessity of keeping track of expenses. It might be well to say that you have been asked to pay for no unexecuted work for many years back, in fact before we made the working drawings for Mount Olive at Wyntoon. You realize thinking back [on] the many projects we have developed together, that I could have had no profit in these years and I have not wanted it. As regards Mr. McClure—on my return this Spring he told me that he wished to remain with the office but would like an arrangement allowing him to come and go at our convenience...."[21]

She was unsuccessful. Hearst replied: "I realize fully that everything has been most delightful and most liberal, and I of course would, if it were possible, prefer to have it continue on the same basis. But circumstances demand the most limited possible expenditure on my part. In fact, for the rest of the year I must not contemplate anything of consequence."[22] Julia not only failed to receive her fee at that time but she also committed to paying Mac's salary herself: "It will be perfectly all right with us, as I have explained to Mr. McClure, if you will pay him for as long as you need him—or I will do so and you can reimburse exactly...."[23]

Julia eventually earned a generous profit on her work at San Simeon, as Mrs. Forney's office ledgers reveal. From 1919 to 1939 she netted $115,000 (equivalent to $1.5 million today). During those twenty years, Hearst spent an estimated $4.7 million on San Simeon's construction (equivalent to $80 million today).[24] This amount may seem relatively small, but at the time an American worker's annual income averaged well under $2,000 a year (equivalent to $31,000 today).[25] When Hearst frequently exceeded his large construction budget, Julia willingly cushioned his losses by paying herself last. Flora explained, "She didn't want to make money. She always thought that if she needed the money she could sell something."[26]

By 1939, it was obvious that W. R. was the one who would have to "sell something." During the next three years, he sold more than half his entire art collection to help defray his debts. Tens of thousands of objects—most of which had been stored in warehouses—were peddled at bargain prices, though the contents of San Simeon and Wyntoon remained largely untouched. After New York's auction houses were inundated, two department stores agreed to turn portions of their sales floors into showrooms. Sak's Fifth Avenue sold Hearst's paintings and Gimbel's sold everything else, from ancient Egyptian statues to medieval English armor to Colonial hooked rugs.[27] W. R. also disposed of real estate, including more than half of San Simeon's ranchland. The federal government purchased the northernmost 153,865 acres for $2.2 million (roughly equivalent to $41 million today; Julia's

Hearst donated Santa Maria de Óvila's stones to San Francisco, to be rebuilt in Golden Gate Park as part of a medieval museum, which Julia designed. Despite her determined efforts, it was never constructed.

ranch buildings—known as the Milpitas Hacienda—are now used as an Army training facility known as Fort Hunter Liggett).[28] With great reluctance, Hearst also resigned himself to liquidating several unprofitable newspapers as well as accepting two cash loans, each for $1 million. The lenders were Marion and—at her request—Eleanor "Cissy" Patterson, the Chicago heiress who was editor of Hearst's *Washington Herald*.[29] Sacramenia—the twelfth-century Spanish monastery W. R. purchased in 1925—was also put up for sale. Having never been shipped west, its thousands of crates had languished in Hearst's block-long South Bronx warehouse. (A pair of Florida businessmen eventually purchased Sacramenia for the bargain price of $50,000, shipping it to Miami, Florida, where

it was rebuilt and ultimately rechristened the Church of St. Bernard of Clairvaux.)[30]

W. R. also realized he could no longer pay the storage fees for Mountolive (Santa Maria de Óvila, the Spanish monastery he purchased in 1931); furthermore, the likelihood of his ever being able to afford to rebuild it was small. He therefore approached San Francisco's city administrators, proposing to donate the monastery stones for use in constructing a medieval museum.[31] This was timely, since John D. Rockefeller's medieval museum, The Cloisters, had opened in New York's Fort Tryon Park on May 10, 1938. Hearst envisioned a similar arrangement: a modern building that displayed the monastery stones on its exterior and showcased a collection of Gothic art inside. After extensive talks, his gift was tentatively accepted. Julia was to be the architect and the proposed site was a small plot of land in Golden Gate Park, between the de Young Museum and the Japanese Tea Garden. These arrangements began a protracted and ultimately unsuccessful effort to build the museum, in spite of Julia's repeated attempts over the next decade.[32]

Hearst's many financial cutbacks saved him from bankruptcy, but the immediate prospect of further construction at San Simeon was dim. In 1940, Julia relayed this news to John Van der Loo, a former hilltop plasterer who was looking for work: "I had hopes for all of those San Simeon groups, as there is much ornamental & decorative design involved.... I do not believe there will be a renewal of Mr. Hearst's projects for some time. You can speculate as well as any one.... Not a cheerful letter, John. But I think we *can* be cheerful & thankful for the comparative safety of our present."[33] With her business again slowing down, Julia booked a freighter trip through the Panama Canal toward the end of 1940.

Before her departure, she accepted an award at the Golden Gate International Exposition, the San Francisco world's fair held during 1939 and 1940 on Treasure Island. California's most famous women had been determined by popular vote, and Julia was selected to represent architects. Other luminaries included novelists Kathleen Norris and Gertrude Atherton; film director Dorothy Arzner; former congresswoman Florence Prague Kahn; and educator Dr. Aurelia Henry Reinhardt, president of Mills College (and a personal friend of Julia's).[34] Though she

accepted this award, Julia typically refused such public accolades as well as interviews.[35] Even when she consented in 1931 to speak with a reporter from the *Christian Science Monitor*, who identified her as "one of our first successful women architects," Julia remained characteristically modest: "I think it is too early to say what contribution women are making in the field of architecture. They have as clients contributed very largely, except perhaps in monumental buildings. The few professional women architects have contributed little or nothing to the profession—no great artist, no revolutionary ideas, no outstanding designs...."[36]

W. R. would doubtless have disagreed. Julia was also not the only female artist whose unique talent he admired. He collected the work of several twentieth-century women sculptors, including American Edith Woodman Burroughs and Parisian Fanny Rozet.[37] Hearst apparently wrote Julia about the persecution of a German Jewish artist, Hanna Gaertner, from whom he had commissioned a fountain for Wyntoon.[38] His letter no longer survives, but Julia's reply, written in the summer of 1939 as war loomed in Europe, provides sufficient context: "Thank you for the drawings of the Bear Fountain and the copy of the letter from Miss Gaertner. While in Italy, I came across a number of such cruel instances of similar treatment of her co-religionists—people of such fine quality, that the cruelty of it all makes one unhappy to think of it, particularly when there is so little a person like myself could possibly do.... If there is anything you can think of that I can do, I would appreciate your letting me know."[39] While in Italy in January 1939, Julia had watched an exiled Jewish family as they listened to the radio broadcast of Hitler's notorious Reichstag speech, predicting "annihilation of the Jewish race in Europe."[40] She wrote afterward in her diary: "The lad now & then hardly able to control his tears, the mother & daughter tense. The father taking notes—requiring gulps of water—These are fine people, cultured, sensitive—especially the mother & children,—of 16 & 18 [I] should judge,—slender, low-voiced, well dressed quiet people. The padrone tells me well to do—the father an owner of some mfg. plant in Germany."[41]

During the final months before America entered the war, an event occurred that ultimately had a detrimental effect on Julia's artistic reputation. On May 1, 1941, Orson Welles's film *Citizen Kane* premiered.[42] This thinly disguised biography of Hearst opens with a padlocked gate that blocks the entrance to Xanadu, Charles Foster Kane's brooding hilltop mansion. Its distant form—which studio artists created by painting a miniature building onto a sheet of glass—was inspired by the medieval abbey of Mont-Saint-Michel in France. Art director Perry Ferguson intended to create lavish interior sets, but money shortages forced a change of plan. Many of *Kane*'s scenes were filmed on a dark and nearly empty sound stage furnished only with a few statues, a large staircase, and an enormous fireplace. The portrait endured. Thereafter, San Simeon was regarded by many as a cold and cavernous

dwelling filled with worthless junk, and Julia was often harshly judged for having created it.[43]

When America declared war on Japan and Germany that December, every other topic became instantly insignificant. Newspapers were suddenly indispensable, which helped W. R. rapidly regain his wealth in the thriving wartime economy. At the age of seventy, Julia decided against pursuing commissions for government war work, explaining matter-of-factly to Bjarne and Eve: "There is a large volume of emergency defense housing [work available] ... which I have ... not tried to get, as [I] have handicaps..., but old clients are constantly asking [for] small items, so that I have full office days anyway—with no help but a part time old-timer, Mrs. Forney."[44]

Instead of undertaking government jobs, Julia embarked on a private project. In the spring of 1942, she took in the twelve-year-old son of her old friends Bjarne and Eve Dahl. Bjarne Jr. (known as B. J.) was living with his parents in Honolulu when Pearl Harbor was bombed, and they feared for his safety. Julia wrote on B. J.'s arrival: "... your lad at first ... was obviously worn out by the trip ... although in good physical condition, & of course home sick, & with an antique stranger."[45]

Many years later, B. J. recalled their first meeting: "It was quite interesting because she was working; she was as busy as all get out.... So I was guided into her presence, and I saw this little old lady. I stayed there until she was finished, and then we took the cable car and went to her house ... [where] she had a room all set up for me." He remembered an early difference of opinion: "Well, coming from Hawaii, we never wore shoes. I decided to go to school bare-footed. Miss Morgan wouldn't have that. She said, 'You're not going to be a savage; you're going to school and be a gentleman.'"[46] Julia wrote the Dahls about this incident: "After the [first] full week together the hurdles are safely over—He knows he can trust me not to ask him to wear what the boys here do not—came up shyly last night & said 'the kids at school never spoke of my clothes'— which was, I realized, an apology....I catch his sensitive little face in repose, can see his quick mind reactions, serious or mischievous, flash over it, & realize how fine & loveable [sic] a little chap he is...."[47]

They soon developed a daily routine, B. J. explained:

" ... Every day after school, when Miss Morgan wasn't home, I would go down to her office, and she would show me books of architecture, and she would give me tracing jobs.... Maybe every other day we would go to the Tele-News theater....and see what was going on in the world. She was very up-to-date.... She ate very conservatively. She was not an ostentatious woman....We would go to Compton's Cafeteria ...or once we went to Bernstein's Fish Grotto....[At home] she would buy these chip steaks....I always remember that, because she ate like a canary and was not very used to big eating."[48]

They frequently viewed Charlie Chaplin films, though it is unlikely Julia told B. J. that she knew Chaplin personally from San Simeon. These they watched twice, at her insistence: once for the story, and once for the art.[49]

During the two months B. J. stayed with Julia, he observed her closely:

"One thing about her, she was absolutely a fearless woman. She wasn't afraid of a doggone thing....She told me once that she went up in an airplane ...Open cockpit. It got stuck in the clouds....they kept going up higher and higher, and they didn't know where in the heck they were....She didn't care; she was a little worried....Finally the guy managed to pull out, and they landed.... in those days it was pretty risky. One day we decided to go to [the amusement park] Playland-on-the-Beach [sic]. I'd never been there....She says, 'Oh, let's go on the roller coaster,' and we did!"[50]

Even after B. J. moved out to stay with his aunt and uncle nearby, Julia remained an encouraging influence, writing him later that summer: "I am glad you are ... finding the useful work you do 'fun'—my 'work' has always been 'fun' to me too."[51]

The war also upended Sachi's life, when in 1942 she and her husband, Kazuo, were sent to a concentration camp in Poston, Arizona. Sachi remembered that during their internment Julia wrote them letters and sent them items they were unable to buy. After their release, they moved to Detroit, where Kazuo could find work in the auto industry. Sachi recalled, "...I told her I can't work for her anymore and that's when she said, 'I bought you a place. Would you come work for me again,' and I said, Sure. I didn't have to live with my in-laws. That would be great."[52] Julia purchased a comfortable Monterey home for them on Hawthorne Street, less than 2 miles from her own cottage. When Sachi and Kazuo returned to the neighborhood, an anti-Japanese petition was circulated in protest, but they moved in regardless. (Sachi lived in that house for more than sixty years, until her death in 2011 at age ninety-five.)[53]

Julia had also given a house to her most trusted employee, Thaddeus Joy, after his home was destroyed in the 1923 Berkeley fire. She "sold" T. J. 2816 Derby Street for $1, the price of the transfer fee.[54] She had constructed this two-story wood-shingled Berkeley bungalow in 1908 as a speculation house, in collaboration with her short-term business partner, Ira Wilson Hoover. Its

narrow front façade contained three tiers of fenestration: a projecting Italianate window at street level, an "eyebrow" window supported by carved balusters on its upper story, and a symmetrically placed small arched window in the attic. T. J. died in this comfortable home in December 1942, at the age of only fifty-nine. He had been ill since 1929, after contracting what was probably paratyphoid, from swimming in the ocean while working on Marion's Santa Monica Beach House. W. R. paid for his specialized medical treatments, and Julia gave him less demanding jobs to perform, but it was all to no avail. She wrote to a former employee, Elizabeth Boyter, in 1931: "Mr. Joy came back with the New Year, but we all see he cannot take hold—It is a serious and very worrying problem."[55]

Julia was unable to attend Thaddeus's memorial service, because early in December

During successful years, Julia shared her profits with her office staff. She also sold her longtime draftsman Thaddeus Joy the Berkeley house at left—at 2816 Derby Street—for $1, the cost of the transfer fee.

1942 she left for Mexico to meet W. R. at Babicora, the far-flung cattle ranch his father, George, had given him in the 1890s. Located in the northern state of Chihuahua on a high-desert plain, Babicora presented a tantalizing building prospect for Hearst. Julia enjoyed her first trip to Mexico, writing to Bjarne and Eve: "The 'center' was on a plateau apparent[ly] about 7,500–8,000 feet in altitude, very cold, but interesting from its absolute primitiveness—No mail, no worrys [sic] no war apparent. . . ." She continued: "The place I was in was miles & miles away from traveled roads—160 miles, in fact . . . . The women folk still washed their familys [sic] & cloths [sic] down on the creek banks, and ground their meal, corn, wheat, and oats, down on the creek beds—& cooked on open fires—, owned their own cows & horses, and dressed as in the Mexican pictures we are used to seeing—[They] Speak Spanish only—as I do not, sign language & grins were in order."[56] Julia and W. R. planned to build a combined residence and ranch headquarters out of adobe brick, but the project was besieged with delays and frustrations caused by the war. She returned to Babicora in June 1943 in hopes of personally inspiring further progress, but without success. The English-speaking superintendent, Edward Ardoin, communicated with her less and less, and construction slowed to a standstill with little but the concrete foundations completed.[57]

In any case, Julia had more immediate concerns during the summer of 1943. Avery had once again disappeared, this time from his care home in Niles Canyon, south of Oakland. She explained to B. J.'s aunt, Mrs. Benedict: "As you suspect, my chief concern has been the search for my brother—It is over three months now with no sure trace of him—not strange perhaps among all the queerly garbed and acting people who have filtered over the state the past two years [during the war]—His trouble is a species of amnesia which remembers its past but leaves its victim adrift in the normal present—I am hoping with the thinning out of the seasonal labor we may succeed in locating him."[58] Julia must have organized a diligent search, but at the age of sixty-eight Avery had embarked on his final journey. His body was found by a wandering transient, nine months after he'd been reported missing. Avery's cause of death was listed as starvation and exposure—a heartbreaking end for the brother Julia had cared for so devotedly. His remains were cremated at Julia's Chapel of the Chimes, then transferred to the family gravesite at nearby Mountain View Cemetery.[59]

Three days after Avery's memorial service, Julia was on a plane to Mexico, likely attempting to follow the advice she had recently given to B. J.: "I am glad you are busy & happy—(one generally is happy, if busy)."[60] While Julia was there, Flora wrote to acquaint her with Emma's response to their brother's death: "Mother [Emma] has pulled around remarkably well, and all our fears were groundless. She has been able to follow some line of rationalizing about Avery and life in general that has satisfied her, evidently, and her only worry now is that perhaps you haven't. Excuse me, there are . . . other things that bother her. One is the fact that she knows you are not getting anything to eat...."[61]

Julia failed to revive Babicora's construction on this third trip. Furthermore, she was having trouble keeping the medieval museum project slated for San Francisco's Golden Gate Park afloat. She wrote Walter regretfully: "You know how much has been put into Santa Maria D'Ovila in the years—interest, study, funds etc.—& of the belief,—brought about by the (to me) failure of the New York 'Cloisters,"—that we could here recreate a spirit, because we knew and felt something of the original builders' urge...."[62] One difficulty came when local administrators reappropriated the monastery's previously designated building funds. Even more disastrously, a series of fires—likely set by protesters who objected to any additional structures within the park—burned the wooden crates containing the stones, and obliterated the construction markings necessary for their reassembly. Nevertheless, Julia continued to visit the site and attempt to recreate plans for the monastery's eventual rebuilding. Walter recalled, "Now there is evidence of the drive of that little lady and the persistence of her dream.... That thing was all in ruins and yet she went out there day after day and made sketches of every little detail she could get to."[63] Julia briefly rehired former employee Dorothy Wormser Coblentz to assist her in preparing the museum's working model, and Dorothy later reflected: "It would have been the cloister to out-cloister all cloisters."[64] Though there were a few more flickers of interest after the war, the project ultimately

After a series of fires burned the crates that held the monastery stones, Julia spent hours among the wreckage, trying to identify salvageable material. The stones were gradually scavenged, though a few remain in Golden Gate Park.

In 1994, The Abbey of Our Lady of New Clairvaux (located in Vina, California) reconstructed and augmented the stones that had once comprised the monastery's medieval Chapter House.

went nowhere. For decades, the stones lay in tumbled piles behind the de Young Museum, where they were scavenged for other projects, including retaining walls and terraced borders for the nearby San Francisco Botanical Garden. (In the 1980s, architectural historian Margaret Burke successfully salvaged sufficient material to rebuild the monastery's 31-by-46-foot-long Chapter House. In 1994 the museum presented these stones to the Abbey of Our Lady of New Clairvaux, a Cistercian order of monastics in Northern California that has successfully reconstructed the building and reinforced it for earthquake protection.)[65]

When the war ended in September 1945, W. R. returned to San Simeon with his prosperity restored and an ambitious building program in mind. He was eighty-two. Julia was seventy-three at this time, and she did not return to the hilltop. Her handwriting appears on some of San Simeon's later drawings, and it is reasonable to assume that she stayed involved in an advisory capacity. Mac, who remained on the hilltop, explained many years later: "San Simeon is truly Miss Morgan's monument. Mr. Hearst's also."[66]

After the war, Julia worked on a few local projects, including the San Francisco transmission tower for KYA, one of Hearst's radio stations, as well as Prospect Court, a Berkeley student-housing complex commissioned by Else Schilling.[67] Mostly she traveled. Mrs. Forney explained, "It was time to go look at the world, so she changed her address to mine, and everything came to my home for quite a few years...." Julia had grown fond of Mexico, to which she returned in 1945 and 1946—albeit with a few misadventures. Mrs. Forney recalled: "She went into one of the churches and she was robbed by a young man.... She realized what was happening, so she chased him up to the back of the church and out. She couldn't find him. He was very fast. He was only about sixteen." On another occasion, "She was approached by a priest in the Catholic Church, and he asked her, what was she doing, was she proselytizing? Of course that would be the last thing in her mind. She said no, she'd been a Baptist all her life and she was only interested in the architecture."[68]

In 1947, Julia toured South America by freighter. Her diary from this trip survives, and though it is less revealing than the diary she kept

In 1947, Julia's sister Emma North (left) and niece Flora North (right) saw Julia off as she sailed from San Francisco to South America.

throughout Italy eight years before, it attests to her continuing independence and her sensitive nature. In Cordoba, Argentina, she wrote: "Had [a] lovely P.M. in [the] Park With . . . a family who 'once spoke English'—beautiful Spring feeling in trees & shrubs just starting to come out—boats of children on dark lakes, a few fruit trees blossomed pink, here & there one white—walked miles—walked back [to the hotel] to be caught in Elevator bet[ween] floors!"[69]

W. R. and Julia both began to experience serious health problems in 1947. At age eighty-four, Hearst had to leave San Simeon when an irregular heartbeat prompted his doctors to advise him to move somewhere lower in elevation and closer to a hospital. Marion bought a home at 1007 Beverly Drive in Beverly Hills, for which he mournfully departed, after stopping all construction at San Simeon. It never recommenced. Julia's final task for W. R. appears to have been some minor remodeling for Marion's Lexington Road residence in 1946. In 1948, Julia noted that an elevator would be installed for W. R. at his Beverly Drive house, but it is unlikely that she herself was involved with the process.[70] By that time, Julia's memory lapses—which were similar to those she had so painfully witnessed among her family members—had begun to worsen.

For a while she attempted to make light of her forgetfulness, writing to Bjarne and Eve: "I [will] take the usual Monterey train

Modêlo S. C. 139

REPÚBLICA DOS ESTADOS UNIDOS DO BRASIL

FICHA CONSULAR DE QUALIFICAÇÃO

Esta ficha, expedida em duas vias, será entregue à Polícia Marítima e à Imigração no pôrto de destino

Nome por extenso ......Julia Morgan......
Admitido em território nacional em caráter: Temporário.
Nos termos do art. 6 letra ---- do dec. n. 7,967, de 1945
Lugar e data de nascimento São Francisco /20/1 / 1872.
Nacionalidade N.Americana Estado civil Solteira
Filiação (nome do Pai e da Mãe) Charles B. Morgan e
Elisa W. Morgan Profissão Arquitéto--
Residência no país de origem Vine St.Berkeley 2388 Calif.

NOME	IDADE	SEXO
FILHOS MENORES DE 18 ANOS		

Carteira de Identidade 4993 expedido pelas Washington
Passaporte n. J autoridades de
Ministério Exterior na data 16-7-1947
visado sob n. 2.768

ASSINATURA DO PORTADOR:

NOTA - Esta ficha deve ser preenchida à máquina pela autoridade consular, sendo as duas vias em original.

Sêlo Cons

Consulado Geral do Brasil em Montevidéu

23 de Outubro de 1947
O Cônsul Geral

Julia continued to travel until 1952, when her worsening dementia prevented further trips. She died quietly at home on February 2, 1957, at age eighty-five.

at 4 P.M. & arrive in Palo Alto at 4.30 . . . where I will be certain to remember to get off!" On her return from South America at the age of seventy-five, she wrote: "It is a couple of weeks since I arrived back here, well, but with so little energy that things I have counted on doing, are still in my hardening skull."[71] North recalled Julia's difficulties with her final project, a remodeling job in Berkeley: "She'd come over and check her measurements, and when she'd go back to the office she'd forgotten everything and was totally frustrated. So as the deterioration took place, her travels got to be more of a mess."[72] Mrs. Forney explained that Julia's struggles had become so evident that she would admit to her after each trip: "'Well now, I don't think that they'll take me again.' In other words, she wouldn't be strong enough. Would have to have a doctor. But she wanted to go."[73]

Julia's final years were troubled ones—since her undimmed spirit persisted in waging a battle against her faltering mind. She remained unsentimental nonetheless, writing to Bjarne and Eve in 1950: "Am closing the office this week for good & all—Not an easy task at that—& then, a few days into the new year, go on another sea voyage—this time to Spain, & only Spain—& home—Probably the last real trip."[74] Mrs. Forney's daughter Lynn recollected having heard about Julia's final day at the office: "When Miss Morgan left her office at the Merchants Exchange Building for the last time, my father [H. C. Forney, who kept Hearst's warehouse records] asked her if she would like to close the door. She said 'nope' and walked down the hall. She never looked back."[75] Julia's final trip to Spain proved problematical, North recalled: "She got lost . . . . She forgot where she was."[76]

After being briefly left behind in Spain when she failed to return to the boat, Julia realized she had taken her last freighter trip. When she had closed her office and sold the Morgan home in Oakland (which she and Emma had retained, though no family member had lived there since 1929), Julia then booked a round-the-world cruise instead. She was seventy-nine when she sailed out of San Francisco on the *Javanese Princess* on Valentine's Day 1951.[77] North and Flora both remembered her saying that she hoped she would be lost at sea. He mused, "She said, 'Maybe sometime when I go on one of these trips I won't come back.' She had a horror of being buried; this was no secret." Flora added, "She didn't want to be a burden since she'd seen her mother and father go out laboriously."[78]

A few months after she returned from the round-the-world cruise (which was indeed her last trip), W. R. died of cerebral thrombosis on August 14, 1951, at the age of eighty-eight. Julia must have mourned him deeply. She understood Hearst, respected his vision, and even defended the lavish estates they created together. Walter remembered her saying, "Of course, this is just temporary for his use. The country needs architectural museums, not just places where you hang paintings and sculpture."[79]

During her last several years, Julia's memory continued to deteriorate. North said, "That was the cruelest thing that could have happened to anybody. She had one of the finest minds going, regardless, and to have it fade out in a horrible way. And she was aware of it, to a degree, at least." In a sad echo of Avery's wandering, at one point Julia decided to take the ferry to Oakland and visit her old neighborhood. Tragically, she was mugged and spent some days in the hospital before her family could locate her.[80]

For the rest of her life, Julia remained at home on Divisadero Street, cared for by nurses as well as by Emma, and seeing almost no one except for Mrs. Forney. Lynn Forney, who was very young at the time, recalled glimpsing Julia as she lay in bed in her living room, wearing a pale blue silk bed jacket—a tiny lady with her hair in braids.[81] Sachi came to visit and explained many years later, "She didn't want people to come, but she recognized me, which surprised me, and she was happy to see me, which made me real happy too. But

I know she didn't want anyone to see her in that position."[82]

Julia's final illness was brief. She had a stroke and lingered for only two weeks, before dying on February 2, 1957, of cerebral thrombosis—the same way that Hearst had died six years before. She was eighty-five.[83] Julia did not want a public funeral, saying merely, "Please give me a quick tuck-in, with my own," so she was quietly buried in the Morgan family plot at Mountain View Cemetery.[84] Several friends raised $15,000 (equivalent to $140,000 today) to honor her with a University of California scholarship, which is still in existence.[85] Walter wrote Julia's obituary for the American Institute of Architects: "Julia Morgan's long and useful life is evidence that even in these frantic times an architect with real ability and dedicated purpose can—without resorting to either publicity tricks or displays of egotism—contribute much to the advancement of the profession and leave a beloved and honored memory."[86]

In the months after Julia's death, the Norths discovered that her long decline had left her business affairs in disarray, with insufficient funds to pay all of her remaining bills. They couldn't locate her will, and therefore assumed she didn't have one. In order to raise the necessary revenue, they decided to sell Julia's large library of architecture books. When they discovered her will not long afterward, they learned to their regret that Julia had wanted her library to be donated to the University of California. This unfortunate loss has impeded a comprehensive understanding of Julia's work, since it is no longer possible to easily trace the sources of her aesthetic inspiration.[87] This fact—combined with the dark portrait of Xanadu presented in *Citizen Kane*, and the overwhelming dominance of modernism by the late 1950s—meant that Julia's name soon faded into obscurity.

Julia's reticence to disseminate her architectural philosophy also exacerbated the situation. Walter explained: "Very little of her work has been published. . . . [She] believed that architecture is an art of form, not an art of words. She was not given to talking, writing, or gesturing about her profession. . . . She was [also] a decade or two ahead of most of her contemporaries in using structure as a means of architectural expression. . . ."[88]

Ten months after Julia's death, the Hearst Corporation donated San Simeon's hilltop buildings, their contents, and 120 acres of landscaped grounds to the State of California. (W. R. had indicated that he wanted it to be presented to the University of California, in memory of his mother. When approached, the university turned down the gift, citing its physical isolation and high operating costs. Instead, it was presented to California's state parks system, ensuring that Hearst's beloved estate would be shared as he had wished.)[89] Though not an immediate success with the critics, Hearst Castle (as it became known) was embraced by the public, more than 45 million of whom have visited since its guided tours began on June 2, 1958.[90]

The previous year, *Life* magazine's August 26 issue had featured a fourteen-page

9. PHOTOGRAPHS/PHOTOSTATS:

The author submits herewith photographs or photostats (size 8" x 10") of several buildings for which he has been the Architect, as follows: (N.C.A.R.B. presentation acceptable.)

```
  I. Ranch Center, 2 prints       IV. Y.W.C.A.Honolulu, 1 print
 II. Country Houses, 1 print       V. Residence Group - California
III. Chinese Y.W.C.A. 3 prints        Mountains, 3 prints
                                  VI. San Simeon views
```

---

10. COLLABORATION WITH JUNIOR ARCHITECTS:

(a) If an established individual or firm, are you willing to collaborate with other firms or individuals which would permit junior architects to qualify and help further their professional careers?

        no

(b) If in private practice at this time, name associates (if additional architects are to be added to your organization) for the purpose of qualifying:

(c) If **not** in private practice at this time, name established architect or firm with whom you have agreed to collaborate, for the purpose of qualifying:

11.(a) I/We wish to be ☒
   – do not wish to be ☐ } included in the **Architects' Roster**

(b) I/We would like to be ☐
   – do not wish to be ☒ } considered for the **Register of Architects Qualified for Federal Public Works**

I/We hereby certify that the above is a true statement of facts.

        Name of Firm or Individual   Julia Morgan

        Signed by all Principals: *Julia Morgan.*

In 1946, while filling out a form for the American Institute of Architects, Julia challenged its assumption that all its practitioners were men.

cover story on Hearst Castle's impending opening. Among the dozens of color and black-and-white photographs and numerous paragraphs of chatty text, the author failed to even include Julia's name.[91] Architecture critic Allan Temko protested this omission in a letter to the editor: "LIFE did not once mention Julia Morgan, Mr. Hearst's architect. This great Californian designed not only San Simeon but more than 700 other buildings during her long career. In American architecture she deserves at least as high a place as does Mary Cassatt in American painting, or Edith Wharton in American letters."[92]

Temko was among the first of Julia's ardent champions. Most significant was architectural historian Sara Holmes Boutelle, who visited Hearst Castle in 1972 and was so eager to learn about its inscrutable designer that she devoted the next dozen years to studying and writing her groundbreaking biography, *Julia Morgan Architect.* Boutelle identified Julia's unattributed buildings and interviewed dozens of her former employees, family, and friends while they were still able to provide firsthand recollections. In this effort she was materially assisted by architectural historians Richard Longstreth and Sally Woodbridge, as well as by Suzanne Riess, who administered the Bancroft Library's Regional Oral History Office's program. The staff at Hearst Castle located and interviewed dozens more employees and guests who had known Julia in her prime. The Norths carefully preserved Julia's personal papers and provided assistance to many interested scholars. In 1980, Flora donated this outstanding archive

to the Robert E. Kennedy Library's Special Collections and Archives at California Polytechnic State University in San Luis Obispo, where the staff have endeavored to make these documents widely available for further scholarship.[93]

Professional approbation for Julia's work took much longer to develop. Curator Susana Torres briefly included Julia in her 1977 retrospective exhibition on female architects, held at the Brooklyn Museum of Art. Social critic Joan Didion, whose 1966 essay "A Return to Xanadu" had extensively analyzed San Simeon's architectural impact without ever mentioning Julia, spoke of her disparagingly in the late 1970s. Didion echoed the conventional wisdom of that time, which regarded Julia's lack of a signature style as a sign of her lack of talent. Didion called her "immensely eclectic—adaptable to a fault. She would construct whatever fantasy a client seemed to require, which is perhaps the only distinctively feminine aspect of her career."[94] Didion's remarks were included in Patricia Failing's 1981 *ARTnews* article titled, "She Was America's Most Successful Woman Architect—and Hardly Anybody Knows Her Name." The author linked Julia with two of her Oakland contemporaries—Gertrude Stein and Isadora Duncan, both of whom had gained world renown—while Julia "is well known only to California architectural historians and real estate brokers."[95] One critical turning point came in 1992, when scholar Diane Favro published a nuanced appreciation of Julia's lifelong dedication to "livability, cost-effectiveness, durability, client satisfaction, and user needs," arguing: "If these aspects of architecture are thought unimportant, then perhaps the priorities of the architecture profession, not the gender of the architect, should be evaluated." [96]

Since then, Julia's reputation has steadily risen, assisted by many scholars. These include social historian Karen McNeill, who along with several others joined architect Julia Donoho in lobbying the American Institute of Architects on Julia's behalf. Their efforts succeeded, and in 2014, the organization awarded Julia a posthumous Gold Medal, as their first female recipient. [97] Some of the twenty-first century's most distinguished architects also penned letters supporting her selection. Michael Graves wrote: "Morgan experimented with formal strategies of place-making and symmetry before Modernism emerged, and she adapted historic motifs with modern ease, showing us how to revere history and design for a new era." [98] Denise Scott Brown declared: "Julia Morgan had a large, well-run office, 46 years of practice, more commissions than we ever saw, the trust, love, and repeat work of her clients, and over 20 books written on her alone. . . . She deserved the Gold Medal in her lifetime." [99] Frank Gehry argued: "Her story tells us not to look at her gender, but to look at her work. . . . one can find her playing with symmetry asymmetrically, slipping forms vertically and horizontally, orienting her buildings for climate and daylight, and expressing structure in new ways, pointing the way to modernism on the horizon." [100]

Julia died more than six decades ago, but San Simeon remains the most remarkable project ever designed by a woman, a distinction it is likely to retain for many years. [101] She created it without any female role models to emulate—and with a predictably modest assessment of her own contributions to the profession. In 1931, Julia told a reporter from the *Christian Science Monitor* that female architects, while not yet having attained greatness, have done "sincere, good work along with the tide; and as the years go on, undoubtedly some greater than other architects will be developed . . . in fair proportion to the number of outstanding men." [102]

Julia Morgan not only became that greater female architect, but she also transcended the need to be identified as such. She was both a sensitive person and a sensitive artist, whose extraordinary attention to the surroundings and comfort of others has left us with an impressive legacy of hundreds of buildings, all of which are strong, useful, and beautiful. She approached her work—and therefore her life—with a fierce joy. She never stopped creating, and she ignored her physical infirmities even as they mounted. She was one of the twentieth century's finest architects, yet she never lost her humility or her desire to improve. In Venice, she admired a carved wooden arch and wrote in her diary: "Whoever did it knew just what the effect [would be] & joyed [*sic*] in the doing. Wish I could leave one thing as beautifully sure." [103] Her wish came abundantly true.

RIGHT: *Julia's designs (including this Berkeley City Club staircase) combine Beaux-Arts elegance with Arts and Crafts individualism—creating her unique Beaux-Arts and Crafts style.*

Acknowledgments

Discovering the story of the fascinating and elusive Julia Morgan has required decades of research, aided by the invaluable expertise and generosity of many people. I am grateful for research assistance from Margaret Rita Cheng and Demetrius Griffin of the County of Alameda Clerk Recorder's office; Susan Snyder of the Bancroft Library, University of California, Berkeley; Waverly Lowell, Miranda Hambro, and Katie Price of the Environmental Design Archives at the University of California, Berkeley; Dorothy Lazard and Emily Foster at the Oakland History Room of the Oakland Public Library; Stacey Behlmer at the Margaret Herrick Library at the Academy of Motion Picture Arts and Sciences; Mary Woodland Gould Tan; Jennifer Watts and Jennifer Goodman at the Huntington Library, San Marino; Thomas Kessler, Kaylee Scoggins-Herring, Eva Ulz, and Erin Wighton of the San Luis Obispo History Center; and Denise Fourie, Ken Kenyon, Nancy Loe, Michael Line, Peter Runge, Courtney Thompson, and Catherine Trujillo—former staff at the Special Collections and University Archives of the Robert E. Kennedy Library, California Polytechnic State University in San Luis Obispo. I have also received essential and unstinting support from its current staff: Jessica Holada, director of Special Collections and Archives; Laura Sorvetti, Library Services specialist; and Zach Vowell, digital archivist.

I appreciate the contributions of many current and former employees at Hearst Castle, including Joann Aasen, Jim Allen, Judy Anderson, Dave Babcock, Jo Barbier, Doug Barker, Karen Beery, George Cartter, Bob Conlen, Tom Craig, Teri Dynes, Dan Falat, Linda Fleming, Victoria Garagliano, Karen Garton, Michael Green, Michelle Hachigian, Andrew Harp, Larry and April Hatchett-Smith, Sandra Heinemann, William Hill, Jerry Howe, Dennis and Michele Judd, Robert Latson, Mary L. Levkoff, Gary Lindquist, Tim Mayer, Debra Mendenhall, Dawn Michals, Bob and Rayena Pavlik, John Porter, Toby Selyem, Beverly Steventon, Jill Urquhart, Eric Weiss, and Frank Young.

A great many others have also graciously shared their knowledge and encouragement, including Syed Ali, Jeanne and Robbie Anderson, Kim Baer, Mitchell Barrett, Margaret Bauman, Gleneva Belice, Pete Bennett, Michael and Katrina Berube, Ted Bosley, Sara Holmes Boutelle, Grey Brechin, Mary Breunig, Tom Brown, Anthony Bruce, John Carpenter, Jill Collins, Riana Collom, Pam Connors, Andrea Danese, Claudia Deutsch, Curt DiCamillo, Susan Doherty, Robert Domergue, Regina and Bruce Drucker, Dawn Dunlap, Jim and Lorna Eisenman, David Evans, Elisa Feingold, Gordon Fuglie, Sarah Gill, Matt Gottesfeld, Paul Gottlieb, Jennifer Halsne, Burks Hamner, Alfred Harrison, Deborah Hatch, Anne Hearst, Alec Heber, Roy Hong, Natalie Howard, Stephen Ives, Jamie Kabler, Anne and Fritz Kasten, Kevin and Dena Kastner, Maggie Latson, Martin Levin, Peter Lyden, Mary Macdonald, Kelly Macleod, Beth Macy, James T. Maher, Marti J. Martin, Peter McGuigan, Jay McInerney, Bill McNaught, Karen McNeill, Tom Michie, Mimi Miller, Michael Murray, David Nasaw, Derek Ostergard, Evelyn Plemons, Wendy Pound, Mary Spletter, Lars Stensland, Annie and Martin Stepanenko, Elias and Isaac Sullwold, Peter Steinberg, Gene Tempest, Elisa Urbanelli, Deborah Wacker, Beverly Walls, Giles Waterfield, Barbara K. Westover, Cecilia White, and Katie Yurchesen.

For their guidance and helpful collaboration in obtaining images, I am grateful to Tanis Pellegrini at the AACA Library and Research Center, Hershey, PA; Mike Prym and Abbot Paul Mark Schwan, OCSO, Abbey of Our Lady of New Clairvaux, Vina, CA; Arlene Baxter and David Mostardi; Eric Abma of Asilomar State Park, Pacific Grove, CA; Diana Reeve at Art Resource, Inc., NY; Lorna Kirwan of the Bancroft Library at the University of California, Berkeley; Bob Cassidy; Anthony Bruce of the Berkeley Architectural Heritage Association; Madison August and Momie Assayag at the Berkeley City Club; Claudia Falconer at the Berkeley City Club Conservancy; Marc Wanamaker at Bison Archives; Lila Coleridge at California Bank and Trust, San Francisco; Debra Kaufman at the California Historical Society; Sue Tyson and Michael Dolgushkin at the California State Library in Sacramento; Father Peter Sanders and Theresa M. Catalano at the New Pentecost Catholic Ministries of Monterey, CA; Ashley Boarman at the Chapel of the Chimes, Oakland; Raphael Marchand at the Fairmont Hotel, San Francisco; Sandra Joy Fisk of the First Presbyterian Church of San Rafael, CA; Michael Fischer at the Georgetown Company; Karine Mnatsakanian at Getty Images; Jackie Burns at J. Paul Getty Museum; Emily Park at Getty Research Institute; Mitch Barrett, Pete Brosnan, Marty Cepkauskas, Cliff Garrison, Ben Higgins, Brian Kenny, Sarah Lemke, Susan Macauley, Kate Magnuson, Lindsay Miller, Bess Parker, Toyia Wortham, and Brennan Zerbe at the Hearst Corporation; Vicki Tom and Clint Reilly at the Julia Morgan Ballroom, San Francisco; Laura Zieg at the Julia Morgan House in Sacramento; Sandra Luna at the Julia Morgan School for Girls in Oakland; Richard Field Levine; Edward and Noelle Long; Laurence Heyworth at the Look and Learn Historical Picture Archive, London; Renee Jadushlever at Mills College in Oakland; Ken MacLennan at the Museum on Main, Pleasanton, CA; Tom Lisanti at the New York Public Library; Joan Clappier and Betzi Hart at the North Star House of Grass Valley; Susan Goldstein at the San Francisco History Center, San Francisco Public Library; Jerry Bruce and Pastor Bill Allison at the Saratoga Federated Church; Karen Pock and Alexandra Nugent at the Saratoga Foothill Club; Yurly Shcherbina at the University of Southern California Digital Library; Elizabeth Dugan and Nan Friedman

LEFT: *When Hearst Castle opened in 1957, Julia's name was seldom even mentioned. But today she is justly celebrated as the first female AIA Gold Medal recipient and a trailblazing and passionate artist.*

at the Wallis Annenberg Beach House; and Kelsey Camello at
the Washington Township Museum of Local History.

I am especially thankful for the wisdom, inspiration, and
support I've received from Marie Alexander, Evelyn Carlson,
Martin Chapman, Muna and Les Cristal, Martha and Rupert
Deese, Lindi Doud, Stephanie Fuller, Stephen and Barbara
Hearst, Lindsay and Peter Joost, Maria Kelly, Jack and Trudi
Rosazza, Marcella Ruble, Owen Seitel, Bruce Smith, Richard
Somerset-Ward, Donna Strauss, Robert Wilson, David Wurtzel,
and Yoshiko Yamamoto. I have been fortunate indeed to work
with Chronicle Books, and particularly with the associate
director of publicity, Diane Levinson; marketing manager
Anastasia Scott; my phenomenal editor, Mirabelle Korn; and
my talented designer, Kayla Ferriera. Alexander Vertikoff's
brilliant photographs have enhanced this volume immeasurably,
and I am grateful beyond expression for the contributions of
my research assistant, Ruth Latson—without whom this book
would not exist.

My final thanks must go to Julia Morgan, who was famously
reticent about being interviewed, since she believed that architecture was an art of form, not an art of words. Nevertheless,
she saved thousands of pages of her personal correspondence
and diaries, making it possible for future generations to be
inspired by the story of her extraordinary life.

RIGHT: *The dining room of the Gimian-Cassidy house in Berkeley
(which Julia designed in 1908, as one of several commissions for Louise Goddard).*

Endnotes

Unless otherwise noted, all correspondence is by letter. Grammatical and spelling errors that do not affect meaning have been silently corrected throughout.

Most of her contemporaries—including W. R. Hearst—called Julia Morgan "Miss Morgan." Close friends and family called her "Julia," as I have done throughout this volume. In her era, she would not have been referred to solely by her last name.

INTRODUCTION

1. Julia Morgan to Arthur Byne, 1 November 1921, Julia Morgan Papers, MS-010, Special Collections, Kennedy Library, California Polytechnic State University, San Luis Obispo (hereafter "Kennedy Library").

2. "Julia Morgan, Her Office, and a House," v. 2, *The Julia Morgan Architectural History Project*, ed. Suzanne B. Riess, Bancroft Library, Regional Oral History Office (Berkeley: University of California, 1976), 170, 173 (hereafter "Bancroft Library"). These two volumes are the best resources for firsthand recollections about Julia. Since I have focused on her personal life, space constraints have unfortunately prevented me from mentioning many of her notable buildings.

3. "Julia Morgan, Her Office, and a House," Bancroft Library, 238–39.

4. J. Morgan to W. R. Hearst, 28 December 1926, Kennedy Library.

CHAPTER 1: GLIMPSING THE FUTURE

1. W. R. Hearst founded the *Los Angeles Examiner* in 1903. Nine years after he died in 1951, it merged with the *Los Angeles Herald-Express* to form the *Los Angeles Herald Examiner*, the name by which the building is still known.

2. "The Work of Walter Steilberg, and Julia Morgan" v. 1 of *The Julia Morgan Architectural History Project*, ed. Suzanne B. Riess, Bancroft Library, Regional Oral History Office (Berkeley: University of California, 1976), 56–57.

3. Jane Sarber, "A Cabbie in a Golden Era, Featuring Cabbie's Original Log of Guests Transported to Hearst Castle" (n.p., n.d.), 4–5, 8; Lynn Forney McMurray, Foreword to Mark Wilson, *Julia Morgan: Architect of Beauty*. (Salt Lake City: Gibbs Smith, 2007), x. Though Zegar was nearly illiterate, family members maintained his records, from which this account was compiled. A five-foot-tall playhouse, designed for Zegar's children, was said to have been a gift from Julia. (It is now part of the Julia Morgan archives at Cal Poly San Luis Obispo's Special

Collections at Kennedy Library.) Lynn Forney Stone, the daughter of Julia's longtime secretary, Lilian Forney, maintains that it was actually designed by one of Julia's draftsmen, Ray Carlson. In either case, it must have been done with her approval, since she oversaw all projects in her office.

4. David Niven, *Bring on the Empty Horses* (New York: G. P. Putnam's Sons, 1975), 291. A close friend of W. R.'s sons, Niven was a frequent hilltop guest in the late 1930s and was one of the Hearst family's final invitees before the estate was donated to California State Parks in 1957.

5. Walter Neale, *Life of Ambrose Bierce* (New York: Walter Neale Publisher, 1929), 90.

6. Wilson, *Julia Morgan: Architect of Beauty*, 17. The author focuses on Julia's residential commissions.

7. Mary McLean Olney, "Oakland, Berkeley, and the University of California, 1880–1895," An Interview Conducted by Willa Klug Baum, Regional Cultural History Project, Bancroft Library (Berkeley: University of California, 1963), 33–36; "Morgan, Her Office, And a House," Bancroft Library, 160; "Julia Morgan Travel Diary, 1938," Julia Morgan-Sara Holmes Boutelle Collection, MS-027, Kennedy Library, 142; Eliza P. Morgan to J. Morgan, 7 June 1895, Kennedy Library.

8. William R. Hearst to Phoebe A. Hearst, c. summer of 1917. William Randolph Hearst Papers, 87/232c, Bancroft Library.

9. Mrs. William Randolph Hearst Jr. (Austine), *The Horses of San Simeon* (San Simeon, CA: San Simeon Press, 1985), 106–8, 114–16.

10. Sarber, "A Cabbie in a Golden Era," 4–5. Julia did ride a horse at San Simeon a few years later. On 5 December 1922 she wrote Hearst: "Risking life and limbs on a horse—seeing you have not provided the camel—I will do my best to see that [the redwoods] are planted in . . . interesting ways. . . ."

11. "Morgan, Her Office, and a House," Bancroft Library, 56, 165.

CHAPTER 2: A CALIFORNIA CHILDHOOD

1. Inge S. Horton, *Early Women Architects of the San Francisco Bay Area: The Lives and Work of Fifty Professionals, 1890–1951* (Jefferson, NC: McFarland & Co., 2010), 314. Among Julia's American contemporaries, at least two architects were more prolific: The visionary Frank Lloyd Wright (1869–1959), who designed more than a thousand structures, many of which became twentieth-century icons; and the pioneering Black architect Paul R. Williams (1894–1980), who overcame societal prejudice and designed more than two thousand projects—primarily residential—throughout the West. A leading female practitioner in the West, Mary Elizabeth Jane Colter (1869–1958), had a highly specialized career, in contrast to Julia's wide-ranging commissions. As exclusive architect of the Fred Harvey Company from 1910 to 1938, Colter designed dozens of picturesque hotels and lodges in the Southwest (including the rustic Bright Angel Lodge, built in 1935 on the South Rim of the Grand Canyon).

2. J. Morgan to Bjarne Dahl, 11 October 1943. MS-027, Kennedy Library.

3. City of Oakland, *Oakland City Tax Assessment Block Books*, Oakland History Room, Oakland Public Library, 1884–85, v. 2–3, pg. 4; 1885–86, v. 2–3, pg. 3; Sara Holmes Boutelle, *Julia Morgan, Architect*, rev. ed. (New York: Abbeville Press, 1995), 160.

4. Sheri Prud'homme, *Gather the Spirit: History of the First Unitarian Church of Oakland, 1869–2000* (Oakland, CA: First Unitarian Church of Oakland, 2019), 13.

5. Eliza Morgan to J. Morgan, 14 February 1897, Kennedy Library.

6. "Julia Morgan Travel Diary, 1938," MS-027, Kennedy Library, 142.

7. "Morgan, Her Office, and a House," Bancroft Library, 170, 176; Flora D. North, "She Built for the Ages," in *Kappa Alpha Theta Journal* 81, no. 3 (spring, 1967), 9.

8. "Morgan, Her Office, and a House," Bancroft Library, 160.

9. Ibid., 176–77; "Course Ended," *Oakland Tribune*, 24 May 1890, 11; Albert C. Aiken and Charles K. Tower, *Register of the Oakland High School.* (Oakland, CA, May 1888), 13. Leo and Gertrude Stein's Paris apartment at 27 rue de Fleurus was located near Julia's beloved Luxembourg Gardens, but the Steins didn't arrive until 1903, one year after she left Paris.

10. George P. Atwater statement of certification, 21 February 1932, of *Grace Church Parish Register*, v. II (24 November 1872), Kennedy Library, 186; David McCullough, *The Great Bridge* (New York: Avon Books, 1972), 528–30. The Parmelee house at 63 Remsen Street in Brooklyn Heights is no longer standing, having been replaced by the Bossert Hotel in 1900. Their five-story Italianate brownstone would have had a subterranean basement; a first-floor kitchen; and a ten-step stoop that led to the main entrance floor, containing the living room and dining room. A large hallway staircase would have led to two additional bedroom levels. For more information, see Charles Lockwood, et al., *Bricks and Brownstone: The New York Row House* (New York: Rizzoli, 2019), 142–45.

11. "Probate Office, District of Litchfield," *Hartford Courant*, 20 May 1817, 4; "Married," *Brooklyn Evening Star*, 20 July 1842; "Morgan, Her Office, and a House," Bancroft Library, 159, 194. Julia's nephew Morgan North recalled that when his grandmother Eliza and her sister Julia Parmelee were young, they occasionally joined their parents Albert and Sarah at the

family's South Carolina home. At those times, a Black slave slept on a mat outside each of the girls' bedrooms.

12. *Eighth Annual Catalogue and Circular of the Brooklyn Heights Seminary, 1858–59* (New York: John F. Trow, Printer, 1859), 4, 12.

13. Eliza Morgan to J. Morgan, 10 July 1890, Kennedy Library.

14. "Married," *Long-Island Star*, 9 April 1835, 3; Reuben H. Walworth, LL.D., *Hyde Genealogy: or the Descendants, in the Female as Well as in the Male Lines, from William Hyde, of Norwich*, v. 1 (Albany, NY: J. Munsell, 1864), 520–21; Ancestry.com. *1850; United States Federal Census*, Colchester, New London, Connecticut; Roll: 48, Page: 48b; "New Spring Goods," *Long-Island Star*, 4 February 1848, 2; Karen McNeill, *Building the California Women's Movement: Architecture, Space, and Gender in the Life and Work of Julia Morgan*, PhD diss., (Berkeley: University of California, Berkeley, Fall 2006), 9. Julia's grandfather William Avery Morgan and his wife Sarah had three children: Charlotte Bill (born in 1836), Charles Bill (Julia's father, born in 1841), and Henry C., born in 1843. Although the established spelling of the family surname is "Bulkeley," Julia's youngest brother, Gardner Bulkley (Sam), omitted the first "e." Morgan North erroneously reported that Eliza had two sisters, Julia and Lucy (in "Morgan, Her Office, and a House," Bancroft Library, 193–94). Lucy Latimer—who married architect Pierre LeBrun in 1880—was Julia's second cousin. Lucy's grandmother was Albert's sister.

15. Nathaniel H. Morgan, *Morgan Genealogy: A History of James Morgan, of New London, Conn. And His Descendants; From 1607 to 1869* (Hartford: Press of Case, Lockwood & Brainard, 1869), 202.

16. Zoë Klippert, ed., *An Englishwoman in California: The Letters of Catherine Hubback, 1871–76* (Oxford: Bodleian Library, 2010), 133. The author—herself a novelist, writing as Catherine Anne Austen—was a niece of the celebrated novelist Jane Austen (1775–1817).

17. Sarah Parmelee to Eliza Morgan, 3 October 1869; Julia P. Thornton to Eliza Morgan, 8 February 1874; Sarah Parmelee to Eliza Morgan, 8 February 1874, Kennedy Library.

18. Ancestry.com. *1870; United States Federal Census*, Brooklyn Ward 3, Kings, New York; Roll: M593_946, Page: 262b; Family History Library Film: 552445.

19. Klippert, ed., *An Englishwoman in California*, 155.

20. "Morgan, Her Office, and a House," Bancroft Library, 160.

21. Eliza Morgan to Charles Morgan, n.d., c. 21 October 1878, Kennedy Library. Though affectionate at times, Eliza's letters to Charles can also be combative and domineering.

22. Eliza Morgan to Charles Morgan, 23 October 1878; 25 October 1878; 17 November 1878, Kennedy Library. Some of Charles's failed mining investments were described by Gertrude Atherton in *California: An Intimate History* (New York:

Blue Ribbon Books, 1914), 275: "These . . . [silver] mines were called the Bonanzas, and practically the whole state invested in them." All but a few lost their money.

23. Eliza Morgan to Charles Morgan, 3 November 1878; 8 November 1878, Kennedy Library.

24. Eliza Morgan to Charles Morgan, 10 November 1878; 17 November 1878, Kennedy Library.

25. Eliza Morgan to Charles Morgan, 24 November 1878, Kennedy Library.

26. Eliza Morgan to Charles Morgan, 6 December 1878, Kennedy Library.

27. Eliza Morgan to Charles Morgan, 10 December 1878; 22 January 1879; 26 January 1879, Kennedy Library.

28. Eliza Morgan to Charles Morgan, 31 December 1878, Kennedy Library.

29. Eliza Morgan to Charles Morgan, 3 January 1879, Kennedy Library. Eliza's sister Julia Parmelee Thornton and her husband Thomas had three surviving children: Celeste (Nina) 1877–1971; Augusta (Cappie) 1879–1968; and Albert (Allie), 1881–1961.

30. Eliza Morgan to Charles Morgan, 5 January 1879, Kennedy Library.

31. Eliza Morgan to Charles Morgan, 12 January 1879, Kennedy Library.

32. Eliza Morgan to Charles Morgan, 12 February 1879; Kennedy Library.

33. Charles Morgan to J. Morgan, 5 September 1897; 29 August 1898; Eliza Morgan to J. Morgan, 23 August 1901; Charles Morgan to J. Morgan, 21 January 1900, Kennedy Library.

34. "Morgan, Her Office, and a House," Bancroft Library, 208; Charles Morgan to J. Morgan, 21 January 1900, Kennedy Library.

35. Eliza Morgan to J. Morgan, 14 December 1901; Eliza Morgan to J. Morgan, 9 September 1901, Kennedy Library.

36. Eliza Morgan to J. Morgan, 8 January 1902, Kennedy Library.

37. Eliza Morgan to J. Morgan, 7 May 1899, Kennedy Library.

38. Eliza Morgan to J. Morgan, 23 August 1901, Kennedy Library.

39. Emma Morgan to J. Morgan, 11 September 1901, Kennedy Library.

40. Eliza Morgan to J. Morgan, 24 June 1891; Avery Morgan to J. Morgan, 7 March 1897, MS-027, Kennedy Library.

41. Eliza Morgan to J. Morgan, 7 May 1899, Kennedy Library.

42. Margaret Fowler to Julia Morgan, 23 May 1929, Kennedy Library.

43. Olney, "Oakland, Berkeley, and the University," Bancroft Library, 28, 33–36.

44. Eliza Morgan to J. Morgan, 19 May 1901, Kennedy Library.

45. Olney, "Oakland, Berkeley, and the University," Bancroft Library, 43.

46. "Morgan, Her Office, and a House," Bancroft Library, 211; New Testament, Julia Morgan, 1883 (1-B-01-04). According to its inscription, Eliza gave Julia this New Testament for her eleventh birthday, 20 January 1883; Sketchbook, Beaux-Arts, 1897 (1-E-05-06), Kennedy Library.

47. "Fine Rooms in Big Houses," *The San Francisco Examiner*, 17 April 1892, 10. A polar bear rug—popular in the 1890s—sat in front of the fireplace. On 21 October 1901, Eliza wrote disparagingly to Julia about a friend's clinker brick fireplace and inglenook seating, which she clearly found inferior to their own.

48. Ibid.

49. David Lowe, "Design Notebook: Madison Square Is a Green Rip in the City's Brick and Stone Carpet," *New York Times*, 15 March 1979, C12; J. Morgan to LeBruns, 19 July 1897; J. Morgan to Lucy LeBrun, 6 July 1896, Kennedy Library. Pierre's father, architect Napoleon LeBrun (1821–1901), opened his Philadelphia office in 1841, where Pierre apprenticed in his teens. In 1866, Napoleon moved his firm to New York City, changing its name to N. LeBrun & Son in 1880, and then to LeBrun and Sons in 1892, when Pierre's brother Michel joined the business. Both sons continued the practice after their father's death. Their best-known building is New York's Metropolitan Life Tower on Madison Avenue and East 23rd, built in 1910.

50. Maryland Historical Trust, "Woodland Hall, K-144, Kent County, Maryland" *Maryland's National Register Properties* (10 December 2008), mht.maryland.gov/nr/NRDetail. aspx?NRID=1556.

51. Mary Woodland Gould Tan and Virginia Carroll, *Woodland Hall: Kent County, Maryland* (Kennedyville, MD: Self-published, 2007), 20–21.

52. Ibid., 17. The house is still owned by Woodland descendants.

CHAPTER 3: SETTING A COURSE

1. Harvey Hefland, *University of California, Berkeley: An Architectural Tour and Photographs* (New York: Princeton Architectural Press, 2002), 3–5, 9.

2. Diana B. Turk, *Bound by a Mighty Vow: Sisterhood and Women's Fraternities, 1870–1920* (New York: New York University Press, 2004), 39.

3. Eleanor Richey, *Eminent Women of the West* (Berkeley: Howell-North Books, 1975), 241; Horton, *Early Women Architects*, 28–29. Richey published two volumes with Howell-North Press, Morgan and Flora North's publishing house. Her personal connection with the Norths gives additional credence to Richey's descriptions. Horton reported that Julia was admitted to the University of California as a Special Student (a category in which students were not expected to earn a degree). Male collegians disparagingly referred to Berkeley coeds as "pelicans," because they wore white shirtwaist blouses with their dark skirts.

4. Eliza Morgan to J. Morgan, 21 June 1891; 12 June 1895, Kennedy Library.

5. Eliza Morgan to J. Morgan, 28 June 1891; 7 June 1895, Kennedy Library.

6. McNeill, *Building the California Women's Movement*, 43, 91; Turk, *Bound by a Mighty Vow*, 71. Julia remained active in the sorority, returning in 1908 to design its large residence house at 2723 Durant Avenue in Berkeley. She also oversaw its 1924 expansion, reorienting the building's entrance and changing its style to English Tudor. Architect Gardner Dailey's 1940 remodel significantly altered the building.

7. Horton, *Early Women Architects*, 28. They were Elizabeth Bragg, who graduated with an engineering degree in 1876; Millie Medbury, who graduated in civil engineering in 1883; and Caroline Baldwin Morrison, who graduated in mechanical engineering in 1892, then earned a PhD in science at Cornell University. She later taught physics at San Francisco's California School of Mechanical Arts (now known as Lick-Wilmerding High School).

8. "The Work of Steilberg and Morgan," Bancroft Library, 32.

9. Kenneth H. Cardwell, *Bernard Maybeck: Artisan, Architect, Artist* (Santa Barbara: Peregrine Smith, 1977), 17; Sally B. Woodbridge, *Bernard Maybeck: Visionary Architect* (New York: Abbeville Press, 1992), 19.

10. Woodbridge, *Bernard Maybeck*, 18; Arthur Drexler, ed. *The Architecture of the École des Beaux-Arts* (New York: Museum of Modern Art, 1975), 80–82.

11. Cardwell, *Bernard Maybeck*, 21–26; Jeffrey T. Tilman, *Arthur J. Brown, Jr., Progressive Classicist* (New York: W. W. Norton & Company, 2006), 17–18.

12. Tilman, *Arthur J. Brown, Jr.*, 19; Kate Montague Hall, "The Mark Hopkins Institute of Art: A Department of the University of California," *Overland Monthly*, v. 30, second series (30 December 1897), 542–43; Birgitta Hjalmarson, *Artful Players: Artistic Life in Early San Francisco* (New Jersey: Princeton Architectural Press, 1999), 151, 157–59; Anthony Bruce, et. al., *Looking at Julia Morgan: Early Residences in Berkeley* (Berkeley: Berkeley Architectural Heritage Association, 2010), n.p., House 5. Arthur F. Mathews and his wife (and former student) Lucia Kleinmans were influential Arts and Crafts designers of murals and furniture.

13. Cardwell, *Bernard Maybeck*, 38–39.

14. "Personal and Social," *Oakland Tribune*, 11 November 1895, 5; Charles Keeler, "Bernard Maybeck: A Gothic Man in the 20th Century," in *Friends Bearing Torches* (n.p., c. 1934), http://berkeleyheritage.com/links.html; Daniella Thompson, "Maybeck's First House Was a Design Laboratory," *East Bay: Then & Now* (Berkeley Architectural Heritage Association, 20 February & 8 March 2007), berkeleyheritage.com.

15. Phoebe A. Hearst to Eliza Pike, 29 July 1868, George and Phoebe Apperson Hearst Papers, MSS 72/204c, Bancroft Library; Judith Robinson, *The Hearsts: An American Dynasty* (New York: Avon Books, 1991), 100. Though she spelled her name Phebe for many years before she began using the Classical Greek spelling, for consistency I've spelled it Phoebe throughout.

16. David Nasaw, *The Chief: The Life of William Randolph Hearst.* New York: Houghton Mifflin, 2000, 6–7; Alexandra M. Nickliss, *Phoebe Apperson Hearst: A Life of Power and Politics* (Lincoln, NE: University of Nebraska Press, 2018), 27–29; Robinson, *The Hearsts*, 41–47, 64–70.

17. Cardwell, *Bernard Maybeck*, 40; Woodbridge, *Bernard Maybeck*, 75; Robinson, 263, 265–68.

18. Woodbridge, *Bernard Maybeck*, 75–76.

19. Cardwell, *Bernard Maybeck*, 42.

20. Emma Bullet, "New Women in France," *Brooklyn Daily Eagle*, 4 April 1897; "In the Art Studios," *Chicago Tribune*, 25 April 1897, 43; J. Morgan to Dr. Aurelia H. Reinhardt, 10 September 1917, MS-027, Kennedy Library.

21. Tilman, *Arthur J. Brown, Jr.*, 24.

22. Richey, *Eminent Women of the West*, 242. Maybeck also called his early residential work "inside-out houses," since their structural beams were often visible.

23. "Woman to Take Degree of Ph.D.," *Oakland Tribune*, 12 April 1900, 8; Jeffrey Edleson, "Our Founding Mother: Jessica Blanche Peixotto," *Berkeley Social Welfare* (8 March 2019), https://socialwelfare.berkeley.edu/news/our-founding-mother-jessica-blanche-peixotto. Julia's friendship with Jessica connected her to other local Arts and Crafts practitioners in the Bay Area. Jessica's older brother Ernest—along with Willis Polk and Gelett Burgess—founded *The Lark* in 1895. They were members of a group of artists who referred to themselves as "Les Jeunes."

24. J. Morgan to Eliza Morgan, n.d., c. March 1896, Kennedy Library.

25. Photograph of Eliza W. Morgan (010-1-h-14-07-20), Kennedy Library.

26. H. De Kératry, *Paris Exposition, 1900: American Cicerone, How to See Paris Alone* Reprint by Forgotten Books (London: FB &c Ltd., Dalton House, 2018), 9, 13–15.

27. David McCullough, *The Greater Journey: Americans in Paris* (New York: Simon & Schuster, 2011), 22.

28. J. Morgan to LeBruns, 8 June 1896, Kennedy Library.

29. Henry James, *Parisian Sketches: Letters to the New York Tribune 1875–1876*, edited by Leon Edel and Isle Dusoir Lind (Washington Square: New York University Press, 1957), 38–40.

30. J. Morgan to LeBruns, 8 June 1896, Kennedy Library; Mildred Stapley, "Is Paris Wise for the Average American Girl?" in *Ladies Home Journal* 23, no. 5 (April 1906), 16, 54; Emily Meredith Aylward, "The American Girls' Art Club in Paris," *Scribner's Magazine*, XVI, no. 65 (November 1894), 598–605.

31. J. Morgan to Beatrice Fox, 11 December 1896, Mary Beatrice Fox Papers, 1789–1961, HM 54391, Huntington Library (San Marino, CA). (Hereafter Huntington Library.) Mary Beatrice Fox was born in Middlesex, England, in 1876. She moved to the Bay Area in 1881 and attended Anna Head School for Girls. She and Julia likely met when Beatrice joined Julia and Emma's Kappa Alpha Theta chapter circa 1894.

32. J. Morgan to Lucy LeBrun, 6 July 1896, Kennedy Library. Julia entered the de Monclos atelier just as American student Fay Kellogg was departing. Julia was unimpressed: "This week I saw the famous Miss Kellogg who came to get her things from the Atelier before going to America—I did not love her, and am mighty glad it's Miss Budd [Katherine Budd, alongside whom Julia worked at the atelier] instead." Fay Kellogg left just before women were admitted to the École's painting and sculpture divisions. For further discussion on Kellogg and other female applicants, see Meredith L. Clausen, "The Ecole des Beaux-Arts: Toward a Gendered History," *Journal of the Society of Architectural Historians* 68, no. 2 (June 2010), 153–61.

33. Tilman, *Arthur Brown, Jr.*, 22; J. Morgan to LeBruns, 8 June 1896; J. Morgan to LeBruns, 4 October 1896, Kennedy Library.

34. Kathleen Adler, Erica E. Hirshler, and H. Barbara Weinberg, *Americans in Paris: 1860–1900* (London: National Gallery Company, 2006), 12. In her letter to Lucy LeBrun on 6 July 1896, Julia mentions seeking out the work of the renowned American portrait painter Cecilia Beaux at the *Salon du Champ de Mars*.

35. J. Morgan to LeBruns, 1 March 1897, Kennedy Library.

36. J. Morgan to Beatrice Fox, 29 December 1896, Huntington Library.

37. J. Morgan to LeBruns, 1 March 1897, Kennedy Library.

38. J. Morgan to LeBruns, 4 October 1896, Kennedy Library.

39. Erica E. Hirshler, "At Home in Paris," in *Americans in Paris: 1860–1900* by Kathleen Adler, et al. 93.

40. J. Morgan to François-Benjamin Bernard Chaussemiche, 27 January 1936, Kennedy Library.

41. McNeill, *Building the California Women's Movement*, 67–69.

42. "May Limit the Number: American Architectural Students Crowding the École des Beaux Arts, the French Government School," *The Boston Globe*, 5 July 1896, 30; McNeill, *Building the California Women's Movement*, 62.

43. "New Women in France," *The Brooklyn Daily Eagle Sunday*, 4 April 1897, 15; "In the Art Studios," *Chicago Tribune*, 25 April 1897, 43.

44. "Female Students at the École des Beaux-Arts," in *The American Architect and Building News*, 56, no. 1121 (19 June 1897), 90.

45. Mary Margaret Kern Garrard, "Over the Desktop," *Kappa Alpha Theta Journal* (Spring 1967), 2; "The Work of Steilberg and Morgan," Bancroft Library, 201; Parmelee Morgan to J. Morgan, 21 March 1897, Kennedy Library.

46. J. Morgan to LeBruns, 24 January 1897, Kennedy Library.

47. J. Morgan to LeBruns, 29 April 1897, Kennedy Library. Filippo Colarossi's Académie was at 10 rue de la Grande-Chaumière, around the corner from the American Girls' Club.

48. J. Morgan to Dr. Aurelia Henry Reinhardt, 10 September 1917, MS-027, Kennedy Library. At Colarossi's studio, Julia sculpted from nude male models and studied with the renowned Jean-Antoine Injalbert (1845–1933). His celebrated works include four allegorical bronzes mounted in 1896 on the sides of the Pont Mirabeau, the bridge connecting Paris's 15th and 16th arrondissements.

49. Gabriel P. Weisberg and Jane R. Becker, eds. *Overcoming All Obstacles: The Women of the Académie Julian* (New Jersey: Rutgers University Press, 1999), 14.

50. J. Morgan to LeBruns, 31 July 1898, Kennedy Library.

CHAPTER 4: REALLY MINE NOW

1. "Julia Morgan Travel Diary, 1899," Kennedy Library, 14, 24; "Travel Memorabilia, Beaux-Arts," Box 11:1, Kennedy Library.

2. J. Morgan to Lucy LeBrun, 6 July 1896, Kennedy Library. The annual Paris Salon became the École's principal exhibition venue in the mid-seventeenth century. Its influence began to wane in 1890, when a splinter group formed to protest William-Adolphe Bouguereau's suggestion that only the artists who had not previously received an award should be allowed to exhibit. Among the secessionists were sculptor Auguste Rodin and mural painter Pierre Puvis de Chavannes. Their breakaway exhibition in 1896 became known as the *Salon du Champ de Mars*, which Julia preferred to the official exhibition (known as the *Salon de la Sociéte Nationale des Beaux-Arts*).

3. J. Morgan to Beatrice Fox, 11 December 1896, Huntington Library.

4. J. Morgan to LeBruns, 8 June 1896; 29 April 1897, Kennedy Library.

5. J. Morgan to Beatrice Fox, 29 December 1896, Huntington Library; J. Morgan to Lucy LeBrun, 5 January 1898, Kennedy Library; Mary Woodland Gould Tan and Virginia Carroll, *Woodland Hall*, 20–21. Julia's maternal grandmother spoke proudly in 1890 about Julia's ability to speak German. On 16 February 1899, Julia mentioned homesickness in her letter to Phoebe Apperson Hearst (George and Phoebe Apperson Hearst Papers, 72/204c, Bancroft Library), but she was evidently reluctant to discuss it with the LeBruns, preferring to use its German equivalent—*heimweh*—instead.

6. J. Morgan to Lucy LeBrun, 6 July 1896, Kennedy Library. On 17 January 1897 (Kennedy Library), Eliza asked Julia about her fellow American student at the Beaux-Arts: "How's Mr. Van Pelt?" On 19 January 1898, Lucy LeBrun wrote Julia: "Carlie was visiting them in Ithaca (the father is a prof. in Cornell) [and] she met your Mr. Van Pelt and he asked particularly about you. . . ." (Kennedy Library). It is not unreasonable to assume that Lucy and Eliza hoped for a romantic attachment between them, but there is no evidence this ever occurred.

7. Tilman, *Arthur J. Brown, Jr.*, 23–24; Eliza Morgan to J. Morgan, 29 December 1901, Kennedy Library. Eliza wrote to Julia about Victoria Brown: "She is quite fond of you—and agrees with me that you ought not to live entirely alone—if you could get a congenial soul to live with you—you'd be happier."

8. J. Morgan to LeBruns, 12 October 1897, Kennedy Library.

9. J. Morgan to LeBruns, 19 July 1897, Kennedy Library; McNeill, *Building the California Women's Movement*, 70. Julia initially—and most uncharacteristically—sent a letter to the École's administrators, requesting that they waive her entrance examinations and admit her into the program as their sole female student. It seems likely that she sent this missive on the advice of Bernard Maybeck. Her request was denied.

10. J. Morgan to LeBruns, 15 August 1897, Kennedy Library.

11. Charles Morgan to J. Morgan, 5 September 1897, MS-027, Kennedy Library.

12. Avery Morgan to J. Morgan, 21 November 1897, Kennedy Library.

13. J. Morgan to LeBruns, 12 October 1897, Kennedy Library; McNeill, *Building the California Women's Movement*, 69. Julia was able to obtain the required letters of recommendation prior to the examination. However, she lacked a history of strong personal connections with socially prominent Americans until she met Phoebe A. Hearst.

14. J. Morgan to LeBruns, 12 December 1897, Kennedy Library. It was typical of Julia to state that she "didn't care much" about this injustice but refused to give up in spite of it.

15. J. Morgan to Lucy LeBrun, 5 January 1898, Kennedy Library.

16. J. Morgan to LeBruns, 27 February 1898; 30 May 1898, Kennedy Library.

17. J. Morgan to LeBruns, 30 May 1898; Morgan North, executor's report for the estate of Julia Morgan, deceased, 31 October 1958, Kennedy Library. François-Benjamin Chaussemiche (1864–1945) was born in Tours, France, and entered the École des Beaux-Arts at nineteen, studying in the atelier of Victor Laloux. In 1893, he won the prestigious *Prix de Rome* and became a specialist in architectural restoration, including at the Palace of Versailles. He and Julia remained lifelong friends. Her 1957 will included a legacy of $500.00 to Chaussemiche's young grandson.

18. J. Morgan to LeBruns, 14 November 1898, Kennedy Library. Julia's admission to the École was one of the defining moments of her life. Her studies there established her design aesthetic, working methods, managerial philosophy, and relentless productivity.

19. "Fame Comes to Julia Morgan," *Oakland Tribune*, 6 December 1898, 5; "America Wins in Paris: California Girl Studies Architecture in Ecole des Beaux Arts," *St. Joseph Gazette-Herald* (Missouri), 1 January 1899, 12.

20. Charles Morgan to J. Morgan, 25 December 1898, Kennedy Library.

21. J. Morgan to Phoebe A. Hearst, 16 February 1899, George and Phoebe Apperson Hearst Papers, 72/204c, Bancroft Library; "Lilian Forney: Working for Julia Morgan, 1923–57," *The Metta Hake Oral History Project* (San Simeon, CA: Hearst San Simeon State Historical Monument Archives, 1977), 23–24. Julia's letter to Phoebe establishes that they met in Paris, not in Berkeley. According to Julia's office secretary, Mrs. Lilian Forney, Julia became very angry several decades later when the press erroneously reported that Phoebe had paid for her Paris education. Mrs. Forney quoted Julia's assertion: "My parents were able and willing to finance all my education."

22. Spiro Kostof, ed., *The Architect: Chapters in the History of the Profession* (Berkeley: University of California Press, 2000), 210–11; 224–28; Mark Alan Hewitt, *The Architect and the American Country House, 1890–1940* (New Haven: Yale University Press, 1990), 38–40; Tilman, *Arthur Brown, Jr.*, 22–24.

23. J. Morgan to LeBruns, 7 May 1899, Kennedy Library.

24. J. Morgan to LeBruns, 14 November 1898, Kennedy Library.

25. Ibid.

26. Charles Morgan to J. Morgan, 21 January 1900; J. Morgan to LeBruns, 25 December 1898, Kennedy Library; Gottlieb, Robert, *Sarah: The Life of Sarah Bernhardt.* (New Haven: Yale University Press, 2010), 141–45. Parmelee accompanied Julia and Avery to Sarah Bernhardt's *Hamlet,* arguably the most controversial role of the famed actress's career. *Lakmé,* an opera by French composer Léo Delibes (1836–1891), was set in India and featured exotic orientalist costumes and scenery.

27. J. Morgan to LeBruns, 7 May 1899, Kennedy Library.

28. J. Morgan to LeBruns, 11 February 1899, Kennedy Library.

29. J. Morgan to the LeBruns, 13 August 1897, Kennedy Library; McCullough, *The Greater Journey,* 446: Mary Ellen Haight, *Walks in Gertrude Stein's Paris* (Layton, UT: Peregrine Smith Books, 1988), 51.

30. Eliza Morgan to J. Morgan, 28 August 1898; Pierre LeBrun to J. Morgan, 2 January 1900; Eliza Morgan to J. Morgan, 21 January 1900; Gardner (Sam) Morgan to J. Morgan, 29 September 1901, Kennedy Library. Emma and Eliza both assured Julia they would visit her in Paris, but they never did. Parmelee and the LeBruns both paid brief visits to Julia and Avery in 1899 and 1900, respectively.

31. J. Morgan to LeBruns, 11 February 1899; Eliza Morgan to J. Morgan, 7 May 1899, Kennedy Library.

32. "Julia Morgan Travel Diary, 1899," Kennedy Library, 5, 20. When Julia and Avery stayed at Brugg, in central Switzerland, she wrote in her diary that they were twice serenaded at dinner by "the same wicked looking old fellow who grimaced and danced," and who on their second night "came in with . . . two women added, & sang & collected, & sang & ditto, until we refused to pay more."

33. Ibid., 32.

34. Eliza Morgan to J. Morgan, 24 June 1891, Kennedy Library.

35. Eliza Morgan to J. Morgan, 1 June 1900, Kennedy Library.

36. Emma Morgan North to J. Morgan, 10–15 July 1900, Kennedy Library.

37. "Morgan, Her Office, and a House," Bancroft Library 112, 191.

38. Ibid., 112.

39. Eliza Morgan to J. Morgan, 1 September 1901, Kennedy Library.

40. Eliza Morgan to J. Morgan, 21 October 1901, Kennedy Library.

41. Eliza Morgan to J. Morgan, 26 October 1901, Kennedy Library.

42. Eliza Morgan to J. Morgan, 22 December 1901, Kennedy Library; Carlhian, Jean Paul and Margot M Ellis, *Americans in Paris: Foundations of America's Architectural Gilded Age* (New York: Rizzoli, 2014), 246–47; Horton, *Early Women Architects,* 47, 225, 394; Clausen, Meredith L., *The École des Beaux-Arts,* 155. Julia's name is not listed in Carlhian's roster of American graduates from the École des Beaux-Arts, because she earned only a *certificat.* Had she been admitted on her second attempt in the fall of 1897, she almost certainly would have earned the full *diplôme.* Instead, the judges deliberately lowered her score (presumably because she would otherwise have qualified), costing her an additional year's delay before she was admitted on her third try. Her achievement was extraordinary, as can be seen by examining the more typical experiences of other female applicants. Kansas City architect Mary Rockwell Hook (1877–1978) failed the École's entrance exam in 1906 and left, after having been badly hazed by the male students. Bay Area architect Helen Louise Douglass French (1901–1994) enrolled only in the École's less demanding summer study program at the Fontainebleau School of Fine Arts in 1926. The first female student to earn the École's full *diplôme* was French architect Jeanne Besson-Surugue (1896–1990), in 1923.

43. Gardner (Sam) Morgan to J. Morgan, n.d., c. December 1901, Kennedy Library; "Gossip of Interest to the Gentler Sex," *Clarion-Ledger* (Jackson, Mississippi, 9 November 1901), 2.

44. "150 Women Doctors in Paris," *Pall Mall Gazette* (London), 10 December 1901, 6.

CHAPTER 5: MAKING A NAME

1. J. Morgan Drawings, "Fearing, Harriet, music salon, Fontainebleau, France 1901–02" (Morgan-Boutelle Collection, MS-027, Box 13:2), Kennedy Library; Boutelle, *Julia Morgan, Architect,* 41; "Mrs. G. R. Fearing Dies in 82nd Year," *New York Times,* 4 March 1931. Harriet Travers Fearing's 34-foot-long *grand salon* was demolished in 1954.

2. "Miss Morgan's Success," *Oakland Tribune,* 28 June 1902, 5; "Personal and Social Notes of Interest," *Oakland Tribune,* 2 August 1902, 6; Georges Seure, H. d'Espouy, *Monuments antiques, relevé et restaurés par les architects pensionnaires de l'Académie de France à Rome* (Paris: C. Massin, 1910).

3. Eliza Morgan to J. Morgan, 6 December 1901; Gardner (Sam) Morgan to J. Morgan, n.d., c. December 1901, Kennedy Library.

4. "Monster Steal to be Boodled Through the State Legislature: Millions of Plunder in the Job Planned by an Unscrupulous Ballot Machine Combine," *San Francisco Chronicle,* 28 December

1898, 1; "Exit North—Enter Backus," *Modesto News*, 30 March 1911, 4; "Clift is Fussed Over Disbarment," *San Francisco Chronicle*, 31 May 1911, 9. Though no crimes were charged, Hart's reputation likely suffered. He did not serve a third legislative term.

5. Avery Morgan to J. Morgan, 5 January 1902, Kennedy Library.

6. "Meddler Tells of the Large Social Affairs," *Oakland Tribune*, 28 December 1901, 6.

7. Eliza Morgan to J. Morgan, 23 October 1898, Kennedy Library.

8. "Boardman Robinson's Widow Dies at 92," *Colorado Spring Gazette Telegraph*, 23 July 1968, 4; Horton, *Early Women Architects*, 252–57. One of Sara and Boardman Robinson's two children died in childhood. Sara Whitney's renouncing her artistic career was not uncommon. Grace Weeks Jory (1889–1973) became the first woman at the University of California to earn a master's degree in architecture and went to work in Julia's office after 1913. She met her future husband, Stafford L. Jory, while they were both still in school. They married in 1920, at which time she left the profession.

9. "Oakland Girl to be Architect," *The Evening Mail* (Stockton), 13 December 1901, 8.

10. Leslie M. Freudenheim, *Building With Nature: Inspiration for the Arts and Crafts Home*, 2nd ed. (Salt Lake City: Gibbs Smith, 2005), 123–25; Eliza Morgan to J. Morgan, 29 September 1901, Kennedy Library. Maybeck may have been a visionary, but nevertheless both Emma and Eliza disapproved of Ben and Annie's eccentric appearance. Eliza wrote to Julia: "Today Emma saw the Maybecks on the Boat dressed in the worst Berkeley clothes—she escaped them as she considers them 'embarrassing acquaintances'—probably at her age I would have felt the same. . . . He is a kind, nice-looking man when dressed decently. . . ."

11. Gray Brechin, et. al., *John Galen Howard & the Beaux-Arts Tradition* (Berkeley: Berkeley Architectural Heritage Association, 1988), n.p.; Sally B. Woodbridge, *John Galen Howard and the University of California: The Design of a Great Public University Campus* (Berkeley: University of California Press, 2002), 3, 12–14, 19.

12. Eliza Morgan to J. Morgan, 22 November 1901; Eliza Morgan to J. Morgan, 29 December 1901, Kennedy Library. Walter J. Mathews was the brother of the celebrated Bay Area artist Arthur F. Mathews, with whom the Morgans had studied in 1895 at the Mark Hopkins Institute of Art. After Avery accompanied Eliza to an opera in San Francisco, Eliza wrote to Julia on 22 November: "Avery was white as a sheet today and unable to work in the morning . . ." On 29 December Eliza wrote that Avery had assisted their newly widowed neighbor, Mrs. Sherman, on Christmas day: "[Avery] went down as soon as he heard of it . . . helped them until afternoon when he came home with such a 'sick headache' he could not brace up, though he tried—had to go to bed and . . . [miss] his Christmas dinner and presents. . . ."

13. "Mrs. Morgan Has Gone South," *Oakland Tribune*, 26 December 1903, 7; "Personal and Social," *Berkeley Daily Gazette*, 28 January 1904, 4; Jack London, "Simple, Impressive Rite at Cornerstone Emplacement of the Hearst Memorial Mining Building," *San Francisco Examiner*, 19 November 1902, 9.

14. Regents of the University of California, *The Cal Performances Centennial, 1906–2006: 100 Years of Performing Arts Presentation at the University of California, Berkeley* (Berkeley: Cal Performances, University of California, Berkeley, 2005), 11.

15. "Mrs. Morgan Has Gone South," *Oakland Tribune*, 26 December 1903, 7.

16. "Greek Theater Dedication on University Grounds Marks Beginning of Large Architectural Plans," *San Francisco Call*, 25 September 1903, 2; "For Twenty Centuries No Theatre Like This," *San Francisco Examiner*, 27 September 1903, 39.

17. Woodbridge, *Bernard Maybeck*, 77, 80; Robinson, *The Hearsts*, 298; Esther McCoy, *Five California Architects* (New York: Praeger Publishers, 1975), 7–10. Phoebe A. Hearst rented a Berkeley house on Channing Way below Piedmont Avenue, hiring Maybeck to build Hearst Hall next door. When this massive building was moved onto campus a few years later, it occupied the present site of Wurster Hall's south wing.

18. Bernard Maybeck, "House of Mrs. Phoebe A. Hearst in Siskiyou Co., Cal.," *Architectural Review* XI, no. 1 (Boston, January 1904), 66. W. R. Hearst finally bought the Wheeler property in 1934.

19. McNeill, *Building the California Women's Movement*, 106–7, 112–13; Beth Bagwell, *Oakland, The Story of a City* (Oakland: Oakland Heritage Alliance, 1996), 110–14. Phoebe A. Hearst maintained her interest in Mills College, hiring Maybeck to develop its campus plan in 1917. See B. Maybeck to P. Hearst, 22 October 1917, Phoebe Apperson Hearst papers. BANC 72/204c 1896–1919, 11.

20. Mills College, *Dedication of El Campanil and Its Chime of Bells at Mills College* (San Francisco: Norman Pierce Co, 1904), 3–5; McNeill, *Building the California Women's Movement*, 120.

21. Carl W. Condit, *American Building: Materials and Techniques from the first Colonial Settlement to the Present* (Chicago: University of Chicago Press, 1982), 171–73, 241; David Gebhard, Robert Winter, and Eric Sandweiss, *The Guide to Architecture in San Francisco and Northern California* (Salt Lake City: Peregrine Smith Books, 1985), 16.

22. McNeill, *Building the California Women's Movement*, 120–22; Mary R. Smith to Mrs. Susan Mills, 29 March 1904, MS-027, Kennedy Library.

23. McNeill, *Building the California Women's Movement*, 12.

24. "New Bell Tower at Mills College Dedicated with Solemn Ceremony," *The San Francisco Call*, 15 April 1904. 6; "The Meddler," *Oakland Tribune*, 16 April 1904, 8; McNeill, *Building the California Women's Movement*, 117–18, note 26.

25. McNeill, *Building the California Women's Movement*, 125. The six buildings Julia designed for Mills College are El Campanil (1904), the Margaret Carnegie Library (1906), the Gymnasium (1909, no longer standing), the Kapiolani Infirmary (1910, now faculty housing), the Student Union (1916, remodeled), and the Ming Quong School for Girls (1925, now known as the Julia Morgan School for Girls).

26. Nasaw, *The Chief*, 89–90.

27. W. R. Hearst to P. A. Hearst, n.d., c. 1884, 72/204c, Bancroft Library; Mrs. Fremont Older, *William Randolph Hearst American* (New York: Appleton-Century, 1936), 45.

28. John William Tebbel, *The Life and Good Times of William Randolph Hearst* (New York: Dutton, 1952), 335.

29. Nasaw, *The Chief*, 43.

30. W. R. Hearst to P. A. Hearst, n.d., c. 1894; 4 February 1895, 72/204c, Bancroft Library; Freudenheim, *Building with Nature*, 173; Nasaw, *The Chief*, 86–94.

31. Richard Longstreth, *On the Edge of the World: Four Architects in San Francisco at the Turn of the Century* (Berkeley: University of California Press, 1998), 53, 56–60, 279–88; Freudenheim, *Building with Nature*, 53. Schweinfurth and Hearst celebrated what they viewed as the hybrid nature of California's early architecture, containing both Native American and Hispanic elements: "The work that they [early Californians] produced has a charm and a sentiment that completely obscures all mechanical defects . . ." Schweinfurth's original design for W. R. called for a square building with an entrance at the back, via a central courtyard. He later modified this somewhat austere plan for Phoebe, increasing its grandeur by adding two additional buildings (containing a dining room and music room) flanking the central core.

32. Boutelle, *Julia Morgan, Architect*, 172–73, 246; Richey, *Eminent Women of the West*, 244–45. Richey described Julia's early conversations with W. R. at Pleasanton, presumably drawing on North family lore: "Then thirty-nine, he was a handsome blond six-footer with piercing blue eyes and a shy but imperious manner. . . . Julia was surprised to find her client's son so knowledgeable about architecture. . . . he told her that later on he would have a commission for her. Although hardly crimped, Hearst was less affluent than he had expected to be at the age of forty."

33. Walter Rice and Emiliano Echeverria, *The Key System: San Francisco and the Eastshore Empire* (Charleston, SC: Arcadia Publishing, 2007), 8.

34. "Wedding of Mr. Kroll," *Oakland Tribune*, 18 February 1905, 9; Boutelle, *Julia Morgan, Architect*, 249. Julia's North Star Mine House may have been influenced by Willis Polk's 1898 design for William Bourn's nearby Empire Mine Company offices. See Richard Longstreth, *On the Edge of the World*, 177–78.

35. "Miss Morgan's Good Work," *Oakland Tribune*, 16 April 1904, 9; "Miss Morgan is Named Architect," *Oakland Tribune*, 9 January 1904, 10.

36. "Morgan, Her Office, and a House," Bancroft Library, 102, 229; "Architecture for Women is Recommended," *The Berkeley Gazette*, 16 February 1912, 2.

37. Horton, *Early Women Architects*, 50, 318. Horton lists three female applicants whom Julia politely turned away, in order to maintain a balance among her office staff: Lutah Maria Riggs (1896–1984), Rose Luis (1901–1993), and Arabelle McKee (Hufbauer) (1914–2005).

38. Ibid., 40.

39. "Women in Business: Women as Architects," *Los Angeles Times*, 4 August 1901, 24; Jean Paul Carlhian and Margot M. Ellis, 246–47. The subject of American women architects is vast (even discounting the unheralded vernacular designs produced by countless numbers of their forbears). Among the earliest are Louise Blanchard Bethune (1856–1913) who trained as a draftsman in Buffalo, New York, where she established a firm with her husband Robert in 1881; Elizabeth Carter Brooks (1867–1951), a Black architect from New Bedford, Massachusetts, who trained at the Swain Free School and later (like Julia) designed for the YWCA; and Marion Mahony Griffin (1871–1961), who was born in Chicago, graduated from Massachusetts Institute of Technology (MIT) in 1894, and was hired as Frank Lloyd Wright's first employee. See Drew Spurlock Wilson, *African-American Architects: A Biographical Dictionary, 1865–1945* (Milton Park, U.K.: Routledge, 2004) and Sarah Allabeck, *The First American Women Architects* (Chicago: University of Illinois Press, 2008).

40. Wayne Craven, *Stanford White: Decorator in Opulence and Dealer in Antiquities* (New York: Columbia University Press, 2005), 53, 127; David Garrard Lowe, *Stanford White's New York* (New York: Watson Guptill, 1999), 86–89, 210–12; John Bryan, *Biltmore Estate* (New York: Rizzoli, 1994), 36–47, 135.

41. "The Work of Steilberg and Morgan," Bancroft Library, 45, 135a, 140.

42. "Morgan, Her Office, and a House," Bancroft Library 67, 139.

43. Ibid., 108.

44. Lynn Forney McMurray, Foreword to Mark Wilson, *Julia Morgan*, viii; ix. McMurray recalled that Julia's hand-tailored suits were often blue or brown, and she always wore a dark hat. "Sometimes she wore a stylish cape, and was embarrassed when some children thought that meant she was a witch." McMurray reminisced: "Mother said she always had a candy bar in her pocket and kept her money in a small wrist purse."

45. Charles Caldwell Dobie. *San Francisco: A Pageant* (New York: Appleton-Century, 1939), 157–58.

46. Simon Winchester, *A Crack in The Edge of the World: America and the Great California Earthquake of 1906* (New York: Harper Collins, 2005), 288–90, 300–301.

47. Ibid., 301–2.

48. Bagwell, *Oakland: The Story of a City*, 174–75; William Bronson, *The Earth Shook, The Sky Burned* (New York: Doubleday, 1959), 60.

49. Winchester, *A Crack in the Edge of the World*, 288, 317.

CHAPTER 6: RUNNING THE OFFICE

1. Claiborne M. Hill, "Our Building: Prepared for Founders' Day, Observed 11 November 1942," Kennedy Library, 5.

2. Pierre LeBrun to J. Morgan, 24 June 1906, Kennedy Library. Julia's destroyed "study abroad notes" may have included the letters she wrote to her family from Paris. She saved their letters to her, and the LeBruns saved Julia's letters to them. The complete absence of the estimated 200 missives that Julia sent to her family over six years makes this a real possibility.

3. "Architects," *Oakland Tribune*, 24 April 1906; "Personal," *San Francisco Examiner*, 25 April 1906, 9; "Miss Morgan's Loss," *Oakland Tribune*, 21 July 1906, 9. A city map from this time shows a building added along the edge of the Morgans' back yard.

4. "Made Land Dangerous, "*The Honolulu Advertiser*, 21 May 1906, 2.

5. Boutelle, *Julia Morgan Architect*, 78–79. Architects James W. Reid and Merritt J. Reid also designed the lavish Hotel del Coronado in San Diego, which opened in 1888.

6. Bronson, *The Earth Shook, The Sky Burned*, 70–71. Julia's alma mater, the Mark Hopkins Institute of Art, was also destroyed by the flames. In 1925, San Francisco architects Weeks and Day built the present Mark Hopkins Hotel on the site.

7. Boutelle, *Julia Morgan, Architect*, 78.

8. Jane Armstrong, "The Young Woman Architect Who Helped Build the Big Fairmont Hotel," *San Francisco Call*, 16 June 1907, 12. Armstrong gushed, "How you must have reveled . . . in this chance to squeeze dry the loveliest tubes in the whole world of color." Julia patiently replied that her work was structural, not decorative, and continued, "It was necessary entirely to replace the glass dome and you have no idea how much important detail is involved in a skylight of such magnitude." Armstrong then asked hopefully, "But I suppose you found the other details of the room more interesting?" Though Armstrong may have been tongue-in-cheek in describing herself as "a mere woman with no more serious problem in life than the construction of a new Easter bonnet," Julia might have been inclined to agree.

9. William Charles Hayes, "Order, Taste and Grace in Architecture," An Interview conducted by Edna T. Daniel, Regional Oral History Office, Bancroft Library, (Berkeley: University of California, 1968), 69–70; "Stewardson Scholarship Awarded," *The Philadelphia Inquirer*, 6 March 1901, 2; "Hoover Wins," *Perrysburg Journal* (Ohio), 15 March 1901, 4.

10. Hayes, "Order, Taste and Grace in Architecture," Bancroft Library, 71; Horton, *Early Women Architects*, 61; Crocker-Langley San Francisco Directory (San Francisco: H. S. Crocker Co., 1907), 1713.

11. "Some Typical California Homes," *St. Louis Star and* Times, 2 January 1910, 47; Bronson, *The Earth Shook, The Sky Burned*, 137.

12. Anthony Bruce et al., "Looking at Julia Morgan: Early Residences in Berkeley" n.p., 3, 11, 13, 18–19, 26; "Unique Exhibition is to be Arranged," *The San Francisco Call*, 27 January 1908, 4; "Design Exhibit is Noteworthy," 31 January 1908, 7.

13. Cholly Francisco, "Among the Swells and Belles: Social Notes," *San Francisco Examiner*, 14 June 1909, 7; "Morgan, Her Office, and a House," Bancroft Library, 102.

14. "Elevation of the Proposed New Home for Incurables," *Oakland Tribune*, 7 April 1906, 19; "Former Co-Ed is to be Architect," *Oakland Tribune*, 12 February 1908, 4; "Girl Designed Oakland's First Baptist Church," *The San Francisco Examiner*, 13 April 1908, 4.

15. Richey, *Eminent Women of the West*, 258.

16. Kathleen Thompson, "Approach of Woman's Clubs," *The San Francisco Call*, 16 March 1908, 6; "Society Notes," *San Jose Mercury-News*, 15 March 1908, 13. Julia's themes echoed those of the City Beautiful movement (largely inspired by the curriculum of the École des Beaux-Arts). This late-nineteenth-century philosophy maintained that civic spaces should be healthful, formal, and magnificent. Its greatest American advocate was architect Daniel H. Burnham, who in 1905 produced a City Beautiful plan for San Francisco that was never implemented.

17. "King's Daughters Vote to Continue," *Oakland Tribune*, 21 May 1910, 20; "Doings of the Women's Clubs," *San Francisco Chronicle*, 12 March 1912, 7; "Colonial Women Will be Pictured," *The San Francisco Call*, 21 September 1911, 8; "Anti-Suffragists Open Quarters: Women Organize to Oppose Campaign to Extend Ballot to Their Sex," *Oakland Tribune*, 23 August 1911, 3; Alexandra M. Nickliss, *Phoebe Apperson Hearst: A Life of Power and Politics*, 383.

18. "Woman Architect Discusses Work: Julia Morgan Says There are Chances for Those of Her Sex Who are Plodders," *The San Francisco Call*, 16 February 1912, 11. Not insignificantly, the criteria Julia uses to determine if a woman architect is suited for the profession are "interest" and "love."

19. Walter Steilberg, "Address to the Historical Guide Association of California," transcribed by Morris Cecil (San Simeon, CA: Hearst San Simeon State Historical Monument Archives, 29 March 1968), 11, 16.

20. "Morgan, Her Office, and a House," Bancroft Library, 71–72; 104; 117; 121. Like anyone, Julia could become impatient. Draftsman Ed Hussey recalled that she "had an aversion to tri-angular scales. . . . One day somebody handed her one of those and she got so angry that she threw it up on top of the cabinets. [She didn't like it] because she had to keep turning it over . . . to find the scale she wanted."

21. "The Work of Steilberg and Morgan," Bancroft Library, 45; 135. Julia was unrealistically confident about her spelling skills. Walter called her "one of the worst spellers I've ever encoun-tered. The funny part of it was that lots of times I would correct something that she had misspelled, and she would gasp and write it back in [her way]."

22. "Morgan, Her Office, and a House," Bancroft Library, 67, 184. North recalled a contractor who had done a poor job of laying the flooring in an apartment project Julia was inspecting. She told him it needed replacing, but he ignored her: "Then, like a vacuum cleaner salesman, he jammed the [sign-off] form in front of her with a fountain pen in his hand. She gave him the coldest look I ever saw anybody give. . . . That was all there was to it, he didn't get his money until he came through."

23. Ibid., 116.

24. Richey, Eminent Women of the West, 247–48; "Morgan, Her Office, and a House," Bancroft Library, 108; 115–16. Dorothy Wormser Coblentz declared, "Nobody could lead a normal life working as she did. She wouldn't have had any private life."

25. "The Work of Steilberg and Morgan," Bancroft Library, 137. On 30 January 1911, the Los Angeles Times reported that Julia and Avery were staying at Pasadena's Hotel Green; on 18 June 1911, the San Francisco Call reported that Julia and Avery were staying at the Hotel La Honda (fifty miles south of San Francisco). The brief interval between these two trips might indicate that Avery was experiencing health problems.

26. Ancestry.com, 1920; United States Census, Oakland, Alameda, California; Roll: T_625_88; 15A.

27. Mildred S. Byne to J. Morgan, 27 November 1928, Kennedy Library.

28. Boutelle, Julia Morgan, Architect, 42.

29. J. Morgan to Bjarne Dahl, 29 May 1931, MS-027, Kennedy Library; "Morgan, Her Office, and a House," Bancroft Library, 223. North recalled: "She would see somebody at the drawing board, and she would go over. At a slight glance she could tell if something was developing the way she wanted it to. She would sit down with that person and they would have a long discussion. She would often put it in the form of 'What do you think?' . . . but very clearly stating what she wanted done."

30. Warren McClure to George Loorz, 22 October 1933; 20 May 1938, George Loorz Collection, History Center of San Luis Obispo County (hereafter History Center).

31. Richey, Eminent Women of the West, 249–50.

32. Louis Schalk to J. Morgan, 20 May 1921, MS-027, Kennedy Library; Wilson, Julia Morgan, 142; "The Work of Steilberg and Morgan," Bancroft Library, 138; "Morgan, Her Office, and a House," Bancroft Library, 106–7, 115. Dorothy Coblentz revealed a consequence of Julia's relentless oversight. Louis Schalk—one of her longtime and best draftsmen—quit in 1921, because "as he grew older and older . . . she was still treating him as a child, and he was grown up and married with children of his own. . . . It had a very bad effect on the office, and things didn't clear up until he left, which was too bad because he had been such a mainstay. . . . there was no job he couldn't do, and do along the lines of her thinking."

33. "Morgan, Her Office, and a House," Bancroft Library, 116, 222.

34. Ibid., 105–6, Bancroft Library; "Julia Morgan '94 Makes Name in Architecture," California Alumni (Berkeley), 23 October 1915, v. 7, n 10. After four years, Dorothy left the office to travel abroad for a year. On her return in 1922, "I went to see her and she said something about 'Are you prepared to work as hard as you know you'll have to work if you come back?' And I said, 'I'm not sure that I am.'" Instead she worked for architect Henry Gutterson, who "would turn over the job to any one of his draftsmen and then it was your job; it wasn't his job anymore. Everything that came out of Julia Morgan's office was Julia Morgan's." Dorothy and Julia remained lifelong friends, and Julia rehired her in 1940 as a modelmaker on the unbuilt medieval museum project planned for Golden Gate Park.

35. Karen A. McNeill, "Women Who Build: Julia Morgan & Women's Institutions," California History 89, no. 3 (2012), 42.

36. "Women's New Hall Awaiting a Site," The San Francisco Call, 8 December 1910, 8.

37. Helfand, University of California, Berkeley, 228–30.

38. "Smart Set Turns Out at Berkeley," Oakland Tribune, 7 April 1912, 7.

39. "Mrs. Hearst Will Entertain Women," Oakland Tribune, 10 April 1912, 22; "Y.W.C.A. Meets in Big Tented City," San Francisco Chronicle, 18 May 1912, 5.

40. Nancy Marie Robertson, Christian Sisterhood, Race Relations, and the YWCA, 1906–46 (Urbana: University of Illinois Press, 2007), 12–14; Amanda L. Izzo, Liberal Christianity and Women's Global Activism: The YWCA of the USA and the Maryknoll Sisters

(New Brunswick, NJ: Rutgers University Press, 2018), 19–20; Olney, "Oakland, Berkeley, and the University," Bancroft Library, 124; "Miss Fisher is Again Honored: Capable Lady Has Been Elected for Third Time President of Y.W.C.A.," *Oakland Tribune*, 24 February 1911, 9. Reaching a definitive total for Julia's YWCA commissions is difficult. Horton estimates forty-six projects, counting Asilomar as twenty-four projects (which includes not only buildings but structures like tennis courts and gates).

41. "Y.W.C.A. Board Discusses Site," *The San Francisco Call*, 21 August 1912, 11.

42. "Y.W.C.A. Home to be Built Soon," *Oakland Tribune*, 21 January 1913, 18. This trip likely commenced Julia's enduring fascination with swimming pools. She designed more than two dozen, ranging from simple exercise pools to the grandly theatrical swimming pools at San Simeon.

43. "Y.W.C.A. Building Site is Selected," *Oakland Tribune*, 11 February 1913, 14.

44. Boutelle, *Julia Morgan, Architect*, 99; "Y.W.C.A. Home to be Built Soon," *Oakland Tribune*, 21 January 1913, 18; Robinson, *The Hearsts*, 364.

45. Richey, *Eminent Women of the West*, 249.

46. "Church Made at Banquet:' Wheeler," *Oakland Tribune*, 24 February 1915, 9; Amanda L. Izzo, *Liberal Christianity and Women's Global Activism*, 16; Nancy Marie Robertson, *Christian Sisterhood, Race Relations, and the YWCA*, 8. The organization's goal was "connecting women across social divides," but this philosophy did not apply to racial divides. YWCAs largely remained segregated until their official adoption of the Interracial Charter of 1946.

47. "Contract for Y.W.C.A. Near Pacific Grove is Awarded," *San Francisco Chronicle*, 5 June 1913, 2; Russell L. Quacchia, *Julia Morgan Architect and the Creation of the Asilomar Conference Grounds* (Albania: Q Publishing, 2005), 125–28; Nickliss, *Phoebe Apperson Hearst*, 338–40; "Work Begun on Y.W.C.A. Building," *Monterey American*, 19 May 1913, 4.

48. Emma Morgan to J. Morgan, 13 November 1898, Kennedy Library; "Morgan, Her Office, and a House," Bancroft Library, 175. Emma wrote Julia in Paris about property for sale at Point Lobos, a scenic coastal bluff seven miles south of Monterey, which Julia apparently dreamed of owning: "You have a rival for the Pt. Lobos lot. . . . Her idea is to rent one of those little cottages there next summer."

49. Quacchia, *Morgan and the Creation of Asilomar*, 127–30.

50. Mrs. Edwin Kurmier, "Conference Days," in *Pacific Coast News*, no. 20 (30 April 1920), 3.

51. "Woman's Work Gains Importance," *Oakland Tribune*, 21 June 1913; Wilson, *Julia Morgan, Architect of Beauty*, 103.

52. "Street Car Hits Fast Automobile," *Oakland Tribune*, 18 March 1913, 13.

53. "Morgan, Her Office, and a House," Bancroft Library, 213.

54. "Husbands Weary and Bachelors Wary Decree Against the Kiss," *The San Francisco Call*, 5 April 1903, 33.

55. Eliza Morgan to J. Morgan, 29 December 1901; Gardner ("Sam") Morgan to Julia Morgan, 29 September 1901, Kennedy Library.

56. "Gardner B. Morgan Buried," *San Francisco Call*, 5 September 1913, 4; "Estate of Fireman is totaled at $10,000," *Oakland Tribune*, 29 September 1913, 9.

57. Julia's first biographer, Sara Holmes Boutelle, personally shared an anecdote during a book signing in 1988, stating that Julia preferred to call this hospital merely "The King's Daughters Home," because she found the rest of its title—"For the Incurables"—too depressing. Julia's archway indeed only states the first part of its name.

58. "Activities of Women," *Oakland Tribune*, 21 August 1922, 7; "Emma Morgan North, Ex-Attorney, Dies at 91," *Oakland Tribune*, 20 November 1965, 4; Boutelle, *Julia Morgan, Architect*, 120.

CHAPTER 7: A LITTLE SOMETHING

1. "Oakland Women and Their Clubs: YWCA Guests," *Oakland Tribune*, 16 May 1915, 31; McNeill, "Women Who Build," 47.

2. "Will Start Work at Once," *San Francisco Chronicle*, 24 March 1914, 16.

3. Boutelle, *Julia Morgan, Architect*, 102–5; Frances A. Groff, "Lovely Woman at the Exposition," *Sunset Magazine* (May 1915), 881.

4. Ben Macomber, *The Jewel City* (San Francisco: John H. Williams, Publisher, 1915), 107; Dianne Sachko Macleod, *Enchanted Lives, Enchanted Objects: Collectors and the Making of Culture, 1800–1940* (Berkeley, CA: University of California Press, 2008), 123–24. Julia's YWCA interior was praised in the press: "The remarkable airy, cheery, welcoming arrangement reflects much credit upon Miss Julia Morgan. . . . On the second floor [is] an assembly hall seating 250 people, which is available free of charge to suitable organizations. Prominent men and women speak here on home-economics, hygiene, physical training and recreation, thrift and economy and kindred subjects." Julia also designed the decorations for New York State's exhibition building—perhaps at the behest of W. R. Hearst.

5. *The Legacy of the Exposition: Interpretation of the Intellectual and Moral Heritage Left to Mankind by the World Celebration of San Francisco in 1915* (San Francisco: Panama-Pacific International Exposition Company, 1916), 76; Taylor Coffman, *Building for Hearst and Morgan: The George Loorz Papers* (Berkeley, CA:

Berkeley Hill Books, 2003) 175; W. R. Hearst to J. Morgan, 4 April 1925, Kennedy Library. Ten years after the fair closed, Julia apparently suggested to Hearst that he should attempt to purchase the San Francisco fair's plaster models and display them at San Simeon. He replied: "It was a wonderful idea that you had about using this material and it is going to make the hill something more distinguished than it possibly could have been under any other circumstances, as we could not have hoped to have all those great artists working for us in any other way." Hearst did purchase some of the plaster models in 1935, but they were not used at San Simeon.

6. "Lavish New Homes in Hillside Region," *Oakland Tribune*, 29 August 1915, 50; Wilson, *Julia Morgan*, 159–61; Boutelle, *Julia Morgan, Architect*, 148–50; Anthony Bruce et al., *John Hudson Thomas and Friends in Claremont Park* (Berkeley: Berkeley Architectural Association, 2017), 2. Stucco was then known as "cement plaster." A major advantage over wooden buildings was its fire resistance.

7. "The Work of Steilberg and Morgan," Bancroft Library, 83.

8. "Pullman Kitchenettes the Latest," *Iola Register* (Kansas), 9 January 1922, 6; "Girls Prepare Own Meals in Y.W. Kitchenettes at Fresno, Calif.," *Arizona Daily Star*, 11 January 1922, 7.

9. "Morgan, Her Office, and a House," Bancroft Library, 138.

10. "War Council Concludes Session; Hostess' Houses to be Maintained at Army Camp," *San Francisco Examiner*, 24 August 1917, 9; "Hue of the Cranberry Tints Kearny Horizon," *Los Angeles Times*, 29 November 1917, 7; "Camp Fremont Hostess House to Be Opened," *Oakland Tribune*, 19 May 1918, 42; McNeill, "Women Who Build," 47; Edna B. Kinard, "In Women's Clubdom," *Oakland Tribune*, 24 October 1917, 6.

11. Cynthia Brandimarte, "Women on the Home Front: Hostess Houses during World War I," in *Winterthur Portfolio*, 42, no. 4 (Winter 2008), 214; Robert H. Moulton, "Women Design Hostess Houses for Army Camps," *McHenry Plaindealer* (Illinois, 8 August 1918), 3.

12. "Y.W.C.A. Home Has Received Last Touches," *San Pedro Pilot*, 16 October 1918, 1; "With the Architects," *The Architect and Engineer of California*, 55, no. 2 (November 1918), 113.

13. See Grace S. Stoermer's 1928 article on the Native Daughters' Home at https://ndgw.org. Julia was a lifetime vice president of the Berkeley City Women's Club.

14. "In Women's Clubdom," *Oakland Tribune*, 26 November 1916, 43.

15. United States Department of the Interior, National Park Service, "Sausalito Woman's Club," *National Register of Historic Places Registration Form* (17 December 1992), Section 7:2. A short distance up the hill from the Foothill Club—at 20390 Park Place—Julia designed the Saratoga Federated Community Church in 1923. It features a Tuscan-style triple-arched square tower. Over the years, many couples have married there, then led their guests down the hill for a reception at the Foothill Club.

16. Walter T. Steilberg, "Some Examples of the Work of Julia Morgan," in *The Architect and Engineer*, 55, no. 2 (November 1918), 60; "The Work of Steilberg and Morgan," Bancroft Library, 52.

17. California Department of Public Health, Death Certificate No. 18-009345 (22 March 1918), Parmelee Morgan; Center for Health Statistics and Informatics, Vital Records, Sacramento; E. E. Southard and H. C. Solomon. *Neurosyphilis: Modern Systematic Diagnosis and Treatment* (Boston: W. M. Leonard, 1917), 80, 103, 250, 452.

18. Ibid.; "County Now Has New Cotton Company," *Calexico Chronicle*, 10 August 1915, 2; "The Work of Steilberg and Morgan," Bancroft Library, 92. Beginning with the Wasserman test in 1907, doctors were able to accurately diagnose the bacterium, though there was little they could do to cure advanced cases of neurosyphilis. Parmelee was treated at Las Encinas Sanitarium for Nervous Disorders. The original buildings—much augmented—still exist, as Pasadena's Las Encinas Hospital.

19. Parmelee Morgan to J. Morgan, 21 March 1897; 1 June 1900, Kennedy Library; "Died," *San Francisco Examiner*, 24 March 1918, 12; "Morgan, Her Office, and a House," Bancroft Library, 167.

20. "The Work of Steilberg and Morgan," Bancroft Library, 57; "Morgan, Her Office, and a House," Bancroft Library, 114.

21. "The Work of Steilberg and Morgan," Bancroft Library, 46; 52. In 1909, Julia designed a house for the Norths at 2414 Prospect Street in Berkeley. It has since been demolished.

22. "Morgan, Her Office, and a House," Bancroft Library, 119.

23. J. Morgan to Phoebe A. Hearst, 26 March 1919, George and Phoebe Apperson Hearst Papers, 72/204c, Bancroft Library; "Mrs. Phoebe Hearst Dies in California," *New York Times*, 14 April 1919, 13.

24. "California Bows Her Head in Mourning for Her Greatest Woman Citizen," *San Francisco Examiner*, 17 April 1919, 15, 18; Nickliss, *Phoebe Apperson Hearst*, 421–22; Kathryn Hearst, *Phoebe Apperson Hearst: The Making of an Upper-Class Woman, 1842–1919*, Ph.D diss. (New York: Columbia University, 2005), 326–28; Robinson, *The Hearsts*, 381; Elbertie Foudray, *United States Abridged Life Tables, 1919–1920* (Washington, D. C.: Government Printing Office, 1923), 8–12.

25. Victoria Kastner, *Hearst Castle: The Biography of a Country House* (New York: Abrams, 2000), 32; Richey, *Eminent Women of the West*, 245.

26. "Morgan, Her Office, and a House," Bancroft Library, 180.

27. "Julia Morgan Travel Records, 1918–1919," Morgan-Boutelle Collection, MS-027, Kennedy Library.

28. Robinson, *The Hearsts*, 381.

29. "The Work of Steilberg and Morgan," Bancroft Library, 57. No correspondence between W. R. and Julia apparently survives from the 1913–1915 construction of the *Los Angeles Examiner* building. It is a virtual certainty, however, that Hearst was as minutely involved in that project as he was in all succeeding collaborations with Julia. She therefore would have been well aware of the implications of designing San Simeon for such a participatory client.

30. W. R. Hearst to J. Morgan, 27 December 1919, Kennedy Library. When W. R. was in California, their letters were usually hand-delivered by a driver (along with the other business communications Hearst received). This substantially decreased the delay between letters.

31. W. R. Hearst to J. Morgan, 31 December 1919, J. Morgan to W. R. Hearst, 8 January 1920, Kennedy Library; Robert C. Pavlik, "Something a Little Different: La Cuesta Encantada's Architectural Precedents and Cultural Prototypes," in *California History*, 71, no. 4 (December 1992), 472.

32. Austin Whittlesey, *The Minor Ecclesiastical, Domestic, and Garden Architecture of Southern Spain* (New York: Architectural Book Pub. Co, P. Wenzel and M. Krakow, 1917), Plates 49, 53; Claiborne M. Hill, "Our Building: Prepared for Founder's Day," 11 November 1942, Kennedy Library, 2.

33. W. R. Hearst to J. Morgan, 10 January 1925, Kennedy Library.

34. J. Morgan to W. R. Hearst, 6 April 1920; J. Morgan to W. R. Hearst, 22 April 1920, Kennedy Library.

35. J. Morgan to W. R. Hearst, 6 April 1920, Kennedy Library.

36. J. Morgan to Arthur Byne, 6 October 1925, Kennedy Library. She began by telling Byne, who had written to her about shipping difficulties he was experiencing in Spain: "Your very interesting letter made me think of our early struggles at San Simeon—hauling fifty-six miles over just such wretched roads—the first year no roads left [for] the last 1800 feet up [the] mountain."

37. "Julia Morgan's Travel Records, 1918–1919," MS-027; J. Morgan to W. R. Hearst, 2 January 1922, Kennedy Library; "Morgan, Her Office, and a House," Bancroft Library, 147. Bad weather also complicated Julia's travel to the hilltop. After a particularly forceful storm, she wrote: "If you would like to break every bone in your worst enemy's body, treat him to the trip between Cayucos to Cambria," referring to the two coastal villages south of San Simeon.

38. David Nasaw, *The Chief*, 529; Steilberg, "Address to the Historical Guide Association," Hearst San Simeon State Historical Monument (hereafter HSSSHM) Archives, 6.

39. J. Morgan to A. Byne, 1 November 1921, Kennedy Library.

40. J. Morgan to A. Byne, 19 September 1921; J. Morgan to A. Byne, 18 November 1921; J. Morgan to A. Byne, 14 March 1925, Kennedy Library.

41. "The Work of Steilberg and Morgan," Bancroft Library, 133.

42. J. Morgan to W. R. Hearst, 3 June 1927; J. Morgan to A. Byne, 30 September 1924, Kennedy Library. There were five warehouses along the coast at San Simeon. George Hearst built the large wooden one in 1878, soon after he bought the property. Julia and W. R. built three metal warehouses (two of which survive) in the late 1920s, and a concrete warehouse that resembles a Spanish mission in 1930.

43. William R. Hearst, "The Lighthouse Keeper's Daughters," film, HSSSHM Archives.

44. Kastner, *Hearst Castle*, 102; J. LeFeaver to W. R. Hearst, 28 February 1935; W. R. Hearst to J. Morgan, 3 August 1930, Kennedy Library.

45. W. R. Hearst to J. Morgan, 25 October 1919; J. Morgan to A. Byne, 19 September 1921, Kennedy Library.

46. J. Morgan to W. R. Hearst, 31 December 1922, Kennedy Library.

47. Bruce Porter, "Report of Mr. Bruce Porter for William R. Hearst, Esquire, Upon His Estate at San Simeon: And Its Improvements" (Jan. 1923), MS-027, Kennedy Library, 10–12.

48. W.R. Hearst to J. Morgan, n.d., c. May 1922, Kennedy Library.

49. Charles W. Moore, *Water and Architecture* (New York: Harry N. Abrams, 1994), 129.

50. Fred Lawrence Guiles, *Marion Davies* (New York: McGraw-Hill, 1972), 391–95. Guiles quotes from *Photoplay*'s review of *The Patsy*: "After two or three reels of this one, the director tossed away his script—maybe his megaphone too—and turned the picture over to Marion Davies. Which was a very smart thing to do, for when Marion cuts loose with clowning, the result is the sort of comedy which reflects its results in crowded theaters."

51. Guiles, *Marion Davies*, 51–52; Marion Davies, *The Times We Had* (New York: Ballantine Books, 1975), 14, 46. Guiles tells of Marion riding a bicycle in Palm Beach, Florida, circa 1920, when she recognized W. R.'s limousine, swerved to the curb, and fell. The vehicle stopped and W. R. got out, pretending not to know her, but asking if she needed help. Millicent was in the limousine, and the two women briefly met at that time.

52. W. R. Hearst to J. Morgan, n.d., c. 2 June 1926; J. Morgan to W. R. Hearst, 3 June 1926, Kennedy Library. In his letter, W. R. continued, "They all wanted to make a picture there [at San Simeon], but they are NOT going to be allowed to do it." The only commercial movie that used the hilltop as its setting was *Spartacus*, filmed in 1960 when Hearst Castle was already open for public tours. Since then, there has been a prohibition on all commercial filming that is not educational.

53. W. R. Hearst to J. Morgan, 14 November 1923; J. Morgan to W. R. Hearst, 22 April 1925, Kennedy Library. In 1923, W. R. suggested creating a game park on the lower hilltop, containing antelope, buffalo, deer, and elk (for effect, not for hunting—a practice that was generally banned at San Simeon). By 1925, more exotic animals began to arrive.

54. J. Morgan to W. R. Hearst, 27 July 1927, Kennedy Library.

55. Victoria Kastner, *Hearst Ranch: Family, Land and Legacy* (New York: Abrams, 2013), 111–16, 151–56.

56. J. Morgan to Walter L. Huber, 14 July 1930, Kennedy Library.

57. W. R. Hearst Jr., *The Hearsts: Father and Son* (Niwot, CO: Roberts Rinehart, 1991), 72; F. Stolte to G. Loorz, n.d., circa November 1933, History Center. In 1933, Fred Stolte, business partner of the newly hired San Simeon construction superintendent George Loorz, wrote to his colleague about Julia's capable leadership: "She is so *little*. But boy, can she see—and remember."

58. Adela Rogers St. Johns, *The Honeycomb* (New York: Doubleday, 1969), 121–22.

59. "Morgan, Her Office, and a House," Bancroft Library, 219.

60. W. R. Hearst to J. Morgan, 13 January 1923; J. Morgan to W. R. Hearst, MS-027, 1 February 1923, Kennedy Library.

61. Horton, *Early Women Architects*, 93; "Morgan, Her Office, and a House," Bancroft Library, 181.

62. "The Work of Steilberg and Morgan," Bancroft Library, 63.

63. "East Bay Vital Statistics," *Oakland Tribune*, 15 February 1924, 43; "Morgan, Her Office, and a House," Bancroft Library, 164.

64. "Course Ended: Twenty-eight Young People Ready for College," *Oakland Tribune*, 11; "More Light Thrown on Ballot Machine Fraud," *San Francisco Chronicle*, 29 December 1898, 1–2.

65. C. B. Morgan to J. Morgan, 22 September 1901, Kennedy Library.

CHAPTER 8: A WIDENING SCOPE

1. Hearst, Jr., *The Hearsts: Father and Son*, 72–76.

2. W. R. Hearst to J. Morgan, 10 January 1925, Kennedy Library; Robinson, *The Hearsts*, 7, 84–85.

3. "Julia Morgan Office Records: Card Files and Lists," Julia Morgan Papers, MS-010, Box 21–27, Kennedy Library; Kastner, *Hearst Castle: The Biography of a Country House*, 134.

4. "Lilian Forney: Working for Julia Morgan, 1923–57," *The Metta Hake Oral History Project* (San Simeon, CA: Hearst San Simeon State Historical Monument Archives, 1977), 5.

5. "The Work of Steilberg and Morgan," Bancroft Library, 52–53, 65.

6. "Heroes of War to Be Honored," *The Marin Journal*, 11 November 1920, 1.

7. Claiborne Hill, "Our Building," Kennedy Library, 4; "Divinity School Dedication to be Held Tomorrow," *Oakland Tribune*, 7 May 1921, 4; "The Work of Steilberg and Morgan," Bancroft Library, 135. An earlier version of the Berkeley Baptist Seminary was located in the First Baptist Church of Oakland from 1890 to 1904. Julia was an active member of this church from 1890 to 1896 and from 1902 to 1904 (when she returned from Paris), and she may well have known Dr. Hill during that time.

8. "Morgan, Her Office, and a House," Bancroft Library, 108, 122–23. Dorothy reminisced about the Emanu-El Sisterhood commission, "They wanted a residence for girls, and they wanted Julia Morgan and nobody else. . . . the Jewish architects of San Francisco started to raise Cain. . . . [Julia] came to the drafting room and said, 'Dorothy, have you got your certificate?' I said 'No!' She said, 'Well, could you get it?' So Walter Steilberg proceeded to give me a course in engineering so I could pass the [licensing] examination. Boy, did I have to work!"

9. "Consider Plans for New Y. W. Building," 28 August 1920, 27; "Woman Architect to Plan Building for Y.W. Homestead," *Honolulu Star-Bulletin*, 15 October 1920, 1; Boutelle, *Julia Morgan Architect*, 107–8; "Julia Morgan, Her Office and a House," Bancroft Library, 78. In 1917, Julia remodeled a small Waikiki house which the Atherton family then donated to the YWCA. In 1921, Julia remodeled the much larger Atherton homestead, Fernhurst, which also became a YWCA residence. In 1925 Julia began designing the YWCA administration headquarters opposite the Iolani Palace. She traveled to Hawaii in 1920, 1924, 1925, and 1928. In the 1930s she also designed the Homelani Columbarium at 388 Ponehawaii Street in Hilo. Though the Tokyo YWCA has been attributed to Julia, her involvement in the project was very slight, according to draftsman Ed Hussey: "Miss Morgan had originally made some preliminary sketches for the [Tokyo] building, but she didn't carry on as architect." Hussey followed his supervision of the Hawaii YWCA by spending three years in Tokyo, overseeing construction on its YWCA building.

10. "The Work of Steilberg and Morgan," Bancroft Library, 72. In 2010, the city of Pasadena acquired the long-derelict Pasadena YWCA through eminent domain. Since then, many proposals have been under consideration for its adaptive reuse.

11. Myra Nye, "What Women Are Doing," *Los Angeles Times*, A7; Lynn Simross, "Studio Club Closes Doors on Memories," *Los Angeles Times*, 9 February 1975, 215, 232–33; Cari Beauchamp, "Sorority of Stars: The Lost History of LA's Women-Only Hollywood Studio Club," *Vanity Fair*, Holiday 2019–2020, 120–30.

12. Thaddeus Joy to W. R. Hearst, 29 July 1925, Kennedy Library.

13. J. Morgan to A. Byne, c. July 1925, Kennedy Library; Pamela Post, "Recreation Center and Margaret Baylor Inn," *Noticias* XXXII, no. 1 (Santa Barbara: Santa Barbara Historical Society, 1986), 6–14. Julia explained afterward: "[I] worked my way down thru the blinding dust to a place in front of an auto salesroom. . . . I could see those great plate glass windows quiver before every wave and shock and the concrete posts of the [auto salesroom] building moved to an angle of at least 20 degrees." The Margaret Baylor Inn closed in the 1940s, and it has since been known as the Lobero Building.

14. "Morgan, Her Office, and a House," Bancroft Library, 150.

15. "Lilian Forney: Working for Julia Morgan," HSSSHM Archives, 4, 39.

16. "Morgan, Her Office, and a House," Bancroft Library, 168–69. Julia's San Francisco residence at 2229 Divisadero Street had previously been numbered 2211 by the city.

17. Ibid., 169.

18. "The Work of Steilberg and Morgan," Bancroft Library, 61f.

19. "Morgan, Her Office, and a House," Bancroft Library, 167–68. In 1964, Eliza's Berkeley house at 2404 Prospect Avenue was moved to nearby 7779 Claremont Avenue.

20. Elinor Richey, *The Ultimate Victorians of the Continental Side of San Francisco Bay* (Berkeley: Howell-North Books, 1970), 161–62.

21. "Morgan, Her Office, and a House," Bancroft Library, 107.

22. Ibid., 91.

23. Hefland, *University of California, Berkeley*, 204; W. R. Hearst to J. Morgan, 15 September 1927, Kennedy Library; "New Hearst Hall to Begin in December," 11 September 1924, 5; "Work to Begin on New Hall at U.C.," *Oakland Tribune*, 30 December 1924, 16; Hearst Jr., *The Hearsts, Father and Son*, 85–86; Gray Brechin, "The Way We (Almost) Were: The Rise and Fall of the Hearst Memorial," *California Monthly* 104, no. 2 (November 1993), 12–15.

24. Hearst Jr., *The Hearsts: Father and Son*, 57.

25. J. Morgan to A. Byne, 27 July 1922, Kennedy Library.

26. J. Morgan to W. R. Hearst, 6 January 1925, Kennedy Library; "Morgan, Her Office, and a House," Bancroft Library, 181. Julia's reminders to W. R. about payments due were often apologetic, for instance, "I dislike to bother you again, but have to."

27. Robert H. Baer, *The Lost Monasteries of William Randolph Hearst* (Merritt Island, FL: Signum Ops, 2012), 69.

28. J. Morgan to A. Byne, 24 February 1925, Kennedy Library.

29. A. Byne to J. Morgan, 4 July 1925, Kennedy Library.

30. J. Morgan to A. Byne, 25 August 1925, Kennedy Library.

31. A. Byne to J. Morgan, 4 July 1925; 14 September 1925; 12 March 1926; 25 March 1926, Kennedy Library; Alice M. Head, *It Could Never Have Happened* (London: Heinemann, 1939), 68. In the summer of 1925, W. R. also purchased St. Donat's, a medieval castle in Glamorganshire, Wales (for which Julia later contributed designs for a swimming pool, built under the supervision of British architect Sir Charles Allom). Hearst delegated Alice Head, editor of his British edition of *Good Housekeeping*, to handle the initial sale. She later recalled, "We were successful, we were prosperous, we were on top of the wave. Out of the current year's profits we bought *The Connoisseur* [magazine], we bought St. Donat's Castle and we bought quantities of antiques."

32. "Morgan, Her Office, and a House," 42; Dorothy Wormser Coblentz Crow to James T. Maher, 10 February 1978, HSSHM Archives; John Madonna, *Bradenstoke's Inimitable History: Hearst, Madonna, and San Luis Obispo* (San Luis Obispo: self-published, 2011), 5–30. Walter recalled joining Julia to examine a medieval tithe barn which Hearst had recently purchased: "They didn't use a round peg in a round hole; they used a square peg in a round hole, so it would never decay because there was ventilation in there. Those old boys knew their stuff. . ." The twelfth-century tithe barn was never reconstructed and is currently owned by John Madonna of San Luis Obispo, California.

33. "Break Ground for New Calif. Crematorium," *Oakland Tribune*, 10 April 1927, 93.

34. "Columbarium Chapel Nears Completion," *Oakland Tribune*, 4 December 1927, 44. Julia added onto the building twice, in 1929 and 1930.

35. W. R. Hearst to J. Morgan, 1 January 1926; 27 January 1926, Kennedy Library.

36. Guiles, *Marion Davies*, 175–76.

37. Arthur Lake and Pat Lake, "Dagwood Bumstead and Marion Davies' Niece," Interview by Metta Hake, edited by Robert C. Pavlik. *Oral History Project* (San Simeon: HSSSHM Archives, 4 April 1984), 12. Marion's niece, Patricia Lake, mentioned that Julia's guest house was often occupied by Patricia's mother, Rose Van Cleve.

38. W. R. Hearst to J. Morgan, 15 June 1926, Kennedy Library.

39. J. Morgan to W. R. Hearst, 23 August 1926, Kennedy Library; Bradley Inman, "The Other White House," *San Francisco Examiner*, 9 April 1995. Julia undertook several additional projects for W. R. at this time. Among them was Marion's fourteen-room bungalow, built in 1928 as her dressing room on the Metro-Goldwyn-Mayer studio lot, then moved to the Warner Brothers lot in 1934. In 1930 Julia designed the Marion Davies Pediatric Clinic at 11672 Louisiana Avenue in Los Angeles. That year she also remodeled W. R.'s eldest son George's residence on El Cerrito Street in Hillsborough. Though originally built in a chalet style by Charles Frederick Crocker in 1878, Julia redid it in a Georgian style, which resulted in it being nicknamed the Western White House by local residents.

40. W. R. Hearst to J. Morgan, 19 February 1927, Kennedy Library.

41. J. Morgan to W. R. Hearst, 15 May 1925; J. Morgan to W. R. Hearst, 21 May 1925; W. R. Hearst to J. Morgan, 27 August 1925; W. R. Hearst to J. Morgan, 25 December 1925; J. Morgan to W. R. Hearst, 13 May 1926; J. Morgan to W. R. Hearst, 11 October 1926; W. R. Hearst to C. C. Rossi, 17 February 1927, Kennedy Library.

42. W. R. Hearst to J. Morgan, 12 August 1926, Kennedy Library.

43. W. R. Hearst to J. Morgan, circa 7 March 1927; W. R. Hearst to J. Morgan, 24 April 1927; J. Morgan to W. R. Hearst, 2 May 1927; W. R. Hearst to J. Morgan, 26 April 1932, Kennedy Library. Julia is fancifully referring to herself as "the other architect." On a few occasions, Hearst jokingly signed his letters to her as either "your assistant architect," or "William Viollet-le-Duc Hearst," referring to the French nineteenth-century architect Eugène-Emmanuel Viollet-le-Duc.

44. J. Morgan to W. R. Hearst, 3 June 1926, Kennedy Library.

45. St. Johns, *The Honeycomb*, 130. The California governor to whom Adela referred was likely "Sunny Jim" Rolph, who presided over the marriage of W. R.'s son George and Lorna Pratt at San Simeon in 1933.

46. "Lilian Forney: Working for Julia Morgan," HSSSHM Archives, 3.

47. "Bjarne Dahl: Working with Julia Morgan," an oral history conducted by Metta Hake, (San Simeon, CA: Hearst San Simeon State Historic Monument Archives, 1983), 26; "Lilian Forney: Working for Julia Morgan," HSSSHM Archives, 26; "Morgan, Her Office, and a House," Bancroft Library, 168.

48. T. Joy to W. R. Hearst, 23 October 1926, Kennedy Library.

49. W. R. Hearst to J. Morgan, 21 December 1926; J. Morgan to W. R. Hearst, 28 December 1926, Kennedy Library.

50. J. Morgan to W. T. Steilberg, 18 August 1927, in Taylor Coffman, *415 Ocean Front: Santa Monica*, (Summerland, CA: Coastal Heritage Press, 2009), 63.

51. "Morgan, Her Office, and a House," Bancroft Library, 118, 197. Flora explained that every one of Julia's clients "always

ended up being very fast friends and very grateful in a sense, that she was able to capture exactly what they had in mind."

52. Boutelle, *Julia Morgan, Architect*, 152–53; "Morgan, Her Office, and a House," Bancroft Library, 199.

53. Ibid., 140, 143. Unfortunately, Montesol was destroyed by fire in 2020.

54. "Lizzie H. Glide," *Oakland Tribune*, 12 October 1952, 63; "Building Contracts Awarded," *Building and Engineering News* 16, no. 40 (4 October 1916), 22; Sara Boutelle, *Julia Morgan House Tour*, sponsored by the Oakland Museum Association Council on Architecture and the Berkeley Architectural Heritage Association (Sarah H. Boutelle Papers, MS-141, Kennedy Library, California Polytechnic State University, San Luis Obispo, 14 March 1976), 1; Dixie Reid, "Miss Morgan's Mark," *The Sacramento Bee*, 23 December 2007, X20–X21, "Public Market Opens Tomorrow," *The Sacramento Bee*, 5 November 1923, 1.

55. Bill Burnett, "Morgan Masterpiece: Berkeley Mansion Has Had 3 Owners Who Knew Enough to Leave It Alone," *SF Gate* (4 May 2003, updated 18 January 2012), http://www.sfgate.com/realestate/article/Morgan-masterpiece-Berkeley-mansion-has-had-3-2618760.php; "Morgan, Her Office, and a House," Bancroft Library, 186.

56. J. Morgan to Bjarne Dahl, 12 December 1927, MS-027, Kennedy Library.

57. J. Morgan to Bjarne Dahl, Jr., 29 December 1928, MS-027, Kennedy Library.

58. J. Morgan to W. T. Steilberg, 18 August 1927, in Coffman, *415 Ocean Front: Santa Monica*, 63; Boutelle, *Julia Morgan Architect*, 122–23. Around this time, Julia designed a women's club, approximately seventy-five miles south of San Simeon. The Minerva Club, at 127 West Boone Street in Santa Maria, is a simple Mediterranean-style building still beloved by its users. In 1927, Julia suggested that the club should establish a chair-selection committee composed of three participants—one extra-tall, one extra-short, and one overweight—to make sure the furniture chosen would be comfortable for all.

59. J. Morgan to W. R. Hearst, 7 August 1928, Kennedy Library.

60. W. R. Hearst to J. Morgan, n.d., c. August 1928, Kennedy Library.

61. J. Morgan to B. Dahl, 28 December 1929, MS-027, Kennedy Library.

62. J. Morgan to B. Dahl, 29 December 1928, MS-027, Kennedy Library. Julia's houses have been separately owned—with the former passage between them blocked—for many years.

63. "Lilian Forney: Working for Julia Morgan," HSSSHM Archives, 15, 26.

64. Ibid., 8.

65. J. Morgan to B. Dahl, 28 December 1929, MS-027, Kennedy Library.

66. J. Morgan to Julian Mesic, 29 December 1929, MS-027, Kennedy Library.

67. "The Work of Steilberg and Morgan," Bancroft Library, 111–12; Sarah Gill, *Julia Morgan's Berkeley City Club: The Story of a Building* (Berkeley: self-published, 2016), 30–31. Julia appointed Walter as the engineer and Herbert Washburn as the construction superintendent (a position he also held for the first few years at San Simeon). Groundbreaking was on 27 December 1929, and on 30 November 1930, the building was ready for occupancy.

68. "Lilian Forney: Working for Julia Morgan," HSSSHM Archives, 6–7, 28; Gill, The Berkeley City Club, 225. In 1930, as an opening gift, Julia gave the Club a Chinese scroll painting of flowers and fruit, dating from the Ming dynasty. (It is displayed in the former Chinese Room, now known as Julia's Lounge.) At the same time, W. R. donated a black lacquer and gold-leafed Japanese Buddhist shrine from the Tokugawa period, in memory of his mother. (It is displayed in the Members' Lounge.)

69. Julian C. Mesic, "Berkeley Women's City Club," *The Architect and Engineer*, v. 105, no. 1 (April 1931), 27, 32; Horton, *Early Women Architects*, 85. Charlotte Mesic (1889–1961) worked as a draftswoman for the San Diego firm Mead & Requa for several years before moving to the San Francisco Bay Area. When one of her employers objected to having a woman's name on the drawings, she changed her name to Julian C. Mesic. She produced the large and intricate model of San Simeon which Julia relied on for many years. It was later donated (by the architectural historian Robert Judson Clark) to the San Luis Obispo History Center.

70. "Lilian Forney: Working for Julia Morgan," HSSSHM Archives, 23; "Bjarne Dahl: Working with Julia Morgan," HSSSHM Archives, 10.

71. Boutelle, *Julia Morgan, Architect*, 49.

72. J. Morgan to B. Dahl, 25 August 1930, MS-027, Kennedy Library.

73. Ginger Wadsworth, *Julia Morgan: Architect of Dreams* (Minneapolis: Lerner Publications Company, 1990), 103–4.

74. "Bjarne Dahl: Working with Julia Morgan," HSSSHM Archives, 6.

CHAPTER 9: DESCENDING FORTUNES

1. "Missing Los Altos Architect Hunted," *The Times* (San Mateo), 28 March 1931, 1; "Missing Los Altos Architect Found," *Modesto News-Herald*, 1 April 1931, 1.

2. Eliza Morgan to J. Morgan, 12 June 1895; Eliza Morgan to J. Morgan, 26 May 1901; J. Morgan to LeBruns, 15 August 1897, Kennedy Library.

3. "Julia Morgan Travel Diary, 1938," MS-027, Kennedy Library.

4. J. Morgan to Bjarne Dahl, 29 May 1931, MS-027, Kennedy Library.

5. "Y.W.C.A. Bulletin," *The San Bernardino County Sun*, 2 December 1928, 10; "The Center of Attraction," *The Sun-Telegram* (San Bernardino), 18 June 1976, 8; McNeill, *Building the California Women's Movement*, 227.

6. United States Department of the Interior, National Park Service, "Japanese YWCA," National Register of Historic Places Nomination Form, 2019. The San Francisco Japanese community organization Soko Bukai (made up of affiliated churches) began raising funds for their separate YWCA in 1912. Julia commenced construction in 1932, with the San Francisco YWCA holding the property in trust (since the Alien Land Law prohibited Japanese ownership). Unfortunately this pact was not upheld. When the San Francisco YWCA tried to sell the property in 1996, Soko Bukai sued the YWCA, and received a settlement in 2002 that allowed the group to purchase the building.

7. The Japanese term Nihonmachi translates as "Japantown."

8. United States Department of the Interior, National Park Service, "Chinese YWCA," *National Register of Historic Places Nomination Form*, 2019.

9. Philip P. Choy, *San Francisco Chinatown: A Guide to its History* (San Francisco: City Lights, 2012), 179–82; McNeill, "Women Who Build," 64.

10. Philip P. Choy, *San Francisco Chinatown*, 182. The Residence's Central Committee of Management announced the end of segregated housing on their 75th anniversary, declaring, "The way to learn to live together is to live together."

11. Philip P. Choy, *San Francisco Chinatown*, 170; "Tooker Presbyterian Home for Chinese Girls to be Built on 3-Acre Tract of Mills College," *Oakland Tribune*, 17 September 1924; "Morgan, Her Office, and a House," 224–25. The Norths listed some of the qualities Julia admired in Chinese art: its continuity, integrity, and richness of color.

12. "The Julia Morgan Legacy Project," online exhibit from the Chinese Historical Society of America: https://chsa.org/exhibits/online-exhibits/julia-morgan-legacy-project/. The CHSA was founded in 1962, "to promote the contribution that the Chinese living in this country have made to their adopted land, the United States of America."

13. "Japanese YWCA," *National Register of Historic Places Registration Form*; Choy, Chinatown, 180–81; McNeill, *Building* the California Women's Movement, 223, 236. In reference to the Japanese YWCA, meeting notes taken on 18 November 1931 state that Julia was donating her services on the project. There is some ambiguity about whether Julia donated her entire services on the Chinese YWCA. McNeill stated that Julia pared down her commission on some YWCA projects, and also on occasion donated her labor.

14. Choy, *Chinatown*, 184–86; Boutelle, *Julia Morgan, Architect*, 64.

15. Erika Lee and Judy Yung. *Angel Island: Immigrant Gateway to America* (New York: Oxford University Press, 2010), 11–15.

16. Lee and Yung, *Angel Island*, 12–13. Walter J. Mathews was dismissed after an inspection revealed construction problems. Avery worked for Mathews in 1901.

17. Boutelle, *Julia Morgan, Architect*, 118, 258.

18. "Morgan, Her Office, and a House," Bancroft Library, 133; "The Work of Steilberg and Morgan," Bancroft Library, 91.

19. "Morgan, Her Office, and a House," Bancroft Library, 225; "The Work of Steilberg and Morgan," Bancroft Library, 90–91.

20. Robert M. Craig, *Bernard Maybeck at Principia College: The Art and Craft of Building* (Salt Lake City: Gibbs Smith, 2004), xxi, 2–3, 189, 210–11, 228–29, 363, 462; J. Morgan to Bjarne Dahl, n.d., c. 31 December 1931, MS-027, Kennedy Library. Mr. Craig incorrectly states that Julia was not responsible for the design of Principia's women's dorms, and that her role as Maybeck's collaborator in this project has been overstated. The endpapers of Mr. Craig's extensive volume show an aerial drawing of the college. While the drawing itself lists "Bernard Maybeck, Architect," it was irrefutably drawn by Julia. Mr. Craig also discounts Julia's involvement as Maybeck's co-architect of the Phoebe A. Hearst Memorial Gymnasium on the Berkeley campus. In addition, he cites Ed Hussey as Principia's collaborating architect; Mr. Hussey was on-site as Julia's representative.

21. Richey, *Eminent Women of the West*, 256; Cardwell, *Bernard Maybeck*, 235.

22. Woodbridge, *Bernard Maybeck*, 85; Nasaw, *The Chief*, 425; Robinson, *The Hearsts*, 333. The cause of the fire has also been attributed to wood shavings, ignited during construction. In her will, Phoebe left Wyntoon to her niece, apparently without realizing that the land was leased, not owned.

23. Wilson, *Julia Morgan: Architect of Beauty*, 135; Taylor Coffman, *Building for Hearst and Morgan* (Berkeley: Berkeley Hills Books, 2003), 8–9, 532; "The Work of Steilberg and Morgan," Bancroft Library, 334.

24. "The Work of Steilberg and Morgan," Bancroft Library, 334, 336; Coffman, *Building for Hearst and Morgan*, 68–70.

25. Arthur Byne to J. Morgan, 27 December 1930, Kennedy Library.

26. Baer, *The Lost Monasteries of William Randolph Hearst*, 58, 165–67. For a comprehensive discussion of the patrimony issues involving Hearst's monastery purchases, see José-Miguel Merino de Cáceres and María José Martínez Ruiz, *La Destrucción del Patrimonio Artístico Español* (Madrid: Ediciones Cátedra, 2012).

27. Baer, *The Lost Monasteries of William Randolph Hearst*, 77.

28. Steilberg, "A Lecture at the San Francisco Museum of Art, Fall, 1941," in "The Work of Steilberg and Morgan," Bancroft Library, 314, 321, 327; W. T. Steilberg to J. Morgan, 10 March 1931, in "The Work of Steilberg and Morgan," Bancroft Library, 325.

29. Maybeck and Morgan Architectural Drawing of Wyntoon, The Environmental Design Archives (Bernard Maybeck Collection, 1956–1); Boutelle, *Julia Morgan, Architect*, 218.

30. Robert M. Clements, Jr., "William Randolph Hearst's Monastery," *American Heritage* 32, n. 3, April–May 1981, 50–59; Alison Sky, Michelle Stone, George R. Collins, *Unbuilt America: Forgotten Architecture in the United States* (New York: McGraw-Hill, 1976), 182–84.

31. W. R. Hearst to J. Morgan, 7 February 1931, Kennedy Library.

32. "Morgan, Her Office, and a House," Bancroft Library, 233–34; Richey, *Eminent Women*, 248–49; J. Morgan to W. R. Hearst, 18 March 1922; 19 May 1924, Kennedy Library; Winter, ed., *Toward a Simpler Way of Life*, 63–72. Julia empathized with the workers' isolation, writing Hearst: "I have tried a moving picture show once a week without asking you, which has been well worth the money in keeping down 'turnover.'" She also overlooked the intentional slights of aggrieved employees, writing about one of the gardeners (whom Hearst immediately fired upon receiving her letter): "I think Hazard has tried very hard to please you, and for that reason I have humored him along, although sometime ago he told me that 'his department on your orders' would have nothing whatever to do with me or my office people."

33. W. R. Hearst to J. Morgan, 18 January 1932; J. Morgan to W. R. Hearst, 20 January 1932, Kennedy Library.

34. C. C. Rossi to J. Morgan, 18 January 1932, Kennedy Library.

35. Coffman, *Building for Hearst and Morgan*, 6, 7.

36. G. Loorz to J. Morgan, 29 February 1932; G. Loorz to A. T. Sokolow, 6 April 1932; G. Loorz, "Recapitulation of Architect's Interview," 6 May 1933; G. Loorz to W. R. Hearst, 2 October 1933, History Center.

37. Boutelle, *Julia Morgan*, 218.

38. Hearst to J. Morgan, 19 August 1933, Kennedy Library; Jeff A. Menges, *Willy Pogány Rediscovered* (Mineola, NY: Dover Publications, 2009), vii–xi, 95, 117. Pogány was born in 1882

in Szeged, Austria-Hungary, and studied art in Budapest. He lived in Paris and London for several years, arriving in America in 1914. He specialized in children's book illustrations, but also produced magazine covers, designed sets for the Ziegfeld Follies and the Hollywood studios, and decorated several ceilings for John Ringling's Sarasota estate, Ca d'Zan. Pogány painted the frescoed murals on Cinderella House and Brown Bear House from 1936 to 1938. He died in 1955 at age seventy-two.

39. Brothers Grimm, *Bearskin*, translated by Margaret Hunt (Copenhagen: Saga Egmont, 2020). W. R. lived at Brown Bear with Marion and may well have chosen this fairy tale with her in mind. His inability to obtain a divorce from Millicent meant that he was unable to remarry.

40. For a further discussion of the origins of The Gables, see Coffman, *Building for Hearst and Morgan*, 86–88.

41. Longstreth, *On the Edge of the World*, 171–76. In the 1880s, miner Justin Sisson bought The Bend property, where he built a fishing resort, Sisson's on the McCloud. He died in 1893, and six years later his widow sold the property to Charles Stetson Wheeler.

42. "Hearst," *Fortune*, October 1935, v. 12, no. 4, 49.

43. G. Loorz to M. McClure, 9 October 1933; G. Loorz to M. McClure, 14 May 1938, History Center.

44. J. Morgan to Grace E. Barneberg, 16 September 1932, MS-027; J. LeFeaver to W. R. Hearst, 24 August 1932, Kennedy Library.

45. In her letter to Grace Barneberg on 16 September 1932, Julia remarked that her healing was "slower than usual." This phrasing may indicate that she had undergone previous ear operations prior to this one.

46. J. Morgan to W. R. Hearst, 16 September 1932, Kennedy Library.

47. J. Morgan to G. Loorz, n.d., c. October 1932, History Center.

48. W. R. Hearst to J. Morgan, 21 September 1932, Kennedy Library.

49. Ibid.

50. G. Loorz to Grace Loorz, 12 June 1937, History Center. In 1937, Loorz and Julia were on an inspection tour in the backcountry of San Simeon when his car broke down. He wrote to his wife, Grace, saying he had wanted to "send a car back for her but nothing doing. She said she was a good walker and if I'd let her put her finger in my rear [coat] pocket she'd like to walk as far as she could anyway. I agreed when she promised she'd let me know when she got too tired. As would be expected with her, she walked straight into [Hearst] camp with me." This was a distance of several miles, much of it uphill.

51. "Morgan, Her Office, and a House," Bancroft Library, 137.

52. Ibid., 204.

53. "Lilian Forney: Working for Julia Morgan," HSSSHM Archives, 28.

54. "Morgan, Her Office, and a House," Bancroft Library, 225.

55. G. Loorz to M. McClure, 9 October 1933, History Center.

56. J. Morgan to G. Loorz, 15 March 1933, History Center.

57. W. R. Hearst to J. Morgan, 23 March 1933, Kennedy Library.

58. M. McClure to G. Loorz, 7 July 1933, History Center.

59. G. Loorz to M. McClure, 12 July 1933, History Center.

60. J. Morgan to Christine Stevens, 9 May 1934, Kennedy Library. Julia's excitement was evident in her missive to the owner of the large house behind her new property: "For some weeks I have hoped to bring down my miscellaneous household items, but each time real work interfered—now 'Bekins' is engaged . . . to [drop] off at the little house Friday morning [with] these possessions, and I plan to be on hand . . . to receive them. The idea is a happy one."

61. "Morgan, Her Office, and a House," Bancroft Library, 234.

62. J. Morgan to A. W. Files, 7 March 1934; 4 February 1936, Kennedy Library.

63. "Lilian Forney: Working for Julia Morgan," HSSSHM Archives, 26–27.

64. "J. Morgan Monterey Cottage Floorplan Sketch," MS 010, Box 10:3, Kennedy Library.

65. "Morgan, Her Office, and a House," Bancroft Library, 231–32.

66. Ibid., 235.

67. Photographs of Monterey Cottage interior, MS-010, Box 37:2, Kennedy Library; J. Morgan to Fred Ruhl, 7 January 1937, Kennedy Library. Julia wrote to a caretaker: "I left some Chinese frescoes in the case [in her outdoor breezeway] and am worried about them. If you are down that way, would appreciate it if you would investigate and if they are damp, set them inside the house. They are of considerable money value."

68. J. Morgan to Doris Day, 26 December 1940, Kennedy Library.

69. "Morgan, Her Office, and a House", Bancroft Library, 139–40.

70. "Sachi Oka," *Oral History Interview* (1995), HSSHM Archives, 5, 6, 14.

71. W. R. Hearst to J. Morgan, 26 October 1934, Kennedy Library.

72. "On the Gangplank: With Lewis Lapham," *San Francisco Examiner*, 9 November 1934, 22.

73. J. Morgan to W. T. Steilberg, 7 October 1928, in "The Work of Steilberg and Morgan," Bancroft Library, 61c.

74. J. H. LeFeaver to G. Loorz, 22 January 1935, History Center.

75. M. McClure to G. Loorz, 4 April 1935, History Center.

76. M. McClure to G. Loorz, n.d., c. July 1935, History Center.

77. J. Morgan to F. B. Chaussemiche, n.d., c. December 1935, Kennedy Library.

78. J. Morgan to W. R. Hearst, 11 November 1936; J. Morgan to W. R. Hearst, 17 November 1936, Kennedy Library; J. Morgan to G. Loorz, 5 June 1936, History Center.

79. W. R. Hearst to J. Morgan, 15 September 1936, Kennedy Library; J. Morgan to G. Loorz, 23 September 1936, History Center.

80. G. Loorz to Fred Stolte, 12 November 1936, in Taylor Coffman's *Building for Hearst and Morgan*, 282–83.

81. J. Morgan to Bjarne Dahl, 10 December 1936, MS-027, Kennedy Library.

82. W. R. Hearst to J. Morgan, 21 May 1937, Kennedy Library.

83. G. Loorz to J. Morgan, 2 July 1937, History Center.

84. J. Morgan to W. R. Hearst, 7 July 1937, Kennedy Library.

85. J. Morgan to G. Loorz, 7 July 1935, History Center.

CHAPTER 10: OUT FROM THE SHADOWS

1. Warren McClure Papers, Hearst San Simeon State Historic Monument Archives, 15. Julia did not have her own bedroom at San Simeon (where in any case she rarely stayed overnight. On the rare occasions when she did, she slept in different rooms, to "try out" their accommodations). She similarly did not have her own office on the hilltop. The "construction shack" to which McClure referred is still located in the east courtyard behind Casa Grande. It is a wooden building which she could have used on her twice-monthly visits, if necessary. Mac McClure used it daily to draft his plans onsite.

2. Coffman, *Building for Hearst and Morgan*, 543–45, 550.

3. J. Morgan to unknown former employee, n.d., c. May 1938, MS-027, Kennedy Library.

4. "Morgan, Her Office, and a House," Bancroft Library, 185.

5. J. Morgan to W. R. Hearst, 30 August 1938; W. R. Hearst to J. Morgan, 31 August 1938, Kennedy Library.

6. "Julia Morgan Travel Diary, 1938," MS-027, Kennedy Library.

7. Ibid., 154.

8. Ibid., 111.

9. Ibid., 91.

10. Ibid., 89–90.

11. Ibid., 80.

12. Ibid., 139.

13. Lynn Forney McMurray in Foreword to Wilson's *Julia Morgan: Architect of Beauty*, vii.

14. J. Morgan to George Loorz, 30 March 1939, MS-027, Kennedy Library.

15. Boutelle, *Julia Morgan: Architect*, 81.

16. "Schilling Girl Injured," *Oakland Tribune*, 3; Lynn Forney McMurray, foreword to *Julia Morgan*, by Wilson, vii; Boutelle, *Julia Morgan, Architect*, 160, 162. Julia and Else referred to each other by the nicknames "Big Fish" and "Little Fish."

17. Boutelle, *Julia Morgan: Architect*, 160–62; "Sachi Oka," *Oral History Interview* (1995), HSSSHM Archives, 7. Sachi Higuchi Oka was born in San Francisco in 1916, but she grew up primarily in Monterey. She initially cleaned the cottage only in Julia's absence, but they soon met and thereafter quickly became good friends.

18. "Sachi Oka," HSSSHM Archives, 3, 6, 15.

19. Ibid., 4–5.

20. "Morgan, Her Office, and a House," Bancroft Library, 185–86, 201.

21. J. Morgan to W. R. Hearst, 9 June 1939, Kennedy Library.

22. W. R. Hearst to J. Morgan, 10 June 1939, Kennedy Library.

23. J. Morgan to W. R. Hearst, 12 June 1939, Kennedy Library.

24. Coffman, *Building for Hearst and Morgan*, 339, 546ff; "The Work of Steilberg and Morgan," Bancroft Library, 93; J. Morgan to T. White, 24 July 1937, Kennedy Library. Julia charged W. R. an 8.5 percent commission on San Simeon (slightly higher than her standard commission, which varied between 6 and 8 percent). Walter explained that she relied on commercial projects to make a profit, because residential work was too time-consuming. The total of $4.7 million for San Simeon's construction was reverse-engineered; Hearst's accountants requested that she come up with a figure near this amount. Nevertheless, it is apparently close to accurate. However, it does not take into account the construction work done from 1945 to 1947, in which Julia did not directly participate. This has been estimated at $1.5 to $2.5 million. See Coffman for a thorough discussion.

25. Statistics of Income, United States (U.S. Government Printing Office, 1926), accessed at https://www.irs.gov/pub/irs-soi/25soirepar.pdf.

26. "Morgan, Her Office, and a House," Bancroft Library, 201.

27. *Art Objects and Furnishings from the William Randolph Hearst Collection*, Hammer Galleries (New York: William Bradford Press, 1941), introduction and appendices.

28. Coffman, *Building for Hearst and Morgan*, 450.

29. Guiles, *Marion Davies*, 294–97; Nasaw, *The Chief*, 535–37.

30. Baer, *The Lost Monasteries of William Randolph Hearst*, 72–73, 142, 166. The two Florida land developers were Stuart Edgemon and Raymond Moss. They intended to turn it into a tourist attraction, but when this failed, they sold it to Colonel Robert Pentland, Jr., who donated it to what became the Episcopal Diocese of Southeast Florida.

31. Coffman, *Building for Hearst and Morgan*, 446–48, Appendix A, 545.

32. Notes from an interview with Walter Steilberg, 6 October 1974, Hearst San Simeon State Historic Monument Archives. Walter remarked that Julia continued to work energetically on her design, even after the fire. "She was no politician," however; and Walter guessed that "her hope was that Hearst would fund it. She always had a certain feeling that it would be done." Sadly, this did not happen.

33. J. Morgan to J. Vanderloo, 15 June 1940, in *Building for Hearst and Morgan* by Coffman, 442–43.

34. "Fair to Honor Famous Women," *Oakland Tribune*, 17 September 1940, 11.

35. "Morgan, Her Office, and a House," Bancroft Library, 230–31.

36. Marcia Mead, "Women's Versatility in Arts Enriches Field of Architecture," *Christian Science Monitor*, 27 November 1931, 5, MS-027, Kennedy Library; Boutelle, *Julia Morgan: Architect*, 46.

37. On the third floor of Casa Grande's north guest wing, Hearst displayed a small bronze *Circe* by the late-nineteenth-century American artist Edith Woodman Burroughs and a silvered bronze Art Deco lamp, titled *Cupid Jailed*, by Parisian artist Fanny Rozet. He also displayed two twentieth-century marble statues in the gardens: *Nymphs Stealing the Pipes of Pan* by Suzanne Muzanne, and *Girl with Parrot* by Madeleine Fessard.

38. J. Morgan to W. R. Hearst, 7 June 1939, Kennedy Library; Boutelle, *Julia Morgan, Architect*, 226; Taylor Coffman, *Hearst and Marion: The Santa Monica Connection* (accessed at coffmanbooks.com, 2010), 272; "Deaths," *New York Times*, 23 October 1964, 39.

39. J. Morgan to W. R. Hearst, 7 June 1939, Kennedy Library.

40. Hitler's notorious Reichstag speech was delivered on 20 January 1939—the same date as Julia's diary entry. In this speech, Hitler predicted the Jews would cause the war, and it would result in "the annihilation of the Jewish race in Europe."

41. "Julia Morgan Travel Diary, 1938," 30 January 1939 entry, MS-027, Kennedy Library, 165.

42. Robert L. Carringer, *The Making of Citizen Kane* (Berkeley: University of California Press, 1985), 117–18. Though *Citizen Kane* was a critical success, it failed to make a profit, and baffled many viewers with its groundbreaking cinematic techniques. The film's short-term impact faded within a year, but interest began to revive in the 1950s, due in part to television screenings.

43. Carringer, *The Making of Citizen Kane*, 54–60.

44. J. Morgan to Bjarne Dahl, 7 July 1942, MS-027, Kennedy Library.

45. J. Morgan to Bjarne Dahl, n.d., c. May 1942, MS-027, Kennedy Library.

46. "Morgan, Her Office, and a House," Bancroft Library, 152, 153.

47. J. Morgan to Bjarne Dahl, n.d., c. May 1942, MS-027, Kennedy Library.

48. "Morgan, Her Office, and a House," Bancroft Library, 153, 154.

49. Boutelle, *Julia Morgan, Architect*, 47.

50. "Morgan, Her Office, and a House," Bancroft Library, 154–55. Julia designed two additional residences for employees. In 1919 she created the Rankin house at 5440 Carlton Street in Oakland. Julia relied on the family's plumbing services on numerous projects, including at San Simeon. In 1925, she built a street-level San Francisco workshop and store, with an upper-story apartment, for the woodcarver Jules Suppo. Located at 2423 and 2425 Polk Street, they retain the intricately carved doors and balcony that Suppo supplied.

51. J. Morgan to Bjarne Dahl, Jr., 8 July 1942, MS-027, Kennedy Library.

52. Sachi Oka to J. Morgan, 5 February 1944, Kennedy Library; "Sachi Oka," *Oral History Interview* (1995), HSSSHM Archives, 3, 10.

53. "Sachi Oka," *Oral History Interview* (1995), HSSSHM Archives, 3, 8–11, 19, 22. Sachi's adult children, who were present during this interview, learned for the first time about the neighborhood petition that had been circulated, protesting their imminent arrival.

54. L. Forney McMurray, in foreword to *Julia Morgan: Architect of Beauty* by Wilson, viii; Anthony Bruce, et al., *Looking at Julia Morgan: Early Residences in Berkeley*, n.p., House 5, 2816 Derby Street.

55. W. R. Hearst to J. Morgan, 29 August 1929; J. Morgan to W. R. Hearst, 30 December 1929, Kennedy Library; "Forney: Working for Julia Morgan," *Oral History*, HSSSHM Archives, 16–17; "Thaddeus Joy, Architect, Dies," *Oakland Tribune*, 3 December 1942, 39; J. Morgan to Elizabeth Boyter, n.d., c. 1931, MS-027, Kennedy Library.

56. J. Morgan to the Dahls, 8 January 1943, MS-027; J. Morgan to unidentified, c. January 1943, MS-027, Kennedy Library; "Mexico Will Take Vast Hearst Ranch," *New York Times*, 16 August 1953, 29.

57. J. Morgan to Mrs. Benedict, 11 October 1943, MS-027; W. R. Hearst to J. Morgan, 4 November 1943; E. Ardoin to J. Morgan, 30 November 1943; W. R. Hearst to E. Ardoin, 6 December 1943; W.R. Hearst to J. Morgan, 12 January 1944, Kennedy Library. Edward Ardoin wrote to Julia: "If Mr. Hearst would only wait until this war is over, we could duplicate what he wants built for at least half the price and do a better job." Hearst continued to attempt to complete the project, despite financial and logistical impediments: "We do not know how long this war is going to last. And we do not know how long I am going to last." For Christmas in 1943, Julia sent W. R. a copy of Garret van Pelt Jr.'s *Old Architecture of Southern Mexico*, perhaps to lift his spirits, or encourage him to revive the project—which never happened.

58. J. Morgan to Mrs. Benedict, 11 October 1943, MS-027, Kennedy Library; "Skeleton Believed Identified," *Oakland Tribune*, 24 March 1944, 15; "Creator of Map Pointing to Skeleton is Held," *Oakland Tribune*, 26 March 1944, 9; "Last Rites Held for Avery Morgan," *Oakland Tribune*, 27 March 1944, 7. The newspaper accounts left little to the imagination: "Remnants of clothing showed the man wore blue herringbone trousers, a light blue shirt, and suspenders. Only one black shoe was on the skeleton. Another, of a different make, was found fifty feet up the hill."

59. J. Morgan to Bjarne Dahl, Jr., 4 August 1942, MS-027, Kennedy Library; Julia Morgan in the *Texas, U.S., Arriving and Departing Passenger and Crew Lists, 1893–1963* (Provo, UT: Ancestry.com Operations, Inc., 2014), 30 March 1944, NARA Roll No. 1; Ancestry.com. *California, U.S., Arriving Passenger and Crew Lists, 1882–1959* (Provo, UT: Ancestry.com Operations Inc, 2008), 10 June 1944, NARA Roll No. 2.

60. J. Morgan to Bjarne Dahl, Jr., 4 August 1942, Kennedy Library.

61. Flora D. North to J. Morgan, 30 May 1944, Kennedy Library.

62. J. Morgan to W. Steilberg, 5 February 1945, Kennedy Library.

63. "The Work of Steilberg and Morgan," Bancroft Library, 81, 313.

64. "Morgan, Her Office, and a House," Bancroft Library, 129.

65. The monastery's rebuilt Chapter House can currently be visited by the public at the Abbey of our Lady of New Clairvaux, in Vina. In 2002, the Fine Arts Museums of San Francisco donated the monastery's sixteenth-century portal—formerly on display in the Hearst Court at the now-rebuilt de Young Museum—to the University of San Francisco, which re-erected it as part of Kalmanovitz Hall, known as the Óvila amphitheater.

66. Coffman, *Building for Hearst and Morgan*, 527–28.

67. Boutelle, *Julia Morgan, Architect*, 234, 260.

68. "Forney: Working for Julia Morgan," *Oral History*, HSSSHM Archives, 11–12; J. Morgan to Doris Day, 27 December 1946, Kennedy Library.

69. J. Morgan, Travel Diary, 20 September 1947, in "Morgan, Her Office, and a House," Bancroft Library, 173a.

70. Boutelle, *Julia Morgan: Architect*, 262; Coffman, *Building for Hearst and Morgan*, 519.

71. J. Morgan to Dahls, 7 July 1948, MS-027; J. Morgan to Dahls, n.d., c. December 1947, MS-027, Kennedy Library.

72. "Morgan, Her Office, and a House," Bancroft Library, 212.

73. "Forney: Working for Julia Morgan," *Oral History*, HSSSHM Archives, 11.

74. J. Morgan to Dahls, n.d., c. 1949, MS-027, Kennedy Library.

75. Lynn Forney McMurray, in *Julia Morgan: Architect of Beauty* by Wilson, viii.

76. "Morgan, Her Office, and a House," Bancroft Library, 173.

77. Alameda County, California, Deed Book 6174 (24 July 1950), 471; Julia Morgan, *New York, U.S., Arriving Passenger and Crew Lists, 1820–1957* (Provo, UT: Ancestry.com Operations Inc, 2010), 13 June 1951, Microfilm Serial:T715, Line 1:119.

78. "Morgan, Her Office, and a House," Bancroft Library, 173a–174.

79. "The Work of Steilberg and Morgan," Bancroft Library, 62.

80. "Morgan, Her Office, and a House," Bancroft Library, 211.

81. Lynn Forney McMurray, in *Julia Morgan: Architect of Beauty* by Wilson, vii.

82. "Sachi Oka," *Oral History Interview* (1995), HSSSHM Archives, 16.

83. California Department of Public Health, Death Certificate No. 57-013519 (2 February 1957), Julia Morgan; Center for Health Statistic and informatics, Vital Records, Sacramento.

84. "Morgan, Her Office, and a House," Bancroft Library, 193.

85. Boutelle, *Julia Morgan: Architect*, 242. Though the original fund has been absorbed into other scholarships, the program continues.

86. "The Work of Steilberg and Morgan," AIA 1957 Bio, Bancroft Library, 135a–135b.

87. "Morgan, Her Office, and a House," Bancroft Library, 192–93; 201; Morgan North, executor's report for the estate of Julia Morgan, deceased, 31 October 1958, Kennedy Library, 10.

88. "The Work of Walter Steilberg and Julia Morgan," AIA Report, Bancroft Library, 135a.

89. Kastner, *Hearst Ranch*, 177–79.

90. Ibid., 185–87.

91. "A Unique Tour of San Simeon," Photographed by Gjon Mili, *LIFE* 43, no. 9 (26 August 1957), 68–84.

92. Allan Temko, "Letters to the Editors," in *LIFE* 43, no. 12 (16 September 1957), 10.

93. The Julia Morgan Papers (Collections 010 and 027) at the Robert E. Kennedy Library's Special Collections are so vast that many unexplored subjects remain for future scholars to investigate.

94. Joan Didion, "A Trip to Xanadu," in *Let Me Tell You What I Mean* (New York: Alfred A. Knopf, 2021), 16–22, quoted in "She was America's Most Successful Woman Architect—and Hardly Anybody Knows Her Name," by Patricia Failing, *ARTNews* 80, no. 6, January 1981, 68.

95. Patricia Failing, "She was America's Most Successful Woman Architect—and Hardly Anybody Knows Her Name," *ARTNews*, 66–71.

96. Diane Favro, "Sincere and Good: The Architectural Practice of Julia Morgan," *Journal of Architectural and Planning Research*, 9, no. 2, (Summer 1992), 125.

97. "Julia Morgan, AIA Nomination for the 2014 AIA Gold Medal," introduction.

98. Michael Graves, Letter of Support in "Julia Morgan, AIA Nomination for the 2014 AIA Gold Medal," 12.

99. Denise Scott Brown, Letter of Support in "Julia Morgan, AIA Nomination for the 2014 AIA Gold Medal AIA nomination," 13.

100. Frank Gehry, Letter of Support in "Julia Morgan, AIA Nomination for the 2014 Gold Medal," 15.

101. Jane Hall, *Breaking Ground: Architecture by Women* (London: Phaidon, 2019), 137. Hall focuses solely—and rather summarily—on San Simeon in this recent treatment. While San Simeon is certain to maintain its significance, future scholarship on Julia's other projects will certainly increase. This is also surely true of growing interest in her extraordinary life. The simple Morgan family tombstone that Julia designed at Mountain View Cemetery is now one of its most visited memorials.

102. Mead, "Women's Versatility in Arts Enriches Field of Architecture," *Christian Science Monitor*, MS-027, Kennedy Library.

103. Julia Morgan Travel Diary, 1938, MS-027, Kennedy Library, 74.

Selected Bibliography

ARCHIVES AND LIBRARIES

Arthur Brown Jr. Papers, 1859–1990. 81/142. The Bancroft Library, University of California, Berkeley.

Bernard Maybeck Collection, 1897–1956. 1956-1. University of California Environmental Design Archives, Berkeley.

George and Phoebe Apperson Hearst Papers. 72/204c. The Bancroft Library, University of California, Berkeley.

George Loorz Collection. History Center of San Luis Obispo County, San Luis Obispo, CA.

Hearst San Simeon State Historical Monument Archives. San Simeon, CA.

Julia Morgan Papers. MS 010. Special Collections. Robert E. Kennedy Library, California Polytechnic State University, San Luis Obispo.

Mary Beatrice Fox Papers, 1789–1961. HM 54330-54451. Huntington Library, San Marino, CA.

Morgan-Boutelle Collections. MS 027. Special Collections. Robert E. Kennedy Library, California Polytechnic State University, San Luis Obispo.

Sarah Holmes Boutelle Papers. MS-141. Special Collections. Robert E. Kennedy Library, California Polytechnic State University, San Luis Obispo.

Walter L. Huber Papers, 1183–1960. C-B 825. The Bancroft Library, University of California, Berkeley.

Warren McClure Papers. Hearst San Simeon State Historical Monument Archives, San Simeon, CA.

William Randolph Hearst Papers. 87/232c. The Bancroft Library, University of California, Berkeley.

MANUSCRIPT AND DOCUMENTARY SOURCES

Dahl, Bjarne. "Working With Julia Morgan." Interview conducted by Metta Hake. *Oral History Project.* San Simeon, CA: Hearst San Simeon State Historical Monument Archives, 3 July 1983.

Forney, Lilian, "Lilian Forney: Working for Julia Morgan, 1923–57." *The Metta Hake Oral History Project.* San Simeon, CA: Hearst San Simeon State Historical Monument Archives, 1977.

McNeill, Karen Ann. *Building the California Women's Movement: Architecture, Space, and Gender in the Life and Work of Julia Morgan.* Ph.D. diss. Berkeley, CA: University of California, Fall 2006.

The Julia Morgan Architectural History Project. Edited by Suzanne B. Riess. The Bancroft Library, Regional Oral History Office. Berkeley, CA: University of California, 1976.

Oka, Sachi. "Sachi Oka: Julia Morgan's Housekeeper." Interview by John Horn and Ted Moreno. *Oral History Project.* San Simeon, CA: Hearst San Simeon State Historical Monument Archives, 1995.

Olney, Mary McLean. "Oakland, Berkeley, and the University of California, 1880–1895." Interview conducted by Willa Klug Baum. The Bancroft Library, Regional Cultural History Project. Berkeley: University of California, 1963.

Porter, Bruce. "Report of Mr. Bruce Porter for William R. Hearst, Esq., Upon His Estate at San Simeon: And Its Improvements." Jan. 1923. Morgan-Boutelle Collection, MS-027. Robert E. Kennedy Library, California Polytechnic State University, San Luis Obispo.

BOOKS, PAMPHLETS, AND ARTICLES

Allaback, Sarah. *The First American Women Architects.* Chicago: University of Illinois Press, 2008.

Armstrong, Jane. "The Young Woman Architect Who Helped Build the Fairmont Hotel." *San Francisco Call* (16 June 1907): 12.

Aylward, Emily Meredith. "The American Girls' Art Club in Paris." *Scribner's Magazine* XVI, no. 65 (November 1894): 598–605.

Boutelle, Sara Holmes. *Julia Morgan: Architect,* rev. ed. New York: Abbeville Press, 1995.

Bruce, Anthony, et al. *Looking at Julia Morgan: Early Residences in Berkeley.* Berkeley: Berkeley Architectural Heritage Association, 2010, no.p., House 5.

Cáceres, José Miguel and María José Martínez Ruiz. *La destrucción del patrimonio artístico español* (Madrid: Ediciones Cátedra, 2012).

Carlhian, Jean Paul and Margot M. Ellis. *Americans in Paris: Foundations of America's Architectural Gilded Age: Architecture Students at the École Des Beaux-Arts, 1846–1946.* New York: Random House, 2014.

LEFT: *The living room of the Baxter-Mostardi house in Berkeley, originally commissioned by Frederick A. and Anna H. Thomas in 1911.*

Clausen, Meredith L. "The Ecole des Beaux-Arts: Toward a Gendered History." *Journal of the Society of Architectural Historians* 68, no. 2 (June 2010).

Coffman, Taylor. *Building for Hearst and Morgan*. Berkeley, CA: Berkeley Hills Books, 2003.

Craig, Robert M. *Bernard Maybeck at Principia College: The Art and Craft of Building*. Salt Lake City, UT: Gibbs Smith, 2004.

Didion, Joan. *Let Me Tell You What I Mean*. New York: Alfred A. Knopf, 2021.

Donoho, Julia, et al. "Julia Morgan, AIA Nomination for the 2014 AIA Gold Medal." Sacramento: American Institute of Architects, California Council, 2014.

Failing, Patricia. "She Was America's Most Successful Woman Architect—and Hardly Anybody Knows Her Name." *ARTNews* 80, no. 6 (January 1981): 66–71.

Favro, Diane, "Sincere and Good: The Architectural Practice of Julia Morgan." *Journal of Architectural and Planning Research* 9, no. 2 (Summer 1992): 112–28.

Freudenheim, Leslie M. *Building with Nature: Inspiration for the Arts and Crafts Home*. 2nd ed. Salt Lake City, UT: Gibbs Smith, 2005.

Fuglie, Gordon, et al. *Julia Morgan: The Road to San Simeon. Visionary Architect of the California Renaissance*. New York: Rizzoli International Publications, 2022.

Gill, Sarah. *Julia Morgan's Berkeley City Club: The Story of a Building*. Berkeley, CA: Berkeley City Club, 2016.

Hall, Jane. *Breaking Ground: Architecture by Women*. New York: Phaidon Press, Inc., 2019.

Horton, Inge S. *Early Women Architects of the San Francisco Bay Area: The Lives and Work of Fifty Professionals, 1890–1951*. Jefferson, NC: McFarland & Co., 2010.

Kastner, Victoria. *Hearst Castle: The Biography of a Country House*. New York: Abrams, 2000.

———. "Julia Morgan and Associates: Julia Morgan's Office Practice as Design Metaphor." In Kiisk, Linda, ed. *20 on 20/20 Vision: Perspectives on Diversity and Design*. Boston: American Institute of Architects, 2003, 44-51.

Longstreth, Richard. *Julia Morgan Architect*. Berkeley, CA: Berkeley Architectural Heritage Association, 1977.

———. *On the Edge of the World: Four Architects in San Francisco at the Turn of the Century*. Berkeley, CA: University of California Press, 1998.

McMurray, Lynn Forney, foreword to *Julia Morgan: Architect of Beauty* by Mark Wilson. Layton, UT: Gibbs Smith, 2012.

McNeill, Karen. "Gender, Race, and Class in the Work of Julia Morgan." *Forum Journal*, 32 no. 3 (2018): 2636.

———. "Julia Morgan: Gender, Architecture, and Professional Style." *Pacific Historical Review* 76, no. 2 (2007): 229–68.

———. "Women Who Build: Julia Morgan & Women's Institutions." *California History* 89, no. 3 (2012): 41–74.

Mesic, Julian C. "Berkeley Women's City Club." *The Architect and Engineer* 105, no. 1 (April 1931): 24–47.

Nasaw, David. *The Chief: The Life of William Randolph Hearst*. New York: Houghton Mifflin, 2000.

North, Flora. "She Built for the Ages." *Kappa Alpha Theta Journal* 81, no. 3 (1967): 9–11.

Pavlik, Robert C. "Something a Little Different: La Cuesta Encantada's Architectural Precedents and Cultural Prototypes." *California History* 71, no. 4 (December 1992): 462–77.

Proctor, Ben. *William Randolph Hearst, 1911–1951*. Oxford, U.K.: Oxford University Press, 2007.

Richey, Eleanor. *Eminent Women of the West*. Berkeley: Howell-North Books, 1975.

———. *The Ultimate Victorians of the Continental Side of San Francisco Bay*. Berkeley: Howell-North Books, 1970.

Sarber, Jane. "A Cabbie in a Golden Era, Featuring Cabbie's Original Log of Guests Transported to Hearst Castle." N.p., n.d.

Stapley, Mildred. "Is Paris Wise for the Average American Girl?" *Ladies Home Journal* 23, no. 5 (April 1906): 16, 54.

Steilberg, Walter T. "Some Examples of the Work of Julia Morgan." *The Architect and Engineer* 55, no. 2 (November 1918): 38–107.

Tan, Mary Woodland Gould and Virginia Carroll. *Woodland Hall: Kent County, Maryland*. Kennedyville, MD: Self-published, 2007.

Whittlesey, Austin. *The Minor Ecclesiastical, Domestic, and Garden Architecture of Southern Spain*. New York: Architectural Book Pub. Co., P. Wenzel and M. Krakow, 1917.

Woodbridge, Sally B. *Bernard Maybeck: Visionary Architect*. New York: Abbeville Press, 1992.

Image Credits

All photographs are by Alexander Vertikoff, except for the following:

AACA Library and Research Center: 101.

Alamy Stock Photos: 76 [Artokoloro], 127 [mauritius images GmbH], 140 [Everett Collection Historical].

Ancestry.com: [Rio de Janeiro, Brazil, Immigration Cards, 1900–1965] 197.

Courtesy of Ray Byram, Annenberg Community Beach House: 148.

Art Resource, New York: [© Beaux-Arts de Paris, Dist. RMB-Grand Palais] 36, [© RMN-Grand Palais] 67.

The Bancroft Library, University of California, Berkeley: 34 [UC Berkeley Campus Views, UARC PIC 93:174], 81 [BANC PIC 1991.064-AX], 84 [Oliver Family Photograph Coll., BANC PIC 1960.010 ser. 2:0249-NEG].

Berkeley City Club Archives: 156.

Courtesy, California Historical Society: 93.

Special Collections and Archives, California Polytechnic State University [Julia Morgan Papers]: Cover left- top and bottom, 2, 6, 9, 11, 18, 21 all, 27 left, 30, 32, 35, 38, 40, 41, 44, 46, 47 bottom, 55, 56, 59, 64 top, 72, 82, 106 top, 110, 118 top, 121, 122, 124 all, 129 top, 131, 139, 162, 175, 177 bottom right, 187, 195, 196. [Julia Morgan-Sara H. Boutelle Collection]: Cover left-center, 27 right, 64 bottom, 100, 142, 159, 167, 189, 200.

Courtesy of the California History Room, California State Library, Sacramento, California: 77.

The Environmental Designs Archives, University of California, Berkeley: [Bernard Maybeck Collection, 1956-1] 37, [Julia Morgan Collection, 1959-2] 54, 70 all, 97, 111.

Courtesy of the First Presbyterian Church of San Rafael, California: 137 [Photo by Sandra Fisk].

Getty Images: 129 bottom [McMullan, Patrick/Contributor via Getty Images].

Digital image courtesy of the Getty's Open Content Program: 47 top.

Getty Research Institute, Los Angeles: 65 left (2838-550).

Library of Congress (Geography and Map Division): 16; (Prints and Photographs Division): 13, 168 [Photographs in the Carol M. Highsmith Archive], 65 right [LC-DIG-ppmsc-05230], 89 [LC-USZ62-26279].

Musée Carnavalet, via Look and Learn: 48.

Newspapers.com: [*San Francisco Examiner*, 17 April 1892, 10] 29.

Milstein Division, The New York Public Library: 19.

Courtesy Oakland Public Library, Oakland History Center: 17.

Courtesy of Pleasanton's Museum on Main: 83.

San Francisco History Center, San Francisco Public Library: 91.

USC Digital Library, California Historical Society Collection: 109.

Marc Wanamaker/Bison Archives, 120.

Courtesy of Washington Township Museum of Local History, Fremont, California: 88.

Wikimedia Commons: 42 [Daniel Vorndran / DXR, Creative Commons, (https://commons.wikimedia.org/wiki/File:Rouen_Cathedral_as_seen_from_Gros_Horloge_140214_4.jpg), Rouen Cathedral as seen from Gros Horloge 140215 4, https://creativecommons.org/licenses/by-sa/3.0/legalcode], 130 [Produced by Metro-Goldwyn-Mayer and supplied to CINELANDIA magazine, public domain].

Index